Gramsci's Pathways

Historical Materialism Book Series

The Historical Materialism Book Series is a major publishing initiative of the radical left. The capitalist crisis of the twenty-first century has been met by a resurgence of interest in critical Marxist theory. At the same time, the publishing institutions committed to Marxism have contracted markedly since the high point of the 1970s. The Historical Materialism Book Series is dedicated to addressing this situation by making available important works of Marxist theory. The aim of the series is to publish important theoretical contributions as the basis for vigorous intellectual debate and exchange on the left.

The peer-reviewed series publishes original monographs, translated texts, and reprints of classics across the bounds of academic disciplinary agendas and across the divisions of the left. The series is particularly concerned to encourage the internationalization of Marxist debate and aims to translate significant studies from beyond the English-speaking world.

For a full list of titles in the Historical Materialism Book Series
available in paperback from Haymarket Books, visit:
www.haymarketbooks.org/category/hm-series

Gramsci's Pathways

by
Guido Liguori

Translated by
David Broder

Haymarket Books
Chicago, IL

First published in Italian by Carocci Editore as *Sentieri gramsciani*, 2006.

First published in 2015 by Brill Academic Publishers, The Netherlands
© 2015 Koninklijke Brill NV, Leiden, The Netherlands

Published in paperback in 2016 by
Haymarket Books
P.O. Box 180165
Chicago, IL 60618
773-583-7884
www.haymarketbooks.org

ISBN: 978-1-60846-692-4

Trade distribution:
In the US, Consortium Book Sales, www.cbsd.com
In Canada, Publishers Group Canada, www.pgcbooks.ca
In the UK, Turnaround Publisher Services, www.turnaround-uk.com
In all other countries, Publishers Group Worldwide, www.pgw.com

Cover design by Jamie Kerry of Belle Étoile Studios and Ragina Johnson.

This book was published with the generous support of Lannan Foundation
and the Wallace Action Fund.

Printed in Canada by union labor.

10 9 8 7 6 5 4 3 2 1

Library of Congress Cataloging-in-Publication data is available.

Contents

Preface to the English Edition   IX

1   **The Extended State**   1
  1   The Extension of the Concept of the State   1
  2   The First 'Extension': Politics and Economics   2
  3   The Second 'Extension': Political Society and Civil Society   8
  4   State and Class Consciousness   9
  5   Dating Texts   14
  6   *Notebook* 6: Definitions   16
  7   The Ethical State   18
  8   Statolatry   20
  9   Unstable Equilibria   24

2   **Civil Society**   26
  1   Bobbio's Interpretation   26
  2   Civil Society in Marx   28
  3   Gramsci's Dialectical Conception   32
  4   'Civil Society' in Contemporary Debates   36
  5   A New Marxist Theory of the State   40

3   **State, Nation, Mundialisation**   42
  1   Mundialisation and Globalisation   42
  2   Gramsci and Taylorism   45
  3   The Myth of Civil Society   48
  4   State and Nation   49
  5   Against 'Passive Revolution'   53

4   **Party and Movements**   55
  1   Gramsci and Lenin   55
  2   Relations with 'the Subalterns'   57
  3   The *Ordine Nuovo* Years   60
  4   *L'Ordine Nuovo* in the *Notebooks*   62

5   **Ideologies and Conceptions of the World**   65
  1   From Marx to Gramsci   65
  2   Gramsci and Marx (and Croce)   70
  3   The Term 'Ideology'   75

4   The Family of Concepts   80
5   Ideology and Will   84

6   **Good Sense and Common Sense**   85
1   Two Meanings   85
2   Spontaneity and Backwardness   89
3   Common Sense, Neoidealism, Misoneism   94
4   Marxism and Common Sense   98
5   Common Sense and Philosophy   102
6   The Re-evaluation of 'Good Sense'   106
7   The Last Notebooks   110
8   Conclusions: The Double 'Return to Marx'   111

7   **Morality and 'Conformism'**   113
1   Marx and Morality   113
2   Gramsci's World   114
3   Universality and Historicity   115

8   **Marx. From the *Manifesto* to the *Notebooks***   120
1   From 'War of Movement' to 'War of Position'   120
2   Marx in the *Notebooks*   121
3   The Re-evaluation of Ideologies   122
4   The National/International Connection   123
5   Politics and the State   125
6   Against the Commodity Form   127

9   **Engels's Presence in the *Prison Notebooks***   128
1   Negative Judgements   128
2   *Anti-Dühring*   133
3   Engels's Anti-determinism   138

10   **Labriola: The Role of Ideology**   142
1   Labriola and Gramsci   142
2   Marx in Labriola's First Essay   146
3   From One 'Essay' to Another   148
4   From Labriola to Gramsci   153

11   **Togliatti. The Interpreter and 'Translator'**   156
1   Between Fascism and Stalinism: 'for Democratic Freedoms'   156
2   'Gramsci's Politics' in Liberated Italy   163

3   After '56: The 'Theorist of Politics'   171
4   The Final Chapter: Gramsci, a Man   173

12   **Hegemony and Its Interpreters**   176
1   After '56: Between Dictatorship and Democracy   176
2   1967: Political and Cultural Leadership   178
3   The 1970s: Hegemony and Hegemonic Apparatus   179
4   1975–6: Hegemony and Democracy   181
5   1977: The Forms of Hegemony   182
6   Hegemony and 'Prestige'   184
7   The 1980s: A Non-modern Gramsci?   186
8   The 1990s: Hegemony and Interdependence   187
9   Hegemony and Globalisation   189
10   The Word 'Hegemony'   190

13   **Dewey, Gramsci and Cornel West**   192
1   Marxism and Pragmatism   192
2   The American Pragmatism of the Prison Notebooks   194
3   Gramsci and Dewey   195
4   Dewey and Marxism   197
5   West's Gramsci   199

14   **The Modern Prince**   202
1   Against Stenterello   202
2   The Machiavelli Question   205
3   The Fourth Notebook: Marx and Machiavelli   209
4   The Eighth Notebook: The Modern Prince   213
5   A Jacobin Force   220

References   223
Name Index   232
Subject Index   236

Preface to the English Edition

The most important theme of the various 'pathways' included in this volume is the study of some of the main concepts, categories and sources of inspiration that appear in Gramsci's work, and especially in his *Prison Notebooks*.

Apart from a couple of more recent texts (Chapters Four and Fourteen, which did not appear in the Italian edition [*Sentieri gramsciani*]), most of the chapters are from the early years of the twenty-first century. Indeed, they were part of a collective work, the International Gramsci Society Italia's 'seminar on the lexicon of the *Quaderni del carcere*',[1] which began in 2001 and continued for over a decade, and whose most mature, abundant fruit was without doubt the *Dizionario gramsciano 1926–37*.[2]

The 'seminar on the lexicon of the *Quaderni*' came about as a reaction to the tendency – which has long been widespread in readings of Gramsci – to 'demand too much of the text', even though Gramsci himself warned against this. This tendency originated in the 'open' character of the *Prison Notebooks*, which were notes and reflections published only after their author's death, and had the same 'dialogical' framework as his thinking itself – almost always proceeding in an interrogative, exploratory, open manner, and not being definitive or closed in character. It moreover originated from the commixture of theory and politics that characterised the *Notebooks* and which inevitably – for a long time fruitfully – accompanied the reading and interpretation of these texts, albeit sometimes with the unavoidable result of encouraging highly polemical positions or politically oriented attempts to bend them out of shape or make them one-dimensional.

We started out from the conviction that it is today possible to read Gramsci as a great contemporary author – not a politically neutral one, but nor one who can immediately be compressed into current-day political debates. Hence the belief that now we need to 'go back to the texts', to 'his' texts, after years and years of interpretations that had built up a long and sometimes fruitful – but now useless – 'battle of ideas' on top of them.

Thus arose the need for a 'lexicon of the *Quaderni*' (an enterprise that had never before been attempted in such vast proportions), to constitute a basis and a web or set of guidelines for understanding this particular 'work'. So we traced out some of the interpretative pathways that also exist amidst the

---

1 See www.gramscitalia.it and www.igsitalia.org.
2 *Dizionario gramsciano 1926–1937*, edited by Guido Liguori and Pasquale Voza, Rome: Carocci.

apparent chaos of the *Quaderni*, and which are possible and perhaps necessary for proceeding through the only apparent non-organicity of Gramsci's thought.

We thus began to reread Gramsci's text with philological rigour, in order to start out again from what Gramsci had left in writing – and from the *way* in which he left it in writing – thus freeing his work of a whole series of dated readings that today risk suffocating its spirit and its capacity to be present in today's world. But we did so fully aware of the fact that *interpreting* is not only unavoidable, but also the only way to understand a text. Ultimately, the result of the 'seminars on the *Quaderni*' was the onset of a new 'Gramscian hermeneutics'; even if there had been some examples of this already (and some of them were important ones) this hermeneutics had never previously, however, been generalised and used continuously and in a programmatic manner.

Many of the essays collected in this volume conform to this 'hermeneutic' method. As such, they mainly stick to following Gramsci's texts, and rarely allow themselves to digress into more general political-cultural considerations. And they seek to take account of the chronological succession of these texts, while always bearing in mind that the *Prison Notebooks* are a diachronic work that also entails contradictions, recapitulations and about-turns.

The chapters that are most directly influenced by the hermeneutic message that I have mentioned are Chapters One, Two, Three, Four, Five, Six and Fourteen. The 'Gramscian terms' examined, here, are the 'extended state' (or 'integral state', as Gramsci put it more precisely), 'civil society', 'ideology', 'conception of the world', 'common sense', 'good sense' and 'modern prince'. Other chapters are devoted to investigating the relation between Gramsci and some of the main 'authors' with whom he established a significant relation (or who established one with him): Marx and Engels, Machiavelli, Labriola and Togliatti, Cornel West, and the main interpreters of his most important category, that of hegemony.

I hope that these 'pathways' and the method that they indicate can provide a useful support to the development of Gramsci studies in English, this today being the most important language after Italian in the international bibliography on the Sardinian Marxist theorist.

CHAPTER 1

The Extended State

1   The Extension of the Concept of the State

'State' and 'civil society' are terms and categories that repeatedly appear together in the *Prison Notebooks*, even though each is autonomous and distinct from the other. Here, we shall study them in conjunction, starting out from the category 'integral' or 'extended' state as a basic interpretative criterion. Gramsci had a dialectical conception of socio-historical reality, within which framework the state and civil society were thought in a nexus of unity-distinction; as such, to address the one without the other is to deny ourselves the possibility of a correct reading of the *Notebooks*. The expression that best denotes this unity-distinction relationship is the 'extended state', which, though not directly coming from Gramsci (who spoke, rather, of the 'integral state'), can be inferred from his writings,[1] and was introduced in 1975 by Christine Buci-Glucksmann, who identified Gramsci's 'expansion of the concept of the state' as his greatest theoretical-political contribution.[2]

What does it mean to use this category, the '*extended* state'? It indicates two things: on the one hand, it grasps the dialectical nexus (unity-distinction) between state and civil society, without 'rubbing out' either of the two terms; on the other hand, it indicates, in context, that such a unity is realised *under the hegemony of the state*. For sure, neither term can be absorbed by the other conceptually, but – in the reality of the twentieth century on which Gramsci reflected and which his theory reflects – the state did play a *protagonist* role. Gramsci, like other Marxist and non-Marxist political thinkers, was able to grasp this.

In the *Notebooks*, the concept of the state is 'extended' in two directions:

a) understanding the new relationship between politics and economics, which Gramsci identified as one of the characteristic traits of the twentieth century, as he reflected on Fascist 'corporativism', the experiences of the Soviet Union, and the situation brought about by the 'Crash' on Wall Street: the many sides of one same coin, which had begun to become clear at least from

---

1   Q6, § 87: Gramsci 1975, p. 763.
2   Buci-Glucksmann 1980.

the time of the First World War and had emerged in the reflection of thinkers such as Walter Rathenau and Otto Neurath. It should be noted that these themes were present in the theoretical debates of the Third International, and so, too, in the Austro-Marxism of the early 1920s – at the same time as Gramsci had cause to stay first in Moscow, then in Vienna. As we have said, it was a new relationship between politics and economics, but for Gramsci, as we shall see, this did not invalidate Marx's and Marxists' thesis as to economics' determining role 'in the last instance'.

b) understanding the new relationship between 'political society' and 'civil society' (in the *properly Gramscian* sense, the 'site of consensus'), which Gramsci arrived at through his fine-tuning of his theory of hegemony. This same relationship between political society and civil society had, according to Gramsci, begun to change even in the nineteenth century, and was fully consolidated in the following century. As we know, Gramsci expressed this change with the spatial metaphor of East and West. Gramsci's reflections were also, inevitably, conditioned by his study of the 'totalitarian' examples which, for different reasons, greatly weighed on his thought – the Italian Fascist state and the Soviet state – even if the conclusions he reached went beyond the terms of such models.

2   The First 'Extension': Politics and Economics

Let us begin on the first front, regarding the relationship between the state and economics. First off, we should sweep aside any doubts: Gramsci situated himself firmly on a Marxist terrain. He did not substitute politics for economics, but simply forcefully reaffirmed the dialectical nexus between – and reciprocal activity of – these two levels of reality; he delved into the very core of the 'superstructure', but on the basis of the fundamental lesson provided by Marx. Though some ambiguities may have appeared in his youthful writings,[3] in the *Notebooks* Gramsci repeatedly polemicised against Gentile and his school of thought, refusing to make the state the subject of history and still less the subject of the capitalist mode of production. Again taking up, in a second draft, a note from the seventh notebook addressing Ricardo and the theory of the state as a 'factor that guarantees property, thus the monopoly over the means of

---

3 See Chapter 3 on Gramsci's positions on the state in the *Ordine Nuovo* years, as Leninist influences at first complemented and then gradually replaced the influences of Gentile.

production',[4] Gramsci adds: 'It is certain that the state as such does not produce but is the expression of the economic situation – but one can however speak of the state as an economic agent in so far as the state is in actual fact synonymous with this situation'.[5]

The state, then, is an 'expression of the economic situation'. Gramsci had already written in the first *Notebook* that 'For the productive classes (the capitalist bourgeoisie and the modern proletariat) the state cannot be conceived except as the concrete form of a given economic world, of a given system of production. The conquest of power and the affirmation of a new productive world are inseparable'.[6]

In the corresponding c text, Gramsci turns to the 'conception of the state according to the productive function of the social classes', repeating the claims of the first draft but stressing that the 'relationship of means to end' (between politics and economics), cannot be said to be 'easily determined' or to take 'the form of a simple schema, apparent at first sight'.[7] There may be a less immediate relationship between the 'economic world' and its expression in the state, for example given an unfavourable historical situation. In the case of the Italian *Risorgimento*, as compared to the French Revolution, there was a weak bourgeoisie, and 'progressive forces' were 'in themselves ... scanty and inadequate'; if, then, 'the impetus of progress' is 'the reflection of international developments which transmit their ideological currents to the periphery', then 'the group which is the bearer of the new ideas is not the economic group but the intellectual stratum, and the conception of the state advocated by them changes aspect; it is conceived of as something in itself, as a rational absolute'.[8] It seems possible to deduce from this that the absolutisation of the concept of the state reflects a backward socio-economic situation: and this of no little significance, since it marks Gramsci's distance from a certain Italian idealist tradition.

The particular dialectic of Gramsci's framework is also evident in the notes in which he speaks of 'economism', in its two variants, the bourgeois (free-trade, liberalism) and the proletarian (theoretical syndicalism) version. Gramsci writes that in the case of the free-traders, 'there is an unconscious speculation ... on the distinction between political society and civil society, it being

4   Q7, § 42: Gramsci 1975, p. 890.
5   Q10II, § 41VI: Gramsci 1975, p. 1310; Gramsci 1995, p. 457.
6   Q1, § 150: Gramsci 1975, p. 132.
7   Q10II, § 61: Gramsci 1971, p. 116; Gramsci 1975, pp. 1359–60.
8   Q10II, § 61: Gramsci 1971, pp. 116–17; Gramsci 1975, pp. 1360–1.

affirmed that economic activity is proper to civil society and political society must not interfere in regulating it. But in reality, this distinction is purely methodological, not organic, and in concrete, historical life, political society and civil society are one and the same thing. After all, even free trade must be introduced by law, that is, by the intervention of political authority'.[9]

This passage is important for its claim that 'this distinction is purely methodological, not organic, and in concrete, historical life, political society and civil society are one and the same thing'. It has been stressed[10] that the civil society *at play*, here, is that proper to the free-trade tradition. Namely, by 'civil society', Gramsci here means 'economic society': the *non-organic* distinction thus only regards the relationship between economics and politics (political society–economic society). Gramsci's text could also give rise to different readings. In any case, to me it seems that we ought play down the significance of Gramsci's strong affirmation as to the 'non-organic' distinction between the different levels of reality. After all, what would it mean to assert the existence of an organic nexus between economic society and political society, and not between civil society (understood in the Gramscian sense) and political society? His many notes on leadership and domination, force and consent, and so on, suggest that the nexus between political society and civil society is also dialectical, a relationship of unity-distinction. This means that the distinction is *not organic*. I do not think that the specificity of Gramsci's theory of hegemony is thus lost, pivoting on consent (a concern that perhaps underlies Texier's and Coutinho's readings), but simply that this contradicts any interpretation of this theory addressing *only* consent, only the 'apparatuses of hegemony'. The complexity of the role of the ('integral') state lies in the fact that it holds force and consent together in a dialectical nexus, one of 'unity-distinction'; and in general, in the 'West', it is the element of consent that prevails – obviously, without this meaning that there is less 'force', just as the extreme examples of fascism and Nazism demonstrate.

An analogous problem arises from Gramsci's statement that civil society and political society are 'one and the same thing'. In the text c,[11] this formulation is replaced with an even stronger one: they are 'identical'. In Q26, § 6,[12] speaking of the 'state as policeman', that is, the state 'in the narrow sense', he even wrote that 'civil society ... is "state" too, indeed is the state itself'. How should we

---

9   Q4, § 38: Gramsci 1975, p. 460.
10   Texier 1988a; Coutinho 2012.
11   Q13, § 18: Gramsci 1975, p. 1590.
12   Gramsci 1971, p. 261; Gramsci 1975, p. 2302.

read this complete superposition of the state and civil society (however this is understood)? I maintain that it would be mistaken to deduce from this or other passages a total *identifiction* – in Gramsci's thought – between economic society and political society, or between civil society and political society: Gramsci's language has here given in to the force of polemic, which, however, if read literally, is incompatible with the 'rhythm' of the author's thought. The relationship remains a dialectical one, one of unity-distinction.[13]

Gramsci's awareness of the lack of 'ontological' separation between state and civil society and between politics and economics was his basis for understanding the novel role politics had taken on in the twentieth century, be that in relation to economic production, or – consequently – in relation to the class composition of society. Gramsci took an interest in the then-new phenomenon of the obligations incumbent on the state, which made the state a powerful 'lung' of finance at the service of capital. Here, we are talking about the years immediately following the 'Great Crash' on Wall Street. Confidence in the capitalist system had been deeply shaken, but the public 'd[id] not refuse its confidence to the state; it wanted to participate in economic activity, but through the state'.[14] And if the state could guarantee savings, Gramsci's farsighted reasoning concluded, it would sooner or later have to enter directly into 'the organisation of production', no less.[15] The state, Gramsci said, would have to intervene if it wanted to avoid a fresh depression. He thus lucidly saw how the capitalist economy was transitioning towards its 'Keynesian' phase in the 1930s, on the same page stating that 'It is not, though, a question of keeping the apparatus of production just as it was at a certain given moment. It is necessary to develop it in parallel with the increase in the population and of collective needs. The greatest danger for private initiative is in carrying out these necessary developments, and it is here that state intervention will be greatest'.

In the corresponding text C,[16] Gramsci specifies that the state is driven to intervene 'to save large enterprises that face uncertainty or are on the road to ruin; that is, as they say, the "nationalisation of industrial losses and deficits"'. Gramsci is not only critical with regard to the fascist version of the new relationship between politics and economics, set in place in response to the worldwide 'great crisis' beginning in 1929. Indeed, Gramsci did not hesitate to

---

13   As is also proven by Q10I1, § 7, where Gramsci criticises Ugo Spirito precisely for failing to make such a distinction. See section 1.8.

14   Q9, § 8: Gramsci 1975, pp. 1100–1.

15   Q9, § 8: Gramsci 1975, p. 1101.

16   Q22, § 14: Gramsci 1975, p. 2176.

note the Fascist state's 'plutocratic structure' and 'links with finance capital',[17] notwithstanding all its 'corporatist' rhetoric. Gramsci also criticised 'state capitalism' *tout court*, considering it 'a means for prudent capitalist exploitation in the new conditions which render impossible ... a liberal economic policy'.[18] Its class character and ultimate end (capitalist exploitation) remained unchanged. And thus the *Notebooks* did not encourage, in this series of notes, the policies of the New Deal, which would only later, across the distance of the twentieth century, be imputed progressive significance. Or, at least, be seen as a 'compromise' following the workers' own struggles and responding to these struggles as well as the needs of the subaltern classes, albeit in a framework that was non-revolutionary and thus, in some senses, a question of 'passive revolution'.[19]

It is worth emphasising, here, that Gramsci noted the state making deep impressions on the class composition of society, for example through its monetary policy acting to reduce or increase the power of parasitic layers.[20] But we could obviously find many other examples, when the state intervenes directly in 'the organisation of production'. Here, we see the *production of society* by the state (bestowing income, directly and indirectly, upon rising proportions of the population – and not necessarily parasitical ones, as Gramsci had thought at the height of Italian Fascism in the 1930s) – which represented the most significant novelty in the twentieth-century relationship between society and state, even if always within the terms of a dialectical relationship of unity-distinction between state and civil society (in all senses, economic and otherwise), as Gramsci teaches us, albeit always basing himself on Marx.

Gramsci was still certain, therefore, that the capitalist mode of production has its 'primary motor' in the economy. He was also still sure that, for a dialectical Marxist, the distinction between structure and superstructure (and between state and civil society, as classically understood) is only methodological and not organic: in a word, it is dialectical. It also remained true, for Gramsci, that in the twentieth century the state, politics, redefined its relations with economics, following capital's need to overcome the crisis into which it had entered. State intervention in savings and in production, introduced in

---

17   Q9, § 8: Gramsci 1975, p. 1101.

18   Q7, § 91: Gramsci 1975, p. 920. But note also the more general objections levelled in Q14, §57 – Gramsci 1975, p. 1716 – on the 'public works' policy and Q15, §1 – Gramsci 1975, pp. 1749–50 – on the birth of the Istituto Mobiliare Italiano, Istituto per la Ricostruzione Industriale, and so on.

19   On this important category of the *Notebooks*, see Voza 2004. On the state-economy nexus, see, too, Cavallaro 1997.

20   Q1, § 135: Gramsci 1975, p. 125.

socialist society as an alternative to the market, was *now* (that is, in Gramsci's own time) being introduced in capitalist society, too, albeit with the opposite objectives.

It has also been noted that Gramsci (more rarely) used a triad schema, namely: economics – civil society – state. Take, for example, Q4, § 49, where we read that 'the relationship between intellectuals and production ... is mediated by two types of social organisation: a) by civil society, that is, by the ensemble of the private organisations of society; b) by the state'.[21] Here, 'production' is clearly distinguished from both civil society (in the 'Gramscian' sense) and from the state – a term here used 'in the narrow sense', in a traditional and not 'extended' sense, not comprising those organisms which Gramsci defines, in the corresponding text C, as 'commonly called "private"'.[22] The word 'commonly' and the quote marks around the adjective 'private' make clear his own position, reaffirming the only-*apparently* 'private' and 'separate' character of civil society. Again in the tenth *Notebook*, Gramsci comes back to the same triad schema: '[b]etween economic structure and the state with its legislation and coercion stands civil society ... the state is the instrument of the adequation of civil society to the economic structure'.[23]

But what does 'civil society' mean, here? It does not seem to be civil society in the 'properly Gramscian' sense, that is, as the apparatus of consent. In this piece of text, entitled 'Noterelle di economia', Gramsci addresses the concept of the 'homo oeconomicus'. The question is how to take this off the field when it no longer corresponds to 'an economic structure' having 'undergone radical change'. Here, then, it seems that Gramsci's use of the term 'civil society' refers to an 'economic world' that extends beyond the 'economic structure' as such. In the same note, moreover, he distinguishes between 'economic structure' and 'economic behaviour', or even between 'economic structure' and 'economic activity'. In any case, the role that Gramsci assigns to the state – and it is worth insisting on this point – seems very significant: namely, adequating civil society to the economic structure.

Let us now return to the schema that we saw in Q4, § 49. Here is the 'structure', while civil society and the state make up part of the 'superstructure'; as Gramsci explains in the corresponding text C, here we find 'Two major superstructural "levels": the one that can be called "civil society", that is the ensemble of organisms commonly called "private", and that of "political society" or "the

---

21   Q4, § 49: Gramsci 1975, p. 476.
22   Q12, §1: Gramsci 1975, p. 1518; Gramsci 1971, p. 12.
23   Q10II, § 15: Gramsci 1975, pp. 1253–4.

State"'.[24] Gramsci – it is fair to say – is the greatest Marxist scholar of super-structures, whose importance, complexity and internal articulations he invest-igated. But this did not mean losing sight of the determining role of the 'base', even within his dialectical conception of its relationship to superstructure.

3   The Second 'Extension': Political Society and Civil Society

Let's turn to the second direction in which Gramsci 'extended the concept of the state'. In his 7 September 1931 letter to Tania, we find an untypically striking portrayal of his theoretical discovery:

> The study I have made of intellectuals is really vast … This study also extends to certain *determinations of the concept of the state*, which is usu-ally understood as political society (a dictatorship, or a coercive apparatus to make the mass of the people conform to the type of production and of the economy of some given moment) and not as a balance of polit-ical society with civil society (or, the hegemony of a social group over the entire national society, exercised by means of the so-called private organ-isations, such as the church, trade unions, schools and so on), and, indeed, intellectuals are especially active in civil society.[25]

Studying the history and role of the intellectuals, and thus clarifying his own theory of hegemony, Gramsci had arrived at a new concept of the state. In this regard Gramsci's attention was particularly addressed to the 'hegemonic apparatuses' (a term that does not actually appear in the *Notebooks*, at least in the plural). These apparatuses were combined with the 'coercive apparat-uses', typical of the state in the narrow sense: the nineteenth-century state to which Marx had devoted his attention – and so, too, Lenin, who acted and made the Revolution in a country whose state was in so many aspects a nineteenth-century one. Flowing from this was the decisive importance that Gramsci assigned to the intellectuals, developing an intellectuals-state nexus that also bore notes of Hegel. 'Civil society' was understood as the ensemble of 'so-called private organisations'. Here reappears an expression similar to that we already saw in Q12, §1 ('organisms commonly called "private"'), which can

---

24   Q12, §1: Gramsci 1975, p. 1518; Gramsci 1971, p. 12.
25   Gramsci 1996a, pp. 458–9.

be found at several points in the *Notebooks*. The use of inverted commas[26] and the adverb 'commonly',[27] as with the expression 'so-called' before 'private', are markers and sign-posts of very great importance indeed. They tell us that, for Gramsci, such hegemonic apparatuses, which are apparently 'private', in reality constitute a fully-fledged part of the state – thus allowing us to speak of the 'extended state'. I have already mentioned that this expression cannot be found in Gramsci – who repeatedly speaks of the 'integral state'[28] – but he does refer to the 'state in an organic and a *wider sense*'.[29]

It is also important to stress one further consideration: if the organisms of civil society, as understood in a Gramscian sense, were 'private' *tout court*, this would open the way for a 'culturalist', 'idealist', 'liberal' reading of Gramsci, tending to emphasise the importance of 'dialogue' or a Habermasian 'communicative action', seen as decoupled from the relations of force: an *ingenuous* vision of democracy and hegemony.[30] The fact that Gramsci instead dialectically posed such organisms – responsible for the formation of consent – as part of the state, allows us to say without ambiguity that he was proposing a broad reading of the morphology of *power* in contemporary society. This meant a hegemonic power – once again, reasoning dialectically – whose twin aspects of force and consent, leadership and domination are indispensible. And it also meant a hegemonic power whose subject is a class; but, as we shall see, this a class that must 'become the state' if it is to be a true hegemon.

4   State and Class Consciousness

Q1, § 47, entitled 'Hegel and associationism', seems to be the first place in the *Notebooks* where Gramsci brings to fruition a conception of the state that also includes the 'organisms' of civil society:

> Hegel's doctrine of parties and associations as the 'private' woof of the state ... Government with the consent of the governed – but with this consent organised, and not generic and vague as it is expressed in the instant of elections. The state does have and request consent, but it also 'educates'

---

26   For example in Q6, § 137: Gramsci 1975, p. 801.

27   For example in Q8, § 130: Gramsci 1975, p. 1020.

28   For instance Q6, § 10 and Q6, § 155: Gramsci 1975, pp. 691 and 810.

29   Q6, § 87: Gramsci 1975, p. 763; Gramsci 1995, p. 18. My italics.

30   On the concept of hegemony, see Chapter 13 and Cospito 2004.

this consent, by means of political and trade-union associations; these, however, are private organisms, left to the private initiative of the ruling class.[31]

For Gramsci, 'civil society' is neither 'base', understood in the Marxian sense, nor the Hegelian 'system of needs', but rather the ensemble of trade-union, political, and cultural associations that are generally termed 'private' in order to distinguish them from the 'public sphere' of the state. Gramsci's dialectical Marxism, as we have already seen, denies any such sharp, 'organic' distinction. Starting out from a distinct reading of Hegel – one that needs several refinements and sometimes seems to force matters somewhat – Gramsci maintained from the first *Notebook* onwards that parties and associations are the moments through which consent is constructed and cultivated. The state is the subject of political-cultural initiative, even if as we know it acts by means of both *explicitly* public channels and *apparently* private ones. The heuristic capacity of this interpretative schema appears all the more clearly today, as the development of the mass media and their politico-cultural weight seems so widely recognised: indeed, together with the old 'hegemonic apparatuses' like schools and the press we also now have television. This new terrain, which is fundamental to the creation of common sense,[32] poses great demands on the nuances of the terms 'public', 'private', 'political' and 'economic'.

The term 'civil society' does not appear in Q1, § 47, but the concept is present there, as we can also tell from reading Q6, § 24:[33]

> civil society as understood by Hegel and in the sense in which it is often used in these notes (viz. in the sense of the political and cultural hegemony of a social group over the whole of society, as the ethical content of the state) ...

We could add that Gramsci repeatedly invoked Hegel in the *Notebooks* as the theorist of the 'ethical state', counterposed to the 'nightwatchman state', that is, in the sense of Humboldt's minimal state. The concept of the 'ethical state' – Gramsci tells us – 'is of philosophical origin (Hegel) and refers ... to the educative and moral activity of the state'.[34] We will return to this point later on.

---

31   Gramsci 1971, p. 259 (translation edited); Gramsci 1975, p. 56.
32   See Chapter 7.
33   Gramsci 1975, p. 703; Gramsci 1995, p. 75.
34   Q5, § 69: Gramsci 1975, pp. 603–4.

Apart from the note on Hegel, in the first *Notebook* (and the second) there are no other notes on this theme that we have not already mentioned. Rather, it is in Notebook 3 that Gramsci repeatedly underlines the role and the function of the state. Firstly, this notebook provides a brief recap of the history of the state: not only the distinction between the ancient/medieval state and the modern one ('The modern state abolishes many autonomies of the subaltern classes ... but certain forms of the internal life of the subaltern classes are reborn as parties, trade unions, cultural associations')[35] but also an important note on the 'modern dictatorship' which 'abolishes these forms of class autonomy as well, and it tries hard to incorporate them into the activity of the state: in other words, the centralisation of the whole life of the nation in the hands of the ruling class becomes frenetic and all-consuming'.[36]

The alterations made in the text C of this note[37] deserve some attention. Not only does 'the modern dictatorship' become 'the contemporary dictatorships', but the final line of the passage cited above is changed to 'the legal centralisa- tion of the whole life of the nation in the hands of the ruling group becomes "totalitarian"'. Certainly, Gramsci is here referring to fascism (and the 1934 text C to plural 'fascisms'). But I would ask whether we cannot also make out the watermark of a reference to the Soviet Union, here – remembering, after all, that Gramsci seems to have seen 'totalitarian' in a generally positive light polit- ically, or at least not a negative or neutral one. There is also the fact that the 'totalitarian' state then making headway in its various forms was a privileged object of inquiry in Gramsci's prison reflections on the state.

The other notes on the state that we find in this *Notebook* serve to emphasise the importance of this concept: 'as soon as a new type of state comes into being, it gives rise [concretely] to the problem of a new civilisation';[38] 'a poor under- standing of the state means a poor consciousness of class';[39] 'The historical unity of the ruling classes is found in the state, and their history is essentially the history of states and of groups of states'.[40] To be precise, for Gramsci, it

---

35   Q5, § 69: Gramsci 1975, p. 303; Gramsci 1996b, p. 25.

36   Ibid.

37   Q25, § 4: Gramsci 1975, p. 2287.

38   Q3, § 31: Gramsci 1975, p. 309; Gramsci 1996b, p. 31. Richer is the text C: 'From the moment in which a subaltern group becomes really autonomous and hegemonic, bringing about a new type of state, is born concretely the need to construct a new intellectual and moral order' (Q11, § 70: Gramsci 1975, pp. 1508–9). For similar statements see Q4, § 3 (Gramsci 1975, p. 425) and Q16, § 9 (Gramsci 1975, p. 1863).

39   Q3, § 46: Gramsci 1975, p. 326; Gramsci 1996b, p. 47.

40   Q3, § 90: Gramsci 1975, p. 372; Gramsci 1996b, p. 91.

seems, the 'class' is only ripe to put itself forward as a hegemonic class when
1) it has an autonomous party, which affirms its own 'complete autonomy'
from the ruling classes[41] and 2) when it proves able to 'consolidate itself in the
state'.[42]

Both Q3, §18 cited earlier on and this Q3, §90 have the same title, 'History
of the subaltern classes'. Gramsci, that is, is trying to understand why a class is
subaltern and how it can become a ruling class. In this vein, he reformulates the
concept of hegemony – already present *in nuce* in the discussions of the Comintern of the early 1920s – and introduces the term 'civil society', though this is not
yet fully developed as a 'Gramscian' concept. Indeed, Q3, §90 continues:

> This unity must be concrete, hence it is the outcome of the relations
> between the state and 'civil society'. For the subaltern classes, the unific-
> ation does not occur; their history is intertwined with the history of 'civil
> society'; it is a disjointed segment of that history.[43]

The corresponding text C is even more explicit:

> The subaltern classes, by definition, are not unified and cannot be unified
> until they become 'the state': their history, then, is intertwined with the
> history of civil society; it is a 'disjointed' and discontinuous function of
> the history of civil society, and, through this, of the history of states and
> groups of states.[44]

It is clear that Gramsci is here describing the path to hegemony, and sees classes
as ready to pose its own challenge for hegemony only insofar as they are capable
of expression and self-expression in a party and of 'becoming' the state.

I will conclude my remarks on the third *Notebook* by drawing the reader's
attention to Q3, §61, which despite certain ambiguities does seem to me to
begin 'extending' the concept of the state:

> every homogeneous social element is 'state' or represents the state insofar
> as it adheres to its programme; if not, the state becomes confused with the
> state bureaucracy. Every citizen is a 'functionary' if he is active in social

---

41   Q3, §90: Gramsci 1975, p. 373; Gramsci 1996b, p. 91.

42   Q3, §90: Gramsci 1975, p. 373; Gramsci 1996b, p. 92.

43   Q3, §90: Gramsci 1975, p. 372; Gramsci 1996b, p. 91.

44   Q25, §5: Gramsci 1975, p. 2288.

life along the lines outlined by the state-government, and the more he adheres to the state's programme and carries it out intelligently, the more he is its functionary.[45]

Gramsci is talking of a 'struggle between generations' (the title of this brief note) and is (if rather cryptically) guarding against 'statolatry'. Here already, we see Gramsci reflecting on the 'totalitarian' experiences of his time. He is talking in particular about the Soviet system, as is clearly apparent if we read Q9, § 69, where – rebutting elitist critiques of democracy and its 'numerical' contents – he comes to speak of the 'representative system, even if [it is] not parliamentary and not fashioned according to the canons of democracy in the abstract': meaning, Soviet democracy. 'In these other systems', Gramsci continues, 'consent ... is assumed to be permanently active, to the point that those who consent could be considered "functionaries" of the state and the elections a means of voluntary enrolment of state functionaries of a certain type'.[46]

In conformity with this argument, we can compare these notes on 'the extension of the concept of the state functionary' to the last note of *Notebook* 2 (which was in reality added much later on, in 1933–4):

> What is the police? It certainly is not just that particular official organ-
> isation which is juridically recognised and empowered to carry out the
> public function of public safety, as it is normally understood. This organ-
> ism is the central and formally responsible nucleus of the 'police', which
> is a much larger organisation in which a large part of a state's popula-
> tion participates directly or indirectly through links that are more or less
> precise and limited, permanent or occasional etc. The analysis of these
> relations helps one understand what the 'state' is, much more than many
> philosophical juridical dissertations do.[47]

Reflection on the history of the ruling classes and of the subaltern classes, and reflection on the contemporary state (and even and above all the 'totalit-arian' state) converge in bringing to light the new morphology of the twentieth-century state.

---

45   Gramsci 1975, p. 340; Gramsci 1996b, p. 59. Translation altered.

46   Q9, § 69: Gramsci 1975, p. 1141.

47   Q2, § 150: Gramsci 1975, pp. 278–9; Gramsci 1992, p. 150. Translation altered.

5   Dating Texts

Before proceeding with our reading of the *Notebooks*, let us open up a paren-
thesis to deal with the temporal scansion with which Gramsci sought to define
the maturation of the new morphology of the state, its process of 'extension'.
The first note that I would like to recall, here, is connected to his new way of
understanding the functions of the 'police':

> Modern political 'technique' has completely changed since 1848, since the
> expansion of parliamentarism, of the system of trade-union association
> and of parties, of the formation of vast state and 'private' bureaucracies
> (political-private ones, for parties and trade-unions) and the transforma-
> tions that have taken place in the organisation of the police in the broad
> sense: that is, not only in the state service devoted to the repression of
> crime, but in the ensemble of organised state and private forces that
> uphold the [political and economic] dominion of the ruling class. In this
> sense, entire 'political' parties and other organisations of an economic or
> some other kind must be considered organisms of a political police of a
> 'repressive' and 'investigative' character.[48]

'After 1848', then. In another note, 1848 is again cited as a parting-of-the waters.
This is Q8, § 52,[49] with regard to 'permanent revolution'. It is a note best read in
its richer second draft:

> The political concept of the so-called 'permanent revolution', which
> emerged before 1848 as a scientifically evolved expression of the Jacobin
> experience from 1789 to Thermidor. The formula belongs to a historical
> period in which the great mass political parties and the great economic
> trade unions did not yet exist, and society was still in many aspects, so to
> speak, in a state of fluidity ... [with] a relatively rudimentary state appar-
> atus, and greater autonomy of civil society from state activity ... In the
> period after 1870, with the colonial expansion of Europe, all these ele-
> ments changed: the internal and international organisational relations
> of the state became more complex and massive, and the Forty-Eightist
> formula of the 'permanent revolution' was expanded and transcended in

---

48   Q9, § 133: Gramsci 1975, p. 1195. Significantly, in the text C, the word 'repressive' is replaced
      with 'preventative' (Q13, § 27: Gramsci 1975, p. 1621).
49   Gramsci 1975, pp. 972–3.

political science by the formula of 'civil hegemony'. The same thing happens in the art of politics as happens in military art: war of movement increasingly becomes war of position, and it can be said that a state will win a war in so far as it minutely prepares for it technically during peacetime. The massive structures of the modern democracies, both as state organisations, and as complexes of associations in civil society, constitute for the art of politics as it were the 'trenches' and the permanent fortifications of the front in the war of position ... This question is posed for the modern states, but not for backward countries or for colonies, where forms which elsewhere have been superseded and have become anachronistic are still in vigour. The question of the value of ideologies must also be studied in a treatise of political science.[50]

The quote is a long one, but it is full of signposts – first of all the last one, which recalls the famous note 16 of *Notebook* 7 on 'war of position and war of manoeuvre or frontal war'. We will return to this, making explicit how his vision of the morphological transformation of the state according to a diachronical axis was corrected in light of the category of 'differentiated development' and a related 'differentiated analysis' applied to contemporary societies and states.

Moreover, we can see how the transformation of the bourgeois state, manifest already after 1848, took on earth-shattering force after 1870. The gradual consolidation of 'democracy' led to a new type of class struggle, at the level of the 'trenches' and 'earthworks' that were rapidly changing the battlefield. Why (bourgeois) democracy? Because, Gramsci wrote in the eighth *Notebook*

> The bourgeois class poses itself as an organism in continuous movement, capable of absorbing the entire society, assimilating it to its own cultural and economic level. The entire function of the state has been transformed; the state has become an 'educator', and so on.[51]

Gramsci then seeks to explain 'how this concept comes to a halt and the conception of the state as pure force is returned to'. For us, however, it is important to establish that the bourgeoisie's line of march – for Gramsci, already grasped (foreseen) in its essentials by Hegel – brings with it a new type of state, ever more complex and based on the organisation of consent. Here and there, Gramsci seems to 'backdate' his discourse on the state-hegemony

---

50   Q13, §7: Gramsci 1975 pp. 1566–7; Gramsci 1971, pp. 242–3. Translation altered.
51   Q8, §2: Gramsci 1975, p. 937; Gramsci 1971, p. 260.

nexus: for example, in Q8, § 227 he asks 'But has there ever existed a state without "hegemony"?'[52] And in Q6, § 87 he recalls a formula of Guicciardini's according to which 'two things are absolutely necessary for the life of a state: arms and religion'; and he translates this into 'force and consent, coercion and persuasion, state and Church, political society and civil society', adding that in the Renaissance 'the Church was civil society, the hegemonic apparatus of the ruling group'.[53] Moreover, the bourgeoisie's process of formation-consolidation lasted for centuries. We will, however, continue to focus our attention on the morphological novelties of the twentieth-century state, noting that for Gramsci the century seems to have begun – from the point of view of the history of the state, that is, of hegemony – not in 1914 (and still less in 1917), but rather in 1870.

6   *Notebook* 6: Definitions

Let's turn back to the *Notebooks*, and follow the development of Gramsci's reflection on the state and civil society. After *Notebook* 3, it is in *Notebook* 6 that we find some of the most pregnant definitions of the 'extended state'.[54] *Notebook* 6, remember, dates from 1930–2, and is a miscellaneous notebook almost entirely comprising B texts. Let's look at some of the passages on the state and civil society.

Q6, § 10: after the French Revolution the bourgeoisie 'could present itself as an integral "state", with all the sufficient intellectual and moral forces needed to organise a complete and perfect society'.[55]

Q6, § 87: As we have already seen, Gramsci translates Guicciardini's formula, rounding off the note with an observation of considerable interest on 'the Jacobin initiative instituting the cult of the "supreme being", which thus appears

---

52   Gramsci 1975, p. 1084.
53   Gramsci 1975, p. 763; Gramsci 1995, pp. 17–18.
54   Here, I overlook the important text of Q4, § 38 (Gramsci 1975, p. 458), much enriched in its second draft Q13, § 17 (Gramsci 1975, p. 1584) to which we shall return, as well as the notes that I mentioned already.
55   Gramsci 1975, p. 691. In continuing the note, Gramsci speaks of the crisis of bourgeois hegemony in terms of '[the process of the] disintegration of the modern state'. Later on he introduces a most interesting comparison between Croce and Gentile ('For Gentile all history is the history of the state; for Croce, instead, it is ethical-political – that is, Croce wants to maintain a distinction between civil society and political society') to which we will return.

as an attempt to establish an identity between state and civil society, to unify in a dictatorial manner the constitutive elements of the state in an organic and wider sense (the state properly speaking, and civil society)'.[56]

Q6, § 88: the general notion of state includes elements that need to be referred back to the notion of civil society (in the sense that one might say that state = political society + civil society, in other words hegemony protected by the armour of coercion).[57]

Q6, § 136: organisations and parties ('in a broad and not a formal sense') constitute 'the hegemonic apparatus of one social group over the rest of the population (or civil society): the basis for the state in the narrow sense of the governmental-coercive apparatus'.[58]

Q6, § 137: *Concept of the state* ... by state must be understood, beyond the governmental apparatus, so also the "private" apparatus of hegemony or civil society'.[59]

Q6, § 155: 'In politics the error occurs as a result of an inaccurate understanding of what the state (in its integral meaning: dictatorship + hegemony) really is'.[60]

At this point in the *Notebooks*, then, Gramsci had arrived at the concept of the 'extended state' which he described in his letter to Tania in September 1931: political society + civil society, governmental-coercive apparatus + hegemonic apparatuses. I would here like to draw attention to the term 'hegemonic apparatus' which appears in Q6, § 136, an expression which to me seems to be of fundamental importance, since it refers to the materiality of the processes of hegemony: it is not only a matter of a 'battle of ideas', but of true and proper *apparatuses* charged with the creation of consent. At the same time, here we can observe how distant Gramsci's conception is from Althusser's ISA (Ideological State Apparatuses), themselves probably derived from the *Notebooks*, even if in a distorted manner. After all, Gramsci's 'integral state' is shot through

---

56   Gramsci 1975, pp. 762–3. Here he speaks of an 'identity between the state and civil society', with civil society undoubtedly to be understood in the 'Gramscian sense'. See section 1.2 above.

57   Gramsci 1975, pp. 763–4; Gramsci 1971, p. 263.

58   Gramsci 1975, p. 800; Gramsci 1971, pp. 264–5.

59   Gramsci 1975, p. 801.

60   Gramsci 1975, pp. 810–11; Gramsci 1971, p. 239.

with class struggle, the processes are never unambiguous, and the state also constitutes the *terrain* of the clash between classes: 'There is a struggle between two hegemonies, always', writes Gramsci.[61] We are far, here, from any structural-functionalist theory: both the state and civil society are shot through by the class struggle, the dialectic is real and open and the outcome is not predetermined. The state is not only an instrument (of a class) but also a site (of the struggle for hegemony) and a process (of the unification of the ruling classes). It is possible to set in motion moments of 'counter-hegemony'; 'a class can (and must) "lead" even before assuming power; when it is in power it becomes dominant, but it also continues to lead'.[62] The leadership function begins first, but the full deployment of the hegemonic function of the class rising to power only comes with its 'making itself the state': the state serves its 'leadership' no less than its 'dominance'.

7   The Ethical State

Gramsci's survey of the state/hegemony and of the crisis of bourgeois hegemony that led to Fascism – but also to the rupture of October 1917 – continues apace. His starting point is the famous East/West distinction that we find in Q7, § 6:

> In the East the state was everything, civil society was primordial and gelatinous; in the West there was a proper balance between the state and civil society, and when the state trembled a sturdy structure of civil society was at once revealed. The state was only an outer ditch, behind which there stood a powerful system of fortresses and earthworks.[63]

On the one hand, 'it is then a question of studying in depth what are the elements of civil society that correspond to the defence systems in the war of position'.[64] On the other hand, he defines the crisis of hegemony as

---

61   Q8, § 227: Gramsci 1975, p. 1084.
62   Q1, § 44: Gramsci 1975, p. 41; Gramsci 1992, pp. 136–7. The corresponding text C (Q19, § 24: Gramsci 1975, pp. 2010–11) does not change the sense of Gramsci's statement, notwithstanding the substitution of the expression 'social group' for the term 'class', a substitution to which there has sometimes been attributed a theoretical significance that it does not seem to me to have, after reading the whole text.
63   Gramsci 1975, p. 866.
64   Q7, § 10: Gramsci 1975, p. 860.

the separation of civil from political society: a new problem of hegemony is posed, that is, the historical basis of the state is shifted. We get an extreme form of political society: either to fight against the new and conserve the unstable, cementing it through coercion, or as the expression of the new for breaking the resistance it meets in its development, and so on.[65]

Revolution and reaction seem to entrust their own fate to the state *stricto sensu*. But the recourse to dictatorship – a possibility that was necessarily very much on Gramsci's mind – does not exhaust the range of possibilities. The theme of the creation of a 'public opinion', for example, if no stranger to the 'totalitarianisms', also very much applied to the liberal-democratic states. Gramsci wrote,

> What is called 'public opinion' is closely connected with political hegemony, and as such is the point of contact between 'civil society' and 'political society', between consent and force. The state, when it wants to begin an activity of little popularity, creates the adequate public opinion in advance, that is, it organises and centralises certain elements of civil society.[66]

Here, too, I would like to note how far Gramsci stood from certain, today rather widespread, conceptions that portray civil society as a free space in which the actors, in dialogue, create the connective tissue of democratic coexistence. Gramsci warned: 'there is a struggle for monopoly over the organs of public opinion – newspapers, parties, parliament – such that a single force might model national opinion and thus its political will, turning those who disagree into individual, inorganic dust'.[67] This is because 'ideas and opinions are not spontaneously "born" in the mind of each individual: they will have had a centre of irradiation and diffusion'.[68]

Behind every 'dialogue' and 'communicative action', there is always, then, a struggle for hegemony. In this sense, the state is an 'educator' (see Q8, §2 and Q8, §62),[69] and in this sense it is 'ethical':

---

65   Q7, §28: Gramsci 1975, p. 876.
66   Q7, §83: Gramsci 1975, p. 914.
67   Q7, §83: Gramsci 1975, p. 915.
68   Q9, §69: Gramsci 1975, p. 1140.
69   Gramsci 1975, pp. 937 and 978.

every state is ethical inasmuch as one of its most important functions is to raise the great mass of the population to a certain cultural and moral level, a level (or type) that corresponds to the productive forces' developmental needs and thus to the interests of the ruling classes.[70]

The state that works to build 'conformism'[71] leaves no room for the *spontaneity* of civil society:

> In reality the state must be conceived as an 'educator', inasmuch as it tends to create a new type or level of civilisation; and how does this happen? Though it is essentially on economic forces that one operates ... one must not deduce as a consequence that superstructural factors should be abandoned to themselves, to their own spontaneous development, germinating sporadically and at random. The state is a 'rationalisation' in this field also: it is an instrument of acceleration and Taylorisation, operating according to a plan, pushing, encouraging, demanding and so on.[72]

The state, then, is here seen in terms of the 'Taylorisation' (more than co-ordination, it means a hierarchical-functional organisation, oriented 'according to a plan') of superstructural activity: schools, newspapers, churches, parties, trade unions, place names – nothing seems to be left to chance. This does not mean to forget that – this being the 'integral state' shot through by the struggle for hegemony – the subaltern class which fights to 'become the state' reacts and seeks to maintain its own 'autonomy' (this being something different, however, from 'the autonomy of civil society' as commonly understood today) and thus also to build its own hegemony, as an alternative to the dominant one.

8   Statolatry

In the eighth *Notebook* (1931–2: one of the periods of Gramsci's sharpest dissent with the USSR) some notes seem to refer, in a more or less veiled manner, to the Soviet Republic. I will limit myself to citing two such texts. The main one is Q8, § 130, entitled 'Encylopaedic notions and questions of culture. Statolatry'. Following some comments on civil society and political society, Gramsci writes:

---

70   Q8, § 179: Gramsci 1975, p. 1049; Gramsci 1971, p. 258, translation altered.
71   On the category 'conformism', see Chapter 6.
72   Q8, § 62: Gramsci 1975, p. 978.

> For some social groups, which before their ascent to autonomous state
> life have not had a long independent period of cultural and moral devel-
> opment on their own ... a period of statolatry is necessary and indeed
> opportune. This 'statolatry' is nothing other than the normal form of 'state
> life', or at least of initiation to autonomous state life and to the creation of
> a 'civil society' which it was not historically possible to create before the
> ascent to independent state life.[73]

As such, the paradox of the October Revolution was that it won in the 'East',
where 'civil society' was not just 'primordial and gelatinous' (as we remember off-by-heart), but apparently even non-existent, as Gramsci emphasises.
From this emerged 'statolary', a totally uncritical attitude of identification with
the state as a means of bridging the backwardness that resulted from the fact
that the Revolution did not follow any 'enlightenment' – any construction of
hegemony. Here come to mind the passages where Gramsci focuses on the
difficulties that the 'new class' has in creating its own organic intellectuals, a
situation from which the limits of Soviet Marxism, as symbolised by Bukharin,
derive. But though Gramsci understood the origin of 'statolatry' and understood well – in another note of this same eighth *Notebook* – that 'The superstructural elements will inevitably be few in number' when 'passing through a
phase of economic-corporate primitivism',[74] this did not mean closing his eyes
to the dangers of such a situation. Rather, he urged a conscious response to it:

> this kind of 'statolatry' must not be abandoned to itself, must not, espe-
> cially, become theoretical fanaticism or be conceived of as 'perpetual'. It
> must be criticised, precisely in order to develop and produce new forms
> of state life, in which the initiative of individuals and groups will have a
> 'state' character even if it is not due to the 'government of the functionar-
> ies' ...[75]

Gramsci perceived the full danger of degeneration in the situation in which
the Soviet system found itself. We are here at the outset of what would later
be called 'Stalinism', where statolatry was not only *not* resisted, but would be
elevated into a whole system. Gramsci wrote this note in 1931–2. He already
had behind him – lest we forget – the clash of 1926, with the concerns he had

---

73   Gramsci 1975, p. 1020; Gramsci 1971, p. 268.
74   Q8, §185: Gramsci 1975, p. 1053; Gramsci 1971, p. 263.
75   Q8, §130: Gramsci 1975, p. 1020; Gramsci 1971, pp. 268–9.

expressed in his famous letters sent to Moscow on the internal struggle among the Bolsheviks' leadership group. 'Statolatry', understandable from a historical point of view – that is, from the conditions in which the Russian Revolution took place – was neither theorised nor accepted without also pointing to the emergence of counter-tendencies that would soon mean being able to do without it. But as we know, the Soviet Union did not follow this programme.

It has also been argued that Gramsci, in his decisive emphasis on the role of the state in twentieth-century modernity, ran the risk of himself falling – or else really did fall – into a statolatrous and/or totalitarian conception. For example, some puzzlement may result from the aforementioned statements telling us that 'police' should not be taken to mean only the organised police force,[76] or suggesting that every active citizen is a state functionary if they 'adhere to' and 'elaborate' the programme of the state.[77] From his Turi prison cell, Gramsci above all looked at two states and two types of state; they were opposite poles, but, for different reasons, both were very much in the forefront of his mind. Namely, the Fascist state that held him prisoner, and the Soviet state in whose cause he recognised himself. His reflection was, of course, interwoven with constant references to the historical experience of each of the two, such as he managed to understand it. Moreover – as we have noted – Gramsci was among the first to grasp the fact that in liberal-democratic states also there were new and significant phenomena of the 'organisation of the masses', of the regulation – even forcibly so – of their ways of living, in search of a new, deep-rooted 'conformism' as was required by the development of the new Fordist production model.

As such, even with the limits imposed by the particular historical time in which he lived and developed his reflection, Gramsci was extremely attentive to the totalitarian drift of the twentieth-century states and the dangers inherent to this, first of all for the communist movement.

The question of statolatry, at a theoretical level, takes us back to a passage to which we have already referred: does the 'identification' of political society and civil society not pose the threat of totalitarianism? If – as we have seen – these are 'one same thing';[78] if 'in effective reality civil society and the state are identical';[79] if civil society 'is also the state, or rather is the state itself'[80] –

---

76   Q2, § 150: Gramsci 1975, p. 279.

77   Q3, § 61: Gramsci 1975, p. 340.

78   Q4, § 38: Gramsci 1975, p. 460.

79   Q13, § 18: Gramsci 1975, p. 1590.

80   Q26, § 6: Gramsci 1975, p. 2302.

then how is it possible to reject the charge of 'statolatry'? These are, it is true, very strong statements – as we have said, they are mistaken, if taken literally. We know that Gramsci wrote the *Quaderni del carcere* as notes, often warning the (presumed future) reader he would need to look at them again, examining and perhaps correcting them, and of the fact that it is necessary to search for the 'rhythm of [his] thought, [which is] more important than single, isolated quotations'.[81] This would seem to be a case in point.

By this I do not mean to say that certain of Gramsci's statements are some-how extraneous to his reflections, but rather that Gramsci – through the brevity of his notes or on account of the 'ardour' of his reaction, since here he was com-batting the theories of those who promoted the ideology of the 'organic' separa-tion of state and civil society – reacted with *excessive* claims. In fact, for Gramsci this relation was a dialectical one, of mutual reference and influence. As all the quotes that we earlier cited already showed us, the state 'properly speaking' and 'civil society' are two distinct moments: they are not identical, but stand in dia-lectical relation and together constitute 'the extended state'. This was similarly made clear in his polemic against Ugo Spirito and his (very 'Gentilian') claims as to the identity of the individual and the state, which Gramsci rejected and attributed to 'the absence of a clear elaboration of the concept of the state, and of the distinction within it between civil society and political society, between dictatorship and hegemony, and so on'.[82]

Gramsci was probably also driven to over-simplification by the influence of certain Gentilian themes, coming from Gentile and his school. In several passages Gramsci passes very critical judgements on Gentile and followers of his (Ugo Spirito and others) who sought to use Gentile as the basis for a 'corporatist' hypothesis working within the terms of Fascism and in polemic against liberals and free-traders. Although Gramsci mocked their verbalism and their incompetent economics, he recognised that Gentile's conception of the state (*all cows are black at night*, since for Gentile 'everything is the state') did at least open the way to overcoming some of Croce's one-sidedness, by which even Gramsci was inspired:

> For Gentile all history is the history of the state; for Croce, instead, it is ethical-political – that is, Croce wants to maintain a distinction between civil society and political society. [For Gentile] hegemony and dictator-

---

81   Q4, §1: Gramsci 1975, p. 419; Gramsci 1996b, p. 138.
82   Q10II, §7: Gramsci 1975, p. 1245.

ship are indistinguishable, and force is just consent: it is impossible to distinguish political society from civil society: all that exists is the state.[83]

Clearly, both these positions were different from Gramsci's. We have repeatedly seen how in Gramsci there are both force and consent, not a *reductio ad unum*: moreover, nowhere in Gramsci is there the undialectical 'distinction' that we find in Croce's 'dialectic of the distinct'. Between Croce and Gentile, Gramsci stands, we could say, for a 'third way': he values Croce's ethical-political moment (hegemony), the moment of civil society, but makes it part of the ('extended') state. As such, we see the unity of, and distinction between, political and civil society.

9   Unstable Equilibria

In Q13, § 17, dating from 1932–4, Gramsci had written that 'the state is conceived of as a continuous process of formation and superseding of unstable equilibria (on the juridical plane) between the interests of the fundamental group and those of the subordinate groups'.[84]

Again in *Notebook* 15 – and here we are in 1933, dealing with a text B – we find a complex, dynamic, captivating and still very open definition: 'the state is the entire complex of practical and theoretical activities with which the ruling class not only justifies and maintains its dominance, but manages to win the active consent of those over whom it rules'.[85] Here, the accent seems to be placed more on processes than on forms. This is not to say, however, that the 'apparatuses' of which we spoke elsewhere are here any less present. In my view, *subjects, processes and forms* all have their place in Gramsci, in a constant cross-referencing of the subjective and objective that makes for a great part of the fascination (and the difficulty) of his work.

Gramsci did not recant, even indirectly, the reflections on and definitions of the state that we have seen up to this point: rather, he re-proposed them, including in many of his last *Notebooks*, as second drafts. But he put forward an interpretative model of the state that was ever more dynamic and processual. 'Unstable equilibria' is an expression that aptly conveys a sense of struggle and the important place of politics. The state is the terrain, means and process

---

83   Q6, § 10: Gramsci 1975, p. 691.
84   Gramsci 1975, p. 1578; Gramsci 1971, p. 182.
85   Q15, § 10: Gramsci 1975, p. 1765; Gramsci 1971, p. 244.

in which this struggle necessarily plays out, but the principal actors in such a struggle are what Gramsci called 'the fundamental classes'. For Gramsci, their 'becoming the state' is an indispensible moment in the struggle for hegemony (and so, too, is having a party that upholds a precise alternative 'conception of the world'). There is no place – in Gramsci – for any 'protagonism of intellectuals' or 'of civil society'; that is, there is no place for considering them in a manner uprooted from these basic co-ordinates.

CHAPTER 2

Civil Society

1   Bobbio's Interpretation

If we want to address the theme of 'civil society' in Gramsci and the relations of contiguity and difference that it has with Marx's homonymous concept as well as with some of the commonplace interpretations of it, it is perhaps useful to begin – always bearing in mind our first chapter's considerations on the parent-concept, the 'extended state' – with a look at Norberto Bobbio's particular reading of civil society in Gramsci. This was perhaps the interpretation, after Togliatti's, that most influenced the reception of the *Prison Notebooks*' author. Indeed, it was above all in the wake of the reading advanced by Bobbio in the mid-1960s that Gramsci became, for many, *the* theorist of civil society. His growing penetration into international philosophical and political-science debates has largely developed under this banner. Tellingly, in the course of the 1980s and 1990s the theoretical rediscovery of civil society often pivoted on Gramsci's thinking, indeed more or less consciously through the mediation of Bobbio's interpretation.

An examination of Bobbio's bibliography offers a clue to understanding how important studying Gramsci was for this author as he developed his classic conception of the dichotomous state/civil society pairing, and, in the first place, his notion of civil society. In the preface to his *Stato, governo, società. Per una teoria generale della politica*[1] a volume that collects together several pieces written for Einaudi's *Enciclopedia*, the same author writes that 'the civil society/state antithesis had already been illustrated to me historically by way of the works of Hegel, Marx and Gramsci'.[2] It was, however, in 1968 that he published his essay '*Sulla nozione di società civile*' ['On the notion of civil society'],[3] a first version of the Einaudi *Enciclopedia* piece later included in that volume. This came in the wake of the international Gramsci studies conference held in Cagliari on 23–27 April 1967, itself largely hegemonised – to put it in Gramscian terms – by Bobbio's intervention on 'Gramsci and the conception

---

1   Bobbio 1985.
2   Bobbio 1985, p. vii.
3   Bobbio 1968.

of civil society'.[4] So Bobbio's interest in Gramsci was of more than secondary importance, not least as regards this theme. And it was a reading of Gramsci that has rightly been judged to have 'influenced his reception more than any other'.[5]

In his Cagliari paper, Bobbio stressed the theme of Gramsci's *autonomy* with respect to the Marxist tradition. Both for Marx and Gramsci, he stated, civil society was the 'true theatre of all history' (as the *German Ideology* famously put it).[6] But whereas for Marx this was part of the structural moment (the 'base'), for Gramsci it was part of the superstructural moment; for Marx, 'the true theatre of all history' was the base, the economy, for Gramsci it was superstructure, culture, the world of ideas. Bobbio quite rightly highlights the difference between the concepts of 'civil society' in Gramsci and in Marx: while Marx identifies 'civil society' with the material base, with the economic infrastructure, 'Gramsci's civil society does not belong to the structural moment, but to that of superstructure'.[7] However, having started on this basis, Bobbio arrives at a mistaken conclusion: while in Marx civil society (the economic base) was the primary factor of socio-historical reality, Bobbio supposes that the transformation carried out by Gramsci shifts this centrality from 'base' to 'superstructure' (and, specifically, to civil society): 'In Marx, this active, positive moment is structural, in Gramsci it is superstructural'.[8]

Gramsci was for Bobbio, therefore, above all the *theorist of superstructures*, in the sense that the ethical-political moment had a foundational position in his theoretical system, without precedent in Marx and Marxism. As such, Gramsci was effectively assimilated to the liberal tradition (as Benedetto Croce had already hypothesised twenty years previously).[9] To build up this thesis, however, Bobbio had to assume and take as a given a *mechanical* reading of the base-superstructure relationship, where the determining role of one of the two terms *in the last instance* instead became a forceful, immediate determination of one level of reality by the other. No longer did there seem to be moments

---

4 Bobbio 1969. Bobbio republished this text in 1976 in a slender volume published by Feltrinelli (in their series 'Opuscoli marxisti' ['Marxist pamphlets'], edited by Pier Aldo Rovatti) and then in a collection, produced by the same publisher in 1990, of his *Saggi su Gramsci* ['Essays on Gramsci'].

5 Vacca 1999a, p. 160.

6 *MECW* Vol. 5, p. 50.

7 Bobbio 1969, p. 85.

8 Bobbio 1969, p. 86.

9 Croce 1947, p. 86.

of both unity and autonomy, and reciprocal interaction, between the different levels of reality, such as we would expect in any dialectical conception – including Gramsci's. Without doubt, Gramsci did place a premium on subjectivity, on politics, but in a different sense to how Bobbio categorises it: the *Prison Notebooks*' attempt to build a theory of politics and of ideological forms always also operated *on the basis of Marx*. Gramsci knew – and wrote – that 'the content of the political hegemony of the new social group which has founded the new type of state must be predominantly of an economic order'.[10]

Besides – and this is a closely connected question – on examining the category of civil society in Gramsci, Bobbio does not see that the concept of 'civil society' is the route through which Gramsci enriches the Marxist theory of the state with new determinations. For Gramsci, the production and reproduction of material life continue to be the primary factor of historical development. And he knew that 'Structures and superstructures form an "historical bloc". That is to say the complex, contradictory and discordant ensemble of the superstructures is the refection of the ensemble of the social relations of production'.[11] To establish this point correctly is essential to any evaluation of Gramsci's position with respect to Marxism, and, indeed, of his concept of civil society: Gramsci did not deny Marx's essential discoveries, but rather enriched, widened and completed them. He did so within the framework of a full acceptance of historical materialism, interpreted in the light of the novelties specific to the reality that he himself faced.

Obviously, this does not mean that their two concepts of civil society were not different – as Bobbio notes. So let's look first of all at how this concept was presented in the works of the 'founder of the philosophy of praxis'.

2   Civil Society in Marx

It is worth clearing the field of one preliminary problem. Wolfgang Fritz Haug, in a (most interesting) 1989 intervention,[12] tried to challenge Bobbio's reading at its roots by maintaining that it is mistaken to translate the German expression *bürgerliche Gesellschaft* with 'civil society', rather than the more literal 'bourgeois society'. As is well-known, the German expression covers both, while almost all other languages distinguish between them. Moreover, this semantic

---

10   Gramsci Q8, §185: Gramsci 1975, p. 1053; Gramsci 1971, p. 263.
11   Gramsci Q8, §182: Gramsci 1975, p. 1082; Gramsci 1971, p. 366.
12   Haug 1995.

double meaning alerts us to a historical reality – 'civil society' did not really exist prior to bourgeois society.

But what sense would it have to translate Marx in such a way as to make him say – in the famous passage from the 1859 'Preface' to *A Contribution to the Critique of Political Economy* – that both 'legal relations [and] political forms ... originate in the material conditions of life, the totality of which Hegel, following the example of English and French thinkers of the eighteenth century, embraces within the term "bourgeois society"'[13] – rather than using the term 'civil society', as in the usual translation? Doesn't this 'following the example of English and French thinkers' tell us that these words typical of Marx's exposition of his theoretical model are referring precisely to the more general – even if not historically indeterminate – use of the term, namely 'civil society' as it was conceptualised in Britain and France (to which he is explicitly referring)? The words that come immediately afterwards in Marx's text (stating 'that the anatomy of this civil society, however, has to be sought in political economy') are, without doubt, more ambivalent in this regard, since here civil society could be substituted with 'bourgeois society'. But the usual translation works on the basis of the phrase that Marx had used immediately beforehand.

Even Gramsci, as is well-known, faltered on this point: as a note in Valentino Gerratana's critical edition comments, in his prison-era works of translation Gramsci had initially rendered this text as 'embraced with the term "bourgeois society"; [but] the anatomy of bourgeois society has to be sought in political economy', before then striking out the word 'bourgeois' and replacing it with 'civil'.[14]

More generally, it hardly seems admissible to translate *'bürgerliche Gesellschaft'* as 'bourgeois society' in this type of context. By 'bourgeois society' we would understand both state relations and those outside of the state. This is, therefore, not an adequate term for rendering the counterposition that Marx makes between 'the forms of the state' and the *other* aspects of society in which these forms sink 'roots'. The term 'civil society' – derived from the Latin *societas civilis* (a medieval translation of the Greek *koinonia politiké*) – has come through a long process of historical definition to mean *societas civilis sine imperio*, as distinct from *cum imperio*: the state.[15]

Let's turn back to Marx. As is well-known, the theme of civil society and the relationship between the state and civil society interested this author even at

---

13   *MECW*, Vol. 29, p. 262.
14   Gramsci 1975, p. 2358.
15   See Portinaro 1999, p. 101.

the time of his youthful works; indeed, this question was one of their central axes. In his 1843 *Critique of Hegel's Philosophy of Right,* Marx – following the course Feuerbach took in his critique of religion, overturning the relationship between subject and predicate – stated that in Hegel the subject is the state and the predicate is civil society, whereas in reality the exact opposite is the case: the subject is to be found in civil society itself. Marx writes:

> Family and civil society are the premises of the state; they are the genu-
> inely active elements, but in speculative philosophy things are inverted.
> When the idea is made the subject, however, the real subjects, namely,
> civil society, family ... become unreal objective elements of the idea with
> a changed significance.[16]

Bobbio is right, then, when he says that the state in Marx is 'a secondary or subordinate moment with respect to civil society'.[17] This position, dating back to 1843, would remain a fixture throughout Marx's entire trajectory. I have already referred to the passage of the *German Ideology* that holds that 'civil society is the true theatre of all history'[18] and to the other, very well-known part of the 'Preface' to the *Contribution to the Critique of Political Economy* where Marx specifically addresses his youthful parting with Hegel in 1843–4.[19]

In Marx's *oeuvre,* nevertheless, we also find elements that draw us towards a more complex reading of the state/civil society dichotomy. This somewhat different reading does not repudiate his 'overturning' of Hegel. However, it does seek to problematise both the concept of civil society and the content on which this concept feeds, and his entire evaluation of the separation between state and society. (I use the term 'society' here to briefly indicate a terminological question which seems to be of some significance: the fact that the mature Marx – the Marx of great works of critique of political economy – no longer used 'civil society', abandoning this term entirely in favour of 'society' *tout court*).

As for the term 'civil society', Gerratana has already raised the point – indeed, replying to Bobbio – that it is not entirely true that the concept of civil society in Marx belongs solely to the structural moment.[20] In his 1843–4 *On the Jewish Question,* for example, Marx wrote:

---

16   *MECW,* Vol. 3, p. 8.
17   Bobbio 1969, p. 41.
18   *MECW* Vol. 5, p. 50.
19   *MECW,* Vol. 29, p. 262.
20   Gerratana 1969, p. 171.

> This secular conflict ... the relation between the political state and its
> preconditions, whether these are material elements, such as private prop-
> erty, etc., or spiritual elements, such as culture or religion ... the schism
> between the political state and civil society – these secular antitheses
> Bauer allows to persist ...[21]

The 'preconditions' of the state, what comes before the state, are thus both
material elements as well as spiritual and cultural ones. And again in the same
work, further on, Marx points to 'on the one hand, the individuals; on the
other hand, the material and spiritual elements', as the 'simple component
parts' of civil society.[22] Moreover, Gerratana adds, referring to the 1859 'Preface', 'When Marx writes that "the anatomy of this civil society ... has to be
sought in political economy", it is not clear why we must identify the part
with the whole, that is, identify the supporting structure, the "anatomy" of civil
society, with the elements which this structure supports and which are functional to it'.[23] According to this view, in Marx's 'civil society' there are both
structural and superstructural elements, even if it is the former that are central.

More generally, to me it seems that the dichotomy in question is, for Marx,
proper to modernity and to bourgeois society itself: parallel to – or even possible to superimpose on – the dichotomy between *bourgeois* and *citoyen*, which
Marx criticises in the name of a higher synthesis and recomposition. That is to
say, Marx does not limit himself to overturning the relationship between state
and society in Hegel, but rejects this counterposition, criticising the dichotomy between the public and private spheres. Moreover, he in some measure
rejects the confinement of politics within the state and of the socio-economic
within society, instead showing how both moments are shot through with
power (and politics). It is this dialectical conception that maintains his connection to Hegel. It is this same dialectic that – to an even greater degree –
marks Gramsci's own perspective.

In other words, we need to step away from a *mechanical* reading of the relation between base and superstructure. Conversely, Bobbio makes this reading
his own. Its classic reference point is the above-cited 1859 'Preface': a text that
Gramsci, however, was able to reinterpret in an anti-deterministic sense. We
need to step back – I repeat – from a conception where the determining role

---

21   *MECW*, Vol. 3, pp. 154–5.

22   *MECW*, Vol. 3, p. 166.

23   Gerratana 1969, p. 171.

in the last instance of one of the two terms (base and superstructure) is transformed into its strong and immediate determination of the other level of reality:
'the true theatre of all history'.

3   Gramsci's Dialectical Conception

If we turn to the *Quaderni del carcere*, this discourse becomes further complicated. Or better, what becomes more complicated is any attempt to read the
Notebooks in all their complexity and richness using the rigidly dichotomous
categorial tools deployed by Bobbio. As Jacques Texier objected, in response to
Bobbio, even at the 1967 Cagliari conference, Gramsci's fundamental concept
was not civil society, but rather 'the historical bloc'.[24] As Togliatti had already
noted ten years previously, picking up on an explicit statement of Gramsci's,
the distinction between the state and civil society is of a *methodological* and
not *organic* character.[25] There are many comments to this effect in the *Notebooks*: passages in which Gramsci turns his focus to the real unity of the state
and society. To pick just one of them, let's look at Q4, § 38:

> [Economism] speculates ... on the distinction between political society
> and civil society and maintains that economic activity belongs to civil
> society and that political society must not intervene in its regulation. But,
> in reality, the distinction is purely methodological and not organic; in
> concrete historical life, political society and civil society are a single entity.
> Moreover, laissez-faire liberalism, too, must be introduced by law, through
> the intervention of political power ...[26]

Here, we have less of a rigid separation between economics, politics and society.
The state and civil society are not autonomous realities, and the liberal ideology
that paints them as such is explicitly rebutted. From this emerges the concept,
central to the *Notebooks*, of the 'extended' state.

Base and superstructure, economy, politics and culture are, for Gramsci,
united and at the same time autonomous spheres of reality. And so there is little
sense in *counterposing* Marx's civil society, principally a site of economic relations, to Gramsci's civil society, principally a site of political-ideological rela-

---

24   Texier 1969, p. 154.
25   Togliatti 2001, p. 179.
26   Gramsci 1975, p. 460; Gramsci 1996b, p. 182.

tions: this would again mean losing the dialectical character of their thought. This is all the more true for Gramsci's thought: when he emphasises certain aspects of civil society, he always does so *starting out from* Marx and his teachings. Gramsci assumes these as his basis and works to *move forward from them* as he inscribes in theory the novelties that have arisen in history.

One of the central points of Gramsci's Marxism is, indeed, the fact that he does not separate out different aspects of reality (the economy, society, the state, culture) in a hypostatised manner. Bobbio, whose political theory is strongly dichotomous and proceeds by way of opposite pairs, instead poses the state/civil society dichotomy as if it were at the very centre of Gramsci's thought, thus denying what is most important in Gramsci: *non-separation*, the dialectical unity between politics and society, between the economy and the state.

Is there something new in Gramsci, as compared to Marx? In part, yes: in terms of the role of the state and of politics. To summarise this very basically: Gramsci completely overcomes (starting from Lenin's teachings) the reductive and instrumental reading of the state that makes for perhaps the very weakest point of Marx's political theory. This means that while Marx considers the dialectical relationship between the state and society on the basis of society, Gramsci considers it on the basis of the state, also in the cause of 'correcting' and 'rebalancing' a prior interpretative imbalance. Marx and Gramsci, however, do agree on one essential point: even civil society is not an idyll, the result of consent and the triumph of democracy and citizenship, such as some commonplace representations would have it, with their tendency to counterpose this reality to the reality of politics, which is seen as more or less despotic and oppressive but always in a negative light. As Joseph Buttigieg has stressed, for Gramsci the history of civil society is the history of the rule of certain social groups over others, hegemony always having been constituted by subordination, corruption, and exclusion from authority:[27] the history of class struggle.

It could also be said that the novelty of Gramsci's elaboration is most visible when it comes to the state. Across Gramsci's entire thought, his reflection on the nation-state was of central importance; and it was also linked to the question of hegemony. The nation-state, the crisis of the bourgeois state, the construction/overcoming of the proletarian state, and internationalism were problematic nodes at the heart of Gramsci's reflection, right from the *Ordine Nuovo* years. This was the moment when the 'primacy of politics' began to take its mature form, gradually subsuming his prior Sorelian influences and lead-

---

27   Buttigieg 1999.

ing him to write (manifestly also influenced by a reading of Hegel and of the Italian Hegelians) that 'the state has always been the protagonist of history'. Gramsci's reflection pivots even more on the state in his *Notebooks*: it is on this point, indeed, that Gramsci makes his most important contribution to the definition of a Marxist theory of politics, the 'integral state' as an *extension of the concept of the state*.[28] Not only does he overcome the reductive instrumentalism also characteristic of some of Marx, 'the state as an instrument in the hands of a class subject endowed with a conscious will',[29] but he redefines the state-*form*, pointing out that this also comprises the hegemonic *apparatus*.[30] And thus he also reveals the non-separateness of 'civil society' from the state, reiterated by Gramsci on countless occasions throughout the *Notebooks*: stating, for example, that 'in effective reality civil society and the state are identical';[31] or that 'civil society ... is also the state, or rather is the state itself'.[32] Not bad, from the supposed theorist of the autonomy of civil society! In Gramsci's thought, the state is configured as the site of a class hegemony, a moment of which – as I have already recalled, there is a 'continuous process of formation and superseding of unstable equilibria (on the juridical plane) between the interests of the fundamental group and those of the subordinate groups – equilibria in which the interests of the dominant group prevail, but only up to a certain point'.[33]

It is important to emphasise that if there is such a moment of theoretical innovation as compared to Marx, it is also because Gramsci's work is bristling with the new, twentieth-century elements of the relationship between economics and politics, including the extension of state intervention in the sphere of production and the organisational and rationalising effort with which politics related to and also *produced* society. Bolshevism, fascism, Keynesianism, and the welfare state were all examples – albeit with obvious differences – of this new relationship between economics and politics emerging after the First World War (as was lucidly grasped by Walter Rathenau in Germany and also debated among social-democratic and communist circles). All this made for a highly novel situation as compared to the capitalism of Marx's day. This was a novelty that Bobbio failed to grasp, due to the idealistic formalisation of his discourse: always moving from theory to theory, without the history of events

---

28   See Chapter 1.
29   Buci-Glucksmann 1980, p. 92.
30   Q6, §137: Gramsci 1975, p. 801.
31   Q13, §18: Gramsci 1975, p. 1590.
32   Q26, §6: Gramsci 1975, p. 2302.
33   Q13, §17: Gramsci 1975, p. 1584; Gramsci 1971, p. 182.

ever entering into this history of ideas, and without their real point of reference ever appearing alongside them – in this case, the societies on which Marx and Gramsci found themselves reflecting. Yet from the end of the nineteenth century, and increasingly so during the twentieth, economics – and not only that – was ever more invaded by politics. As Marco Aurelio Nogueira has written, 'politics overflowed, flooding many different spaces. The "politicisation of the social" was followed by the "socialisation of politics"'.[34] Gramsci was among those on the terrain of Marxism who best grasped this phenomenon politically and theoretically.

Would what we have said up until now take us to the point of saying that Gramsci was a theorist of 'the autonomy of the political'? I do not believe so. I cannot agree with the readings that, giving excessive emphasis to Gramsci's youthful 'Sorelianism', run the risk of making him a theorist of the 'autonomy of the social'. But the dialectical character of his thought (as well as his whole human and political biography) also guard against the opposite error. The modernity of Gramsci's thought consists in the fact that the state life and politics portrayed in his conception *include* society, even in the sense that they feed on society, as opposed to negating it or separating themselves from it. His notes on the subaltern classes, on folklore, on the struggle for hegemony, and so, too, his youthful 'spirit of cleavage', refer back to an 'extended conception of politics', as well as of the state. Whoever divides society from the state, politics from economics, or society from politics, and sets off in whatever other direction, is no longer in the groove of his thought.

For the author of the *Notebooks*, then, civil society is a moment of the 'extended state', a space in which power relations are determined, even if this is a space that enjoys a certain autonomy with respect to 'political society'; meaning, 'the coercive state'. Therefore, Gramsci does not accept a dualistic, Manichean position that counterposes 'civil society' to 'the state' (conceived as intrinsically coercive): civil society is not homogeneous, but rather is one of the principal theatres of the struggle between classes, and intense social contradictions are manifest within it. And civil society is a moment of the political-ideological superstructure, conditioned 'in the last instance' by the material base of society; and, as such, it is not at all a sphere 'beyond the market and the state', as has been claimed in recent years.

---

34   Nogueira 1997.

4   'Civil Society' in Contemporary Debates

From Bobbio onwards, many interpreters have formulated a reading of 'civil
society' in Gramsci that attributes it a strongly anti-statist stamp. An important
example of this tendency was on display in 1997, a 'Gramscian year' in the
pattern of scholarly conferences organised by the Fondazione Istituto Gramsci
upon each ten-year anniversary of the great Sardinian thinker's death. The
materials arising from the conference were published in 1999 with the title
Gramsci e il Novecento ['Gramsci and the Twentieth Century'],[35] offering a
telling panorama on how the concept of 'civil society' is today internationally –
above all, but not only, in the US and UK – mainly inflected with what we could
call a liberal-democratic slant.[36]

Today's Anglo-American studies (Robert Cox, Jean L. Cohen, Stephen Gill
and Anne Showstack Sassoon were present in Cagliari)[37] principally draw on
Gramsci's concepts of 'international hegemony' and 'civil society'. These are
inserted into a reading of the prevalent political framework that takes as a given
the tendency towards the weakening of the political-state moment in the face
of economic globalisation. These two phenomena (which are real, although
often highly exaggerated)[38] are accepted as positive, as a new opportunity
for liberation. And the reflection in the *Notebooks* is also subsumed into this
framework. This risks two errors. On the theoretical level, it runs the risk of a
mistaken reading of Gramsci, undervaluing his concept of the extended state.
And on the political level, there is the risk of too-quickly renouncing the very
political and state tools that thus far have proven the only instruments that it
is possible to deploy as an alternative to the logic of the market.[39]

In Cagliari, it was Robert Cox's intervention that most explicitly connected
the current-day debate to Gramsci's elaboration. It was unsurprising that he
drew on Bobbio's reading and compared Gramsci with Tocqueville. Cox admit-

---

35   Vacca (ed.) 1999b.

36   The contribution in Vacca (ed.) 1999b by Carlos Nelson Coutinho (who has an utterly
      different theoretical-political perspective) is devoted to the philosophical origins of the
      concept of civil society. See Coutinho 1999.

37   See Cox 1999 and Showstack Sassoon 1999 for the Anglophone bibliography on this topic.
      Also particularly worth highlighting is *Gramsci, Historical Materialism and International
      Relations* – Gill (ed.) 1993 – whose contributors include Cox and Gill.

38   See Chapter 3.

39   See Nogueira 2000. Though specifically referring to the Brazilian situation, the essay in
      question is rich in more general theoretical and political insights.

ted, in fact, that the current reduction of the role of the state may be a defeat for the oppressed classes, but from this he deduced a new opportunity. Namely, to relaunch the subaltern layers' 'complex of autonomous collective activities'.[40] These, according to him, constitute civil society: NGOs, volunteering and interstitial forms autonomous of the market should be compared to Gramsci's civil society, because in the *Notebooks* these are 'the ambit within which cultural changes take place'[41] – these cultural changes being understood as alterations of subjectivity. On this basis, the author hopes for a new participatory democracy and a 'global civil society', the basis for an alternative world order. Though recognising – for example – that NGOs are in reality ever more bankrolled by state subsidies (hence a function of public spending) and thus rendered ever more 'conformist', the author sees the possibility of a global alternative to capitalism in this heterogeneous voluntary and non-economic mix. Here what we have is a disarticulation of Gramsci's own theoretical approach (pivoted on the dialectical unity of state and society) and an anti-institutional conception of politics that we could define as 'Sorelian'. While Gramsci (in the first place, the Gramsci of the *Notebooks*) profoundly redefined the Marxist conception of the state, he never ceased to consider the political-state moment as a lever for the redistribution of power and resources. The extended state, of which civil society is part, therefore does not escape class contradictions, but rather is the very site in which they play out.

Jean L. Cohen also promotes the redefinition of civil society as the *whole set* of voluntary associations.[42] For this author, it is easy to situate Gramsci in such a cultural climate, since to her it seems that the Sardinian thinker insisted above all on the autonomy of society *from the state*. Again, here, we lose the dialectical vision with which Gramsci held together state and society. The author is explicit about her points of reference: her sympathies lie with a certain kind of sociology (Touraine, Melucci) that has 'exalted' pre-political or pre-state voluntary activity. An interesting and very well-known perspective; but what's important for our discourse, here, is that such an outlook is improperly extended to Gramsci, who is quite mistakenly converted into an author of reference or 'elder statesman' for the tendency to counterpose civil society to the state.

Similarly, albeit with more radical political tones, Stephen Gill entrusts *intellectuals* the task of bringing about an alternative collective *consciousness*.[43] No

---

40   Cox 1999, p. 242.
41   Cox 1999, p. 240.
42   Cohen 1999.
43   Gill 1999.

place for classes and parties – a fixture in the *Notebooks*' theoretical perspective – in this discourse.

Some Italian scholars have also shifted in a direction that converges with these authors in certain aspects. In his intervention at the conference 'Il giovane Gramsci e la Torino d'inizio secolo' ['The Young Gramsci and Early-Twentieth-Century Turin'], Giuseppe Vacca spoke of 'a new season of Gramsci studies' and of 'scholars contributing to the renewal of the interpretations of Gramsci's thought', a renewal characterised by 'the elaboration of new interpretations of the *Quaderni del carcere*'.[44] On the basis of 'Americanism and Fordism' and the thesis of a sharp separation between Gramsci's prison-era reflection and his previous elaborations, Vacca reads Gramsci as a theorist of globalisation, of the crisis of the nation-state, and of the formation of an 'international civil society'.[45] 'The nation', Vacca writes, interpreting Gramsci, 'can no longer be limited within the horizon of state life', and even politics is diverging from the state. The anchor of Vacca's discourse is Gramsci-as-theorist of 'a new conception of politics', which seems to situate him in a horizon of thought far from that of the communist tradition.

To return to the Cagliari conference, Marcello Montanari was there in agreement with Vacca's framework. He held that Gramsci was above all the theorist of the crisis of the state, having grasped 'the exhaustion of the progressive role historically played by nation-states', even to the point of reaching the conclusion that 'the modern idea of democracy transcends the nation-state form'.[46] The end of the national state, a post-national democratic horizon, the centrality of international civil society, even the recognition of the market – *in Gramsci* – such are the cornerstones of this interpretation, which is thematised in a more structured manner in the introduction to *Pensare la democrazia* ['Thinking Democracy'], an anthology of Gramsci's writings that Montanari edited for the publisher Einaudi.

To these theses we could also add the position Mario Telò expressed in Cagliari, stating that 'doubt as to the possibility of the state serving as a lever of modernisation runs throughout Gramsci's prison notes, but it seems that he ultimately leaned towards critical acceptance [of this possibility]'.[47] While this author warns against any undervaluation of the role of political institutions in Gramsci's prison reflection or disregarding the distance that separated

---

44   Vacca 1998, p. 239.
45   Vacca 1998, pp. 244–5.
46   Montanari 1999, pp. 25, 35.
47   Telò 1999, p. 55.

the mature Gramsci from Sorel, he ends up claiming that the category 'extended state' is of no lasting strategic value. According to Telò, though Gramsci laid down his theoretical roots in the pan-statist thought of the 1930s, he managed to transcend this by having his sights on the long term: thus he could ultimately see only the liberal state as the 'institutional form adequate to the type of economic-political modernisation and internationalisation coming into view'.[48]

The considerations advanced by Anne Showstack Sassoon seem to have been an 'outpost' of the 'renewal of the interpretations of Gramsci's thought' here in question. On the one hand, this author is very attentive in reconstructing accurately the positions of the Sardinian thinker and his reflection on the expansion of the state sphere from the First World War onwards. And she seeks to bring into focus the changes that have taken place since. For example, according to Showstack Sassoon, volunteering, non-profits, NGOs and the 'third sector' constitute 'the new weft of relations that link the state to the individual'. That is, they are not 'civil society' liberated by the retreat of the state, but rather part of the extended state, albeit a redefined one. They are a means of reclassifying the tasks and roles of welfare in supporting the capitalist market, though this latter will disappoint a great number of needs if it is left to its own devices.

Other interventions at Cagliari appeared to be marked by a partially or entirely different tone. For the American Benedetto Fontana, for example, 'the current usage of the term "civil society" in political-cultural debate, whether in the Gramscian, Hegelian or liberal sense, is nothing but the reflection of the gradual embourgeoisement of the world, of globalisation and of the spread of economic forces within the markets, as well as the proliferation of private bodies and associations ever more concentrated upon single interests'.[49] Remo Bodei recalled the new phenomena of the 1920s–30s, which had a sharp observer in the person of Gramsci: 'The state took on demands and tasks that had previously been outside of its purview'.[50] He added: 'Today a sort of "poor man's Popperism" is spreading, one that thinks it can defend and salvage the heritage of Gramsci by forcing him into the guise of a liberal'.[51] Roberto Racinaro, for his part, recalled that the civil society that Gramsci deduced from Hegel 'no longer designated the sphere of economic relations *as separate* from that of political

---

48   Telò 1999, p. 68.
49   Fontana 1999, p. 290.
50   Bodei 1999, p. 185.
51   Ibid.

relations. It designated a situation that did *not* correspond to the *distinctions* of the liberal state'.[52] What Gramsci grasped with his category of the extended state was the process of politics spreading.

Racinaro also made explicit reference to the conference that the Istituto Gramsci had staged in Florence in December 1977. The Cagliari conference of 1997 – some of whose significant aspects we have recalled here – seemed poles apart from this event, almost as if connecting up again with the 1967 Cagliari conference and Bobbio's famous intervention on 'Gramsci and Civil Society'. The intention, here, is not to stick some label on all the contributors to either one of these assemblies, but only to bring to light their most characteristic themes. In 1977 the question of 'the working class becoming the state' (the Communist Party in search of a 'third way') had led to a reading of the *Notebooks* in some aspects exaggeratedly crushed into the framework of politics, but at least it was precise in clarifying fundamental categories like the extended state and passive revolution. In 1997, in a different socio-political and cultural climate, it was no chance thing that civil society made a major comeback – from Cagliari to Cagliari, that is.

5   A New Marxist Theory of the State

Certainly, hegemony is in the last analysis defined on the terrain of the relations of force, of actual political struggle, whether in 'grand' or 'small' politics. However, as Gramsci knew well when he insisted on the 'solidity of popular beliefs', one must not underestimate the role of the battle of ideas in defining the relations of force. In this sense, redeeming the full meaning of Gramsci's concept of 'civil society' – in order to counterpose it to 'apolitical' versions of this term – is no abstract question.

In fact, in Gramsci's view, as we have seen, 'civil society' is a privileged arena of the struggle between classes, a sphere of social being where there is an intense struggle for hegemony; and for precisely that reason, it is not the 'other' of the state, but rather – together with 'political society' – the 'coercive state' – one of its indispensible constitutive moments. For Gramsci, not everything that makes up part of civil society is 'good' (after all, doesn't the 'law of the jungle' prevail, here?) and nor is everything that comes from the state 'bad' (since it can express universal needs that originate in the struggle of the subaltern classes, it can serve as a dam against the excesses of 'big powers', and it can be

52   Racinaro 1999, p. 378.

an instrument for the redistribution of resources in the name of justice). From the viewpoint of the subaltern classes, which were always Gramsci's reference point, only a concrete historical analysis of the relations of force present at any given moment can define the function and positive or negative potential of either civil society or the state.

Without doubt, in order to drive forward this redemption of Gramsci's concept of 'civil society', accurately understood, we need not only the theoretical acumen and philological rigour to reconstruct the rich and complex categorial weft elaborated in the *Notebooks*, but also to investigate the work of his principal interlocutors. And, above all, to remember that Gramsci was Gramsci precisely because he dialectically surpassed the concepts of his 'creators' and constructed a most original notion of 'civil society': the scaffolding of a new Marxist theory of the state. The correct definition of the theoretical status of 'civil society' and the 'state' is one of the most important themes of the ideological-political debate of our time.

CHAPTER 3

State, Nation, Mundialisation

1   **Mundialisation and Globalisation**

The debate surrounding 'globalisation' has been central to the cultural and political panorama of the last few years. It is widely felt that we are living in the 'age of globalisation'. For some, given this new discursive order, it is necessary to profoundly rethink strategies and philosophies. The question that we must try to answer, therefore, is the following one: how can Gramsci's thought be situated in relation to the socio-economic phenomena that are today most debated – globalisation and post-Fordism first among them?

First off, what do we mean by 'globalisation'? What definition, even if a very general one, can we offer, before we attempt to inflect it in relation to Gramsci's thought? It seems to me that we can define 'globalisation' as a hypothesis on the contemporary modality of capitalism – or of modernity – according to which the relation between economics and space, politics and territory has radically changed. From this, another question immediately emerges: is globalisation a series of quantitative changes (which do not change the substance of the capitalist model we have in front of us, or the substance of its laws of functioning) or is it a qualitative leap, comparable to the passage from *laissez-faire* to organised (Fordist and Keynesian) capitalism? Some students, above all Anglophone ones, have insisted on the 'rupture', the element of discontinuity. Others, instead, reject the term globalisation, preferring to speak of 'mundialisation'. This slight difference results from the hypothesis that since industrialised economies were already integrated and internationalised in the nineteenth and twentieth centuries, the acceleration of trade that can today be observed at various levels (financial, productive and consumer goods) is taking place above all within macro-regional spheres and not homogeneously at a global scale. Scholars such as Étienne Balibar and Serge Latouche often repeat that capitalism has always been global. Others recall how even Marx always observed capital as a global phenomenon. We could add what Gramsci himself wrote in the notebooks:

> The whole economic activity of a country can only be judged in relation to the international market, it 'exists' and is to be evaluated insofar as it is inserted into an international unity ... there is no purely national 'balance

sheet' of the economy, neither taken as a whole nor for any one particular activity.[1]

However, we should avoid the trap of an exaggerated sense of continuity. We need to deploy analytical tools that allow us to read the changes with which we are faced. This is what, for example, the two English authors Hirst and Thompson have sought to do, elaborating two different models relating to an *international* and to a *global* economy respectively.[2] The protagonist of this latter model is a new actor, the transnational enterprise, characterised by no longer having any main national base (as a multinational would do), and operating on global markets by way of global operations. Hirst and Thompson do not, then, refuse to note and to emphasise the great changes that have taken place in the world economy in recent decades, but they do maintain that a world economy characterised by a high and rising level of trade and international investment is not necessarily a *globalised* economy. In their work, the point of contrast between the partisans of the term 'mundialisation' and those who choose 'globalisation' is clearly apparent. The stakes of this semantic difference is the national state. While many[3] claim that, faced with processes of socio-economic globalisation, the function of the national state is becoming superfluous, according to these authors multinational corporations 'still rely on their "home base" as the centre for their economic activities, despite all the speculation about globalization'.[4] In reality, there seem to be a whole series of counter-indicators that raise doubts as to whether capitalism has indeed been transformed in a *globalising* sense. Following Hirst and Thompson, we can say that the state and states continue to play a front-rank role in the current inter-national economy, by way of the indispensible legal framework that they provide. I have elsewhere made the argument that what we today face, therefore, is a process of *redefinition* and *evolution* of the state,[5] and not its 'disappearance', as some have even tried to claim. The terms of social reproduction have changed, but the image – advanced by some of the most ardent upholders of the idea of globalisation – of the mass of people defining themselves individually and collectively with reference to some transnational corporation, rather than to a nationality and a state, seems for now to be nothing more than

---

1   Q9, § 32: Gramsci 1975, p. 1115.
2   See Hirst and Thompson 1996.
3   See Ohmae 1990 and 1995; Horsman and Marshall 1994; and Hardt and Negri 2000.
4   Hirst and Thompson 1996, p. 84.
5   I will take the liberty of referring the reader to two of my texts: 'Fine o Metamorfosi dello Stato-nazione?' and 'Lo Stato non è morto' (Liguori 2002a and 2002b).

science fiction. This is not to ignore the processes of internationalisation that today exist and the growing strength of supranational powers, but rather to try to make out to what extent the *myth of globalisation* corresponds to real processes and how much of it is an ideological excess corresponding to the interests and axioms of neoliberal policies.

According to the US economist Susan George – who, not by chance, prefers the term 'mundialisation' – this is also a function of 'ideological lobbying': 'Each year, hundreds of millions of dollars are invested in order to produce and spread neoliberal ideology. Thousands of intellectuals and dozens of think tanks, periodicals, newspapers, radio and TV programmes and so on receive enormous sums of private money in order to develop the ideological infrastructure that underpins mundialisation. It is above all thanks to them that "There Is No Alternative" has triumphed'.[6] She adds, 'Often we speak of "deregulation"; for sure, this does exist, but it applies only to the rules established by nation-states, in particular to those designed to protect citizens and the environment and set limits to the operations of the market. In reality, though, the new actors need rules to govern mundialisation. They simply seek to establish ones more advantageous to themselves'.[7]

I do not believe that the organised voluntary activity of a certain social subject can alone explain the somersault in hegemony performed by the international bourgeoisie since the 1970s, the so-called 'triumph of neoliberalism'. Technological developments and related changes in class composition have made a 'bloc' together with cultural changes and subjective actions such as those mentioned above. George's observations do, however, introduce a theme that is decisive for explaining the current triumph of the *myth* of globalisation – this being situated entirely within the terms of the neoliberal revolution, which has at its ideological core the end of ideologies, the return to *laissez-faire*, and the demand that the state be abruptly brought down to size.

Globalisation is, then, perhaps a 'mundialisation' *enriched* by an ideological surfeit, proper to neoliberalism. All this is connected to a contiguous idea of the 'triumph of civil society', or what some call 'international civil society'.[8] And this gives us the opportunity directly to interpellate Gramsci. Now, though, faced with the radical reduction of the state by the ideology of globalisation, we surely find ourselves on a horizon of political thought rather different from that of the *Notebooks*.

---

6   George 1998, p. 18.

7   Ibid.

8   See Chapter 2.

2   Gramsci and Taylorism

Beyond the processes of globalisation, the crisis of the Fordist model has – according to some – heavily reduced the importance of the state and of national states. This is said to have been to the advantage of civil society and the economic forces – or, in any case, pre- or non-state forces – that operate within it, and which seem to have taken on fresh centrality, above all since the collapse of 'actually-existing socialism' and the various Keynesian-type models of welfare. Various different political hypotheses can take their lead from this assumption, such as those contained in *La sinistra sociale* by Marco Revelli, or Bruno Trentin's *La città del lavoro*.[9] On the one hand, Revelli considers finished any possibility of founding the processes of social, individual and collective identity on labour; on the contrary, Trentin still identifies labour as standing at the centre of the processes of identity and political strategy, albeit within a markedly post-Fordist panorama. As well as noting this fundamental divergence, it is, however, also possible to see some ways in which the two converge: both authors agree on the fact that the Left must radically rethink itself, starting from the critique-overcoming of what has been its attitude towards politics and the state up until now. What interests me in particular, here, is to follow the thread of Trentin's reasoning, because it is in large part grounded on the author's theoretical engagement with Antonio Gramsci. Although Trentin offers a sympathetic reading of various authors who were historically in the minority in the twentieth-century socialist tradition, from Luxemburg and Korsch to Bauer and Weil – all having in common a marked anti-state and anti-institutional instinct – he engages most deeply and broadly with the author of the *Notebooks*, by way of a complex reading rich in both light and shadow.

Trentin uses Gramsci, in this book, in two ways – one more obvious, the other less so. In the first case, I am referring to the second part of his book entitled 'Gramsci e la sinistra europea di fronte al "fordismo" nel primo dopoguerra' ['Gramsci and the European Left faced with post-WWI "Fordism"']. The other concerns a more discrete yet equally important use of Gramsci – and perhaps this is even more important to the overall discourse of his book – that links Gramsci to the concept of civil society, which is central throughout the whole volume. The Gramsci that Trentin sets his target on in the second part of his book is the Gramsci of both *L'Ordine Nuovo* and 'Americanism and Fordism', the Gramsci – the author stresses – who apparently 'assumed as rational, and thus

---

9   Revelli 1997; Trentin 1997.

immutable, the historical forms of organisation and subordination of human labour'.[10] Though Trentin recognises that Gramsci was less 'productivist' than Lenin, he nonetheless claims that he was caught by a fascination for the bourgeois mode of production. That is, he claims that Gramsci remained wholly within the culture of the Third International (and not only that) in which the production process and the scientific organisation of labour were ferried across from capitalism to socialism without being subjected to almost any critique. This is the Gramsci of *L'Ordine Nuovo*, who exhorted the workers to substitute themselves for the bosses, but without *overturning* the factory – before and together with society and the state.

Is Trentin's critique of Gramsci, here, a fair one? To me, it seems, it is not without foundation: even in *L'Ordine Nuovo* there appeared the theme (widely prevalent in the communist culture of the time) of the priority and need to preserve and increase labour *discipline* and production *after the revolution*, with the workers' weak productivity being *blamed* only on the presence of capitalists. From this followed the claim that once the capitalist was eliminated, so, too, would this problem be resolved:

> The world needs a multiplied production, intense and feverish labour; the workers and peasants will rediscover their capacity and will to work only when the person of the capitalist is eliminated from industry, when the producer has won his economic autonomy in the factories and fields and his political autonomy in the state of councils of workers' and peasants' delegates.[11]

Moreover, it fostered the illusion (of Leninist derivation) of the possibility of a non-Taylorist use of Taylorism,[12] of a 'form of "Americanism" accepted by the working masses', as Gramsci himself described in the *Notebooks* in his discussion of *L'Ordine Nuovo*.[13] In any case, the thesis put forward by Trentin is not a new one.[14] And even a researcher who did investigate – with interesting

---

10   Trentin 1997, p. 172.

11   Gramsci, 'Vita politica internazionale [IV]', *L'Ordine Nuovo*, 7 June 1919, now reproduced in Gramsci 1987, p. 68.

12   See the articles by Carlo Petri, 'Il sistema Taylor e i Consigli dei produttori' ['The Taylor system and producers' councils'], 25 October, 1 November, 8 November, 15 November and 22 November 1919.

13   Q22, § 2: Gramsci 1975, p. 2146.

14   See, for example, Asor Rosa 1973; Revelli (ed.) 1998.

results – the specific theme of Gramsci's attitude toward the organisation of production, from the *biennio rosso* to the *Notebooks*, and in general (rightly) upholding the thesis that Gramsci cannot be reduced to the industrial-productivist culture of the Third International, had to recognise that 'there is not, in Gramsci, any intensive reflection on the peculiar contradictions connected to Taylorism'.[15]

That said, it should also be remembered that the factory that Gramsci had in front of him was still in part a pre-Fordist one: Fordism and Taylorism were fully consolidated in Italy only much later, and certainly it is no chance thing that a new sensibility in the workers' movement towards the organisation of labour would emerge only with the 'second *biennio rosso*' of 1968–9.[16] But above all it should be remembered that the councilism particular to *L'Ordine Nuovo* – original with respect to the Soviet experience, in its tendency to strongly connect the state and the factory, politics and the site/subject of production – already in itself represented an objective obstacle to, and implicit insubordination against, the 'scientific organisation of labour'. It should be remembered how Gramsci saw – and in some measure, experienced – the *ensemble* of *producers*, workers and technicians, as a *community*, a collective body, which also has implications in the sense of giving new appreciation to the worker-subject, not considering it only in the purely *quantitative* aspect, which Trentin rightly stigmatises.[17] And apart from other possible considerations on Gramsci's 'Taylorism', there is another aspect of the *Ordine Nuovo* years that Trentin – from his point of view – could have made more of: namely, Gramsci's theoretical construction of a model of the state not founded on the citizen, but rather on the producer, thus attempting a recomposition of *citoyen* and *bourgeois*.[18] After all, Gramsci fully embraced Marx's well-known discourse in *On the Jewish Question* denouncing the abstraction of the category 'citizen'. This is a theme that also speaks to our theoretical-political present, as we lament the fact that the horizon of citizenship stops short at the factory gates. But to me it seems that this is a threshold it cannot cross, because it is a category constitutively alien to any discourse of classes and the division of society into classes, which is most demonstrably on display precisely in the factory. Unless,

---

15   Dubla 1986, p. 175.

16   On this point, I refer the reader to Trentin 1999.

17   For a reading opposite to Trentin's (and those of Asor Rosa and Revelli) see Burgio 2002, pp. 211 et sqq., and Baratta 2004.

18   See, for example, Gramsci's 'Cronache dell'"Ordine Nuovo" [III]', in *L'Ordine Nuovo*, 7 June 1919, now reproduced in Gramsci 1987, p. 54.

that is, the term 'rights' (always correlated, in a contradictory manner, to the theme of 'citizenship')[19] is used to mean what the working class has really managed to extract for itself on the terrain of class struggle. As history teaches us, when the relations of force change, presumed 'rights' fall apart. In reality, rights are a weak and far from irresistible limit on private powers.

3   The Myth of Civil Society

Trentin's second, equally important use of Gramsci – indeed, perhaps even more important to the overall discourse of his book – links Gramsci to the concept of civil society. If, on the one hand, Trentin criticises Gramsci on themes concerning the factory and the organisation of work, on the other hand it seems that he substantially wants to accept his teachings as regards the primacy of 'civil society'. However, it is apparent that what Trentin believes to be Gramsci's theses on civil society are in fact the interpretation that Norberto Bobbio made of Gramsci's concept in his famous intervention at the 1967 Cagliari conference, which we already studied in Chapter 2.[20] Why does Bobbio's reading have a central role in Trentin's theoretical construction? It is, in my view, one of the many signs of the fact that the interpretative categories of socialist thought after 1989 have become ever more contiguous with the central categories of liberal thought and subject to its hegemony. This is based on a heavy undervaluation of the role of politics, to the advantage of 'civil society', within the terms of an (obviously unconscious) renewed process of 'passive revolution'.[21]

Evidently, the collapse of actually-existing socialism and the defeats also suffered by the welfare state cannot but produce questions, critiques and self-critique. And it remains true that the history of the twentieth-century Soviet experience also encourages reflection as to the validity of certain points of liberal theory concerning the limits of power. Trentin's book is a considered series of charges against a certain type of Marxism that is excessively statist and centred on politics. Yet there remains the fact that the 'return to civil society' was the slogan of choice for 1980s neoliberalism: enough with the state –

---

19   The contradiction results from the fact that rights are supposed to be universal, while the historically-determined character of citizenship is apparent – and even more so in recent years.

20   See pp. 26–8.

21   On the concept of passive revolution, I refer the reader to Voza 2004.

first of all, the welfare state, obviously – and leave society to its own devices. Enough politics, enough professional politicians, and let the representatives of civil society do as they will.

Naturally, there are two versions of this 'return to society', both rotating around the critique of the political and both strengthened by the *leitmotiv* of globalisation. One is a *right-wing* version, placing the 'animal spirits of capitalism' at the centre of its universe. And then there is the *left-wing* version, which wants to guarantee rights and widen citizenship, but which – at the very moment that it poses these categories as being central – embraces a vision proper to *liberalism*. That is to say, such a theoretical horizon has at its basis an inevitably liberal anthropological conception of the subject: the individual as *prius*, prior to her being in society, and a bearer of rights as such. However, Marx (following Hegel), Marxism and Gramsci had a quite different conception of the individual, one that was fundamentally relational, one that does not deny the individual but rather considers them *fundamentally* and *necessarily* existing in relation with others, and thus part of socio-cultural contexts on which that individual in large measure depends and is partly affected by.[22]

It is no chance thing, then, that in the wake of Bobbio, Trentin would read in Gramsci a contradiction between the centrality of the social and the legitimising role of the state. He underestimates the significance of the fact that Gramsci lay great political-cognitive importance on social subjects and the forms in which they are opposed and inter-related (questions of ideology – common sense and hegemony), and *at the same time* placed the state at the centre of his reflection. This combination of hegemony and the state was certainly no coincidence.

4   State and Nation

Reflection on the nation-state was central to Gramsci's entire thought, and intrinsically linked to the question of hegemony. The nation-state, the crisis of the bourgeois state, the construction/overcoming of the proletarian state, and internationalism were problematic nodes that defined the heart of Gramsci's reflection from the *Ordine Nuovo* years onward, when the 'primacy of politics' began to take its mature form, gradually subsuming the elements of his previous 'Sorelianism'. 'The state has always been the protagonist of history', Gramsci

---

22   See Finelli 1992 and Chapters 6 and 7 of this book.

wrote in 1919.[23] He shared in the Marxist – and Karl Marx's – idea of the gradual overcoming of the state by the 'proletarian international', but seems already to have gone beyond any purely instrumental idea of the state, and stressed that

> the socialist and proletarian movement is against the state, because it is against capitalist national states, because it is against national economies, which have their life-spring and take their form from the national state. But if in the communist international *national states were suppressed, this would not mean suppressing the state*, understood as the concrete 'form' of human society. Society as such is a mere abstraction.[24]

The communists, therefore, are not against the state. And Gramsci strongly opposed anarchist and anarcho-syndicalist tendencies[25] – accused of continuing the liberal tradition – and demonstrated how 'the whole liberal tradition [is] against the state'.[26] The communists, instead, Gramsci writes on the same page – riding the wave of the 'soviet' experience – hold that it is necessary that there be a transition to a 'national and class state' different from the bourgeois state above all because it would be based on participation.[27] The state form, then, seems to be impossible to overcome so long as the commodity form exists: 'the national state is an organ of competition: it will disappear when competition is eliminated and a new economic custom is brought about by way of the concrete experiences of socialist states'.[28]

Gramsci's reflection in the *Notebooks* hinged even more on the state: indeed, it was on this point that Gramsci made his most important contribution to defining a Marxist theory of politics, the 'extension of the concept of the state' or the 'integral state', which we focused on in Chapter 1. Not only did he overcome a reductive instrumentalism also apparent in Lenin, namely 'the state as an instrument in the hands of a class subject endowed with a conscious

---

23   Gramsci, 'La conquista dello Stato,' *L'Ordine Nuovo*, 12 July 1919.

24   Gramsci, 'Lo Stato e il socialismo', *L'Ordine Nuovo*, 28 June 1919, reproduced in Gramsci 1987, p. 128 (my italics).

25   Gramsci, 'Lo Stato e il socialismo', *L'Ordine Nuovo*, 28 June 1919, reproduced in Gramsci 1987, p. 116.

26   Gramsci, 'Lo Stato e il socialismo', *L'Ordine Nuovo*, 28 June 1919, reproduced in Gramsci 1987, p. 117.

27   See, on this, Suppa 1979, pp. 258–60.

28   Gramsci, 'Lo Stato e il socialismo', *L'Ordine Nuovo*, 28 June 1919, reproduced in Gramsci 1987, p. 117.

will',[29] but he gave a new definition of the state-*form*, indicating that this also comprises the hegemonic *apparatus*. It was also by this route (and not only in relation to 'national economies') that Gramsci definitively uncovered the non-separateness of 'civil society' from the state, which he reiterated on countless occasions throughout the *Notebooks*.

Certainly, Gramsci was acutely aware of the supranational dimensions of the problems that he addressed. The national/international relationship is one of the central themes of his thought. Every national history is read through its relationship of oneness and difference with the supranational context in which it is situated, starting with Italy's *Risorgimento*, the birth of the Italian national state. Could we say, then, that what was at the centre of Gramsci's reflection in the *Notebooks* was not the question of the state, but rather that of its crisis and overcoming – and thus that Gramsci proposed a 'new theory of politics untying it from its identification with the state'?[30] It seems to me that when in the *Notebooks* Gramsci speaks of 'the crisis of the state as a whole', he is really speaking of the 'crisis of hegemony of the ruling class' given the 'great masses" exit from passivity.[31] To my eyes, that is, in Gramsci there is always an overall theoretical-political framework pivoting on the division of society into classes and on the class struggle. This is far, then, from any possibility of reformulating his problematic field 'based not on antagonisms without solution or a totalitarian perspective, but on the principle of interdependence'[32] and a 'unitary and sympathetic vision of the human race'.[33] If we attempt – faced with mundialisation, or globalisation – a non-state refoundation of the political, refusing to seek any horizon other than that dominated by the commodity form[34] and the division of society of classes, then the perspective we are setting out is one quite different from that indicated in the *Notebooks*. It is a possible political choice, and can be debated like any other – but it is not present in Gramsci, because in his thinking the state is essential precisely as a site of class hegemony, a moment in which there is 'a continuous process of formation and superseding of unstable equilibria (on the juridical plane) between the interests of the fundamental

29   Buci-Glucksmann 1980, p. 92.

30   Vacca 1994, p. 20. These theses are also developed by Montanari 1997.

31   Q13, § 23: Gramsci 1975, p. 1603.

32   Vacca 1994, p. 20.

33   Vacca 1994, p. 171.

34   According to Montanari 1997 (p. xi), Gramsci managed in prison to pose himself the question of 'governing the modes of penetration and the spread of the commodity-form into ever new sectors and territories, and certainly not that of its overcoming-elimination'.

group and those of the subordinate groups-equilibria in which the interests of the dominant group prevail, but only up to a certain point'.[35]

As far as I can see, the fact that the *Notebooks'* reflections on the crisis of the nation-state do not amount to advancing a hypothesis of the elimination of the state, its role and its functions, is also demonstrated by Gramsci's specific treatment of the theme of nations and 'the national'. In note 68 of *Notebook* 14 (a text B, from 1932–5), Gramsci looks into the national-international connection and how 'the international situation must be considered in its national aspect'. In a passage taking its cue from some of Stalin's statements and explicitly addressing the theoretical relationship between Marx and Lenin, he comments:

> In reality, the internal relations of any nation are the result of a combination which is 'original' and (in a certain sense) unique: these relations must be understood and conceived in their originality and uniqueness if one wishes to dominate them and direct them. To be sure, the line of development is towards internationalism, but the point of departure is 'national' – and it is from this point of departure that one must begin. Yet the perspective is international and cannot be otherwise. Consequently, it is necessary to study accurately the combination of national forces which the international class [the proletariat] will have to lead and develop, in accordance with the international perspective and directives [i.e. those of the Comintern].[36]

The twisting and turning of Gramsci's sentences are ample demonstration that the author wanted to define a dynamic situation. Internationalism was fixed as the necessary future objective, but for now the national moment could not be disregarded – since, for Gramsci, *hegemony is possible only in this sphere.* Indeed, further on our author continues:

> It is in the concept of hegemony that those exigencies which are national in character are knotted together ... A class that is international in character has – in as much as it guides social strata which are narrowly national (intellectuals), and indeed frequently even less than national: particularistic and municipalistic (the peasants) – to 'nationalise' itself in a certain sense.[37]

---

35   Q13, § 17: Gramsci 1975, p. 1584; Gramsci 1971, p. 182.

36   Q14, § 68: Gramsci 1975, p. 1729; Gramsci 1971, p. 240.

37   Gramsci 1975, p. 1729; Gramsci 1971, p. 241.

Ultimately, 'non-national concepts (i.e. ones that cannot be referred to each individual country)' are 'erroneous', Gramsci concludes.[38] Indeed, within the terms of Gramsci's struggle against 'cosmopolitanism' – that is, the undervaluation of the importance of belonging to a national community[39] – we can say that the nation appears to him as a difficult-to-avoid passage in the long march towards the 'reunification of the human race'. I do not believe that we today face the elimination of the question of nationality, but rather its redefinition in a multi-ethnic, multicultural key. Just as I do not think that today's processes tending toward the constitution of a new multi-national European state will wipe away the question of nationality: on the contrary, they complicate and intensify it. All this does, of course, entail great innovations, for analysis and politics, never addressed by Gramsci: but it does not tear up his general theoretical framework. In any case, today's positions and problems cannot simply be placed on his shoulders, through a facile 'bringing Gramsci up to date' that ends up denaturing his thought.

5   Against 'Passive Revolution'

It seems, ultimately, that in reflection concerning globalisation there is often the risk of heavily under-valuing the role of politics and the state, to the advantage of the political-interpretative category of 'civil society' (in some cases, 'international civil society'). There is the risk that even the emphasis today placed on globalisation ends up endorsing a definitive albeit bogus 'end of politics'.

Certainly, there is politics and there is politics – there is the state and there is the state. Gramsci himself – we have seen – did not fail to stress repeatedly the dangers of 'statolatry'.[40] Obviously there is no need to deny or ignore the errors and the horrors of the twentieth century. Rather, we need to seek a politics and a state order that are linked to the social as much as possible. But this search must always have the same dialectical perspective that drove Gramsci to think and write – at the very moment when he was promoting and theorising the councils – that it was also necessary to 'conquer the state', that is, create a new type of state. It is true that today this expression 'conquest of the state'

---

38   Gramsci 1975, p. 1730; Gramsci 1971, p. 241.

39   See Raimondi 1998, pp. 166 et sqq. On 'the national' in Gramsci more generally, see Durante 2003.

40   See Chapter 1.

sounds deeply alien. But it was first of all the Gramsci of the *Notebooks* who overcame this problem, in profoundly redefining the concept of the state and the concept of revolution, making them something processual and complex, just as the society and the reality of 'the West' are complex.

Gramsci teaches that it is not possible to separate economics and politics, the factory and the state. The forms by which the dynamics of businesses and companies' strategies tend to play out can change. But it does not seem that this means the end of the political: that is, the action directed at defining norms and rules, relating the corporatist struggle between classes to the wider and more general level of the answers to the problems that a national community faces. The nation continues to be a fundamental moment of collective life, even if subject to dynamic processes and often dynamic tensions that redefine its role. And the state – states – not only don't seem to be disappearing, but they continue in their complex dialectic with the socio-economic, and, unfortunately, in their 'imperial' efforts. It is mistaken to separate and counterpose society and politics, society and the state.[41] Gramsci is still important for this reason: because he redefined the meaning of politics, enriching it precisely with the understanding that politics forms a single whole with activity in society, in the factory, in culture, and everywhere where the game of power is played.

---

41   See Nogueira 1997, which underlines the need to break with a 'hypostasised modality of civil society, seen as the virtuous "opposite" or negation of the state, which can be resorted to as the stimulus for the renewal of everything. Civil society is virtuous only when it proves able to condition the state by way of politics' (p. 79).

CHAPTER 4

Party and Movements

1   Gramsci and Lenin

In my view, addressing the theme of Gramsci's conception of popular or social movements – in the first place the Turin workers' movement – requires that we speak of the relation between these movements and the political party of the working class, or of the proletariat, or of the 'subalterns'. That is to say, in short, the party as it was conceived in the twentieth century by the socialist and communist tradition to which Gramsci belonged. Indeed, it was in relation to the political party of the working class that Gramsci read the question of movements, or more specifically the Turin workers' movement, with which he was historically most involved. And he *always* located the party-movement dialectic at the centre of his political thought, even in his *L'Ordine Nuovo* and councilist period: in the 1919–20 *biennio rosso*, which is sometimes wrongly considered a phase of his thought characterised by a sort of workerist and spontaneist 'Sorelianism'. During the years of the councils and the occupation of the factories, Gramsci continued to be a party leader, perhaps feeling himself to be a militant of a party bigger than the Italian Socialist Party (PSI), namely the Communist International born in 1919 in Moscow, capital of the revolution, at the Bolsheviks' instigation. From the defeat of the councils, Gramsci – who even at the beginning of the workshop occupations had lucidly warned against any facile revolutionary illusions[1] – must have drawn certain lessons that would help him devote his energies to the battlefront of building a revolutionary party.[2] Already in the wake of the defeat of the 'clock-hands strike'[3] he believed that this party would have to be 'a homogenous, cohesive party with its own doctrine, its own tactic, an implacable and rigid disci-

---

1   See Gramsci's 'L'occupazione', *Avanti!*, Piedmont edition, 2 September 1920, reproduced in Gramsci 1987, pp. 646–8.

2   Gramsci, 'Il Partito comunista', in *L'Ordine Nuovo*, 4 September 1920 (Part I) and 9 October 1920 (Part II), reproduced in Gramsci 1987, pp. 651–61.

3   [*Sciopero delle lancette*, an April 1920 Turin strike against the imposition of daylight saving time, forcing workers to set off for work in the dark. The workers at Fiat Bravetta set the clocks back an hour in protest, hence the name of this event. The series of strikes and occupations also involved the creation of factory councils.]

pline'.[4] So it would be a Leninist party, the opposite of the 'Barnum circus' that leftist critics saw in the chaotic and quarrelsome PSI. From this resulted Gramsci's adherence first to the communist fraction, then to the 'Livorno split'[5] led by Bordiga.

Here, I will seek above all to investigate the party-movement link, without being able to address the question of the party itself in the manner that it deserves. I am referring not only to the theme of the 'Modern Prince',[6] but also to the wider theme of 'collective will', which is, indeed, also 'collective social will' as he wrote as a young man in 'The Revolution against *Capital*'.[7] As concerns Gramsci's concept of 'collective will', Carlos Nelson Coutinho demonstrated aptly how Gramsci was influenced by neoidealism and how he overcame this, as well as the differences Gramsci had with Sorel's 'spontaneism'.[8] As such, I refer the reader to Coutinho's fundamentally important considerations also in regard to many aspects of this current discussion.

As for the theme that I here propose to address – even if summarily – namely Gramsci's vision of mass movements and their relationship with the 'class' party typical of the socialist and communist tradition, it seems opportune to take our cue from note 48 of the third *Notebook*. In this 1930 note, Gramsci reflects on a classic aspect of Lenin's Marxism, namely the relationship between spontaneism and organised consciousness, committed to paper in many classic passages of *What Is To Be Done?*

As is well-known, people rightly see in some of Lenin's writings, especially *What Is To Be Done?*, a rather rigid counterposition between 'spontaneity' and 'consciousness'. I want to note, however, that in *What Is To Be Done* – almost at the start of the second chapter, entitled 'The Spontaneity of the Masses and the Consciousness of the Social Democrats', where the masses/party dichotomy is substantially translated into that of spontaneity/consciousness – Lenin himself recognises that there are different, historically determinate, forms of 'spontaneity'. He explains that within some 'spontaneous' protest movements there are also significant elements of consciousness, such that – Lenin writes – 'the "spontaneous element", in essence, represents nothing more nor less than consciousness in an *embryonic form*'.

4   Gramsci, 'Per un rinnovamento del Partito socialista', *L'Ordine Nuovo*, 8 May 1920, reproduced in Gramsci 1987, p. 515.

5   [That is, the foundation of the Communist Party of Italy (PCd'I).]

6   See Chapter 14.

7   Gramsci, 'La rivoluzione contro il "Capitale"', *Avanti!*, 24 December 1917, reproduced in Gramsci 1982, p. 514.

8   Coutinho 2009.

Lenin puts 'spontaneous element' in quote marks, signifying – I believe – that it is 'spontaneous' only as a manner of speaking, always containing some element of 'consciousness'. This statement is an important one, allowing us to glimpse a *continuum* between spontaneity and consciousness. It is the same *continuum* that is apparent – on a partly but not wholly different plane – in the *Notebooks*, for example between common sense and philosophy.[9] When Gramsci writes – to take another example belonging to this same problematic field – that 'all men are philosophers',[10] he is by no means denying that there are significant and even fundamental differences between a 'simple man' and a 'great intellectual'. But he is emphasising that this difference is only 'quantitative', not 'qualitative', and thus, in prospect, possible to bridge – obviously on condition of a new historical situation, of a new society that *wants* to reduce the gap between 'intellectuals' and 'simple men'. Equally, in saying that there is 'consciousness in an *embryonic form*' in the 'spontaneous element', Lenin, too, I believe, was essentially portraying a *continuum* able to unite 'spontaneity' and 'consciousness' dialectically, these not being juxtaposed. It remains true that *What Is To Be Done?* gives strong priority to *organised* consciousness – and thus there is an inevitable, symmetrical undervaluation of spontaneity. And it is also true that this tendency was further accentuated over time, whether in the ambit of Lenin's Marxism or in the ambit of the twentieth-century communism that took its lead from Bolshevism.

It would be interesting to go back over this history, as, indeed, to step back and study the links between *What Is To Be Done?* and Kautsky (there are links of affinity and even derivation) and between *What Is To Be Done?* and Luxemburg's so-called 'spontaneism' (a largely inappropriate term). But here is not the place for that.

2   Relations with 'the Subalterns'

Returning to Gramsci and note 48 of the third notebook, the text that we are here considering is entitled 'Spontaneity and Conscious Leadership', a single-draft text B not brought up again in a second draft, for reasons that are not clear. It is, however, a very important note, for our present discussion, and in my view more generally for the *Notebooks* as a whole. Like Lenin, the Sardinian thinker also himself began to distinguish between different forms of spon-

---

9   See Chapters 6 and 7.
10   Q8, § 204: Gramsci 1975, p. 1063.

taneity. Gramsci, like Lenin, said that there is no 'pure' spontaneity without some degree of 'consciousness', which he designates as 'conscious leadership'.[11] Even 'in the "most spontaneous" of movements', Gramsci writes, there are 'elements of conscious leadership', but they 'cannot be ascertained, simply because they have left no verifiable document'.[12] The 'element of spontaneity', Gramsci continues, is 'characteristic of the "history of subaltern classes" and, especially, of the most marginal and peripheral elements of these classes, who have not attained a consciousness of the class per se'. They remain at the level of 'common sense', Gramsci contends, at the level 'of the [traditional] conception of the world of a given social stratum'.[13]

Gramsci speaks, here, of the 'history of subaltern classes', an important theme of the *Notebooks*,[14] and, indeed, the title – or rather, subtitle – of *Notebook* 25, which Gerratana dates to 1934, towards the end of Gramsci's creative arc in prison (the Sardinian communist wrote nothing after 1935, except a few letters). Thus from the beginning to the end of his prison reflection, running from 1929 to 1935, Gramsci reflected on the subalterns, on their 'common sense', on their 'spontaneity', on the movements that they managed to bring forth in order to fight the hegemonic class. On their limits, above all – on the limits of the subalterns, of their conception of the world limited to 'common sense'. But also on their tenacious resistance and opposition, on their more or less fleeting traces of autonomy from the 'conception of the world' proper to the hegemonic class by which they are daily *colonised*.

In the note that we are here examining, Gramsci proceeds by way of a short side-polemic against De Man, which is of interest to us here primarily because, in polemicising against this anti-Marxist Belgian socialist, Gramsci counterposes him to 'Ilyich' – Lenin. It is a passage with much to say about the topic with which we are here concerned. Gramsci writes, among other things: 'Nonetheless, De Man has an incidental merit: he demonstrates the need to study and work out the elements of popular psychology'. Which for Gramsci, however, must be done 'actively (that is, in order to transform them by means of education into a modern mentality) and not descriptively as he [De Man] does – a necessity that was at least implicit (and perhaps also explicitly stated) in Ilyich's doctrine, of which De Man is totally ignorant'.[15]

---

11   Gramsci 1975, p. 328; Gramsci 1996b, p. 49.

12   Ibid.

13   Ibid.

14   I will take the liberty of referring the reader to my article 'Three meanings of the "subaltern" in Gramsci' (Liguori 2011).

15   Gramsci 1975, p. 329; Gramsci 1996b, p. 49.

Gramsci makes two important statements in this passage. In the first place, the subalterns' way of thinking, their psychology, but also their conception of the world and their common sense (invoked in the lines immediately above this), are studied and worked through *actively*, 'that is' – Gramsci explained – 'in order to transform them by means of education'. Here, in polemic against De Man, his attention is mostly directed towards psychology – mentality. Yet we find the same attitude in the *Notebooks* in the relation that Gramsci establishes with regard to common sense, with folklore.[16] There is never, in Gramsci, any 'subaltern' just as they are. There is no 'populism', understood in this sense. If the subaltern want to become hegemonic, they must first of all change themselves. They must change without losing their autonomy – even if this is a relative and intermittent autonomy – and without being assimilated and hegemonised; but in the first place, by transforming themselves, acquiring consciousness. How would this be possible? Who would help them in such a transformation, eventually making the subaltern layers into a hegemonic class or alliance of classes? I will return to these crucial questions.

The second significant point in the passage of Q3, §48 here cited regards the fact that Gramsci read Lenin seeing in him this same 'dialectical' attitude, that of attention to the 'conception of the world' proper to the subalterns – but a dialectical attention, with the perspective of 'transforming' it. Where both moments, 'attention' and 'transformation', are important, both of them similarly indispensable.

The philological accuracy or otherwise of this reading is not of importance, for now. Gramsci was not practicing philology in prison: he was *doing politics*. He was producing new political theory, for the purposes of understanding the defeat of the 1920s and the possibility of a new departure, a recovery, a new strategy taking account of the difference between 'East' and 'West', as was signalled by Lenin as early as 1918.[17]

After the aside on De Man, the note proceeds almost as a paraphrase of the short text from *What Is To Be Done?* that I mentioned above. Lenin had writ-

---

16   See Chapter 7.

17   See Lenin's March 1918 political report at the Seventh Congress of the Bolshevik Party, which was published in 1923 when Gramsci was in Moscow. Lenin said 'The revolution will not come as quickly as we expected. History has proved this, and we must be able to take this as a fact, to reckon with the fact that the world socialist revolution cannot begin so easily in the advanced countries as the revolution began in Russia ... In such a country it was quite easy to start a revolution ... But to start without preparation a revolution in a country in which capitalism is developed and has given democratic culture and organisation to everybody, down to the last man – to do so would be wrong, absurd'.

ten – comparing various moments of 'spontaneous' rebellion taking place in nineteenth-century Russia – 'Which proves that the "spontaneous element", in essence, represents nothing more nor less than consciousness in an *embryonic form*'. Gramsci writes of 'The presence of a rudimentary element of conscious leadership, of discipline, in every "spontaneous movement"'.[18] Gramsci repeats the words of *What Is To Be Done?*, simply substituting 'conscious leadership' for 'consciousness'. And 'spontaneous' appears between quotation marks, as did 'spontaneous element' in Lenin.

3   The *Ordine Nuovo* Years

The Gramsci of the *Notebooks* was thus still influenced by Lenin's thinking. The 'revolution against *Capital*', the October Revolution, had moreover – as is well-known – heavily marked the cultural-political activity of the Sardinian communist, from 1917 onwards. But the encounter with Lenin, of particular significance after his stay in Russia – where Gramsci also had the opportunity to meet the Bolshevik leader in person – did not diminish Gramsci's prior formation and elaborations. It was from the encounter between Leninism and this prior cultural formation, made up of many and varied influences from Bergson and Sorel to Mosca and Pareto, from Croce and Gentile to pragmatism and his fundamental studies of linguistics at university, that the mature Gramsci and the peculiarity of his reinterpretation of Marxism were born.[19]

Already in the period of *L'Ordine Nuovo* (1919–20) there was a fruitful encounter between the Russian example (the soviets, a different model of democracy) and the specific formation and sensibilities of Gramsci. Many accounts describe the Turin-based Gramsci who led that great, struggling social movement – culminating in the occupation of the factories – as a leader 'able to listen' to the workers, one who tried to understand their problems, their psychology, their daily life both within and outside the factory walls. The *Ordine Nuovo* group lived in symbiosis with the Turin workers in struggle; it studied the organisation of labour in the great Fiat plant; it went to school with the working class which it *simultaneously* led. The educator was educated, as Gramsci wrote in *Notebook* 7, reading Marx's *Theses on Feuerbach*.[20] The political van-

18   Gramsci 1975, p. 329; Gramsci 1996b, p. 49.

19   Here I will take the liberty of referring the reader to my article 'Teoria e politica nel marxismo di Antonio Gramsci', in the forthcoming volume *Marxismo: Una Storia Globale*, edited by S. Petrucciani.

20   Q7, § 1: Gramsci 1975, p. 854.

guard led the movement, but learnt from it. For example, Battista Santhià, one of the workers in the vanguard of the movement together with the *Ordine Nuovo* intellectuals, commented:

> I would like to remember Gramsci, speaking above all of his links with the Turin working class. This is not very easy. Because they were deep and reciprocal links: between the working class, above all its vanguard, which felt itself attracted to him, and Gramsci, who personally managed to establish a particular relationship with us ... demonstrated that he was different from the others: because he was able to listen.[21]

L'Ordine Nuovo was, at root, a small party (a group at loggerheads with the majority of the PSI and the reformist union, but also very different from the communist group led by Bordiga) that related to a great movement of struggle, tried to lead it, and supplied it with a theory and political perspective. But it learnt from it. The weekly *Ordine Nuovo* saw its sales multiply out of all proportion. The workers read it, even if it was not always written in an easy manner. In Gramsci, they saw a 'leader', and a leadership group in *L'Ordine Nuovo*. But *L'Ordine Nuovo* was not wholly external to them: the relationship between the 'vanguard in the factory' and Gramsci was a strong one, having been built during the years of struggle against the War and in the Turin population's 1917 revolt, a true and proper insurrection. These were years in which Gramsci 'listened to the workers',[22] years that interrupted his journalistic work every time that the workers came into his room and talked to him about their problems. These were years in which he was in dialogue with them, got to know them, educated them and was educated by them. Through this, Gramsci, the young socialist student and later militant journalist at the start of the First World War, became Gramsci, the well-known and recognised revolutionary socialist political leader – in Turin, at least. Inevitably, though, only in Turin.

This would be the limit of the early Gramsci, the limit of the factory councils and factory occupations movement of 1919–20, and so, too, the limit of the Communist Party of Italy, which for this reason was born in 1921 under the leadership not of Gramsci, but of Bordiga.[23]

---

21   In Paulesu Quercioli (ed.) 1977, p. 131.

22   Ibid.

23   Still valuable on both Gramsci's Turin years and the foundation of the PCd'I is the research of Paolo Spriano, for instance *Gramsci e l'Ordine nuovo* (Spriano 1965). But see also the more recent introduction by Angelo d'Orsi to *La nostra città futura. Scritti torinesi (1911–1922)*: D'Orsi 2004.

4   *L'Ordine Nuovo* in the *Notebooks*

Gramsci does mention the *Ordine Nuovo* movement in the *Notebooks*, again in
this same note (Q3, § 48) with which we started. After the first part, on which
we focused before, the note continues with a close *theoretical* reading of 'spontaneism', with critical references to Sorel and to anarcho-syndicalism.[24] Thus
Gramsci speaks of *L'Ordine Nuovo* and of the 'Turin movement', as he terms
the workers' councils and factory occupations movement of the 1919–20 *biennio rosso*. These are important, richly textured pages.[25] I will try to summarise
Gramsci's main points in this text:

a) the 'leadership' of the 'Turin movement' (the work, it is implied, of the *Ordine
   Nuovo* group), accused by the reformists of being simultaneously 'spontaneist' and 'voluntarist', was not in fact 'abstract'. Indeed, it was well aware
   that the relationship it had with the workers was with 'real people in specific historical relations with specific sentiments, ways of life, fragments of
   worldviews, etc., that were outcomes of the "spontaneous" combinations of
   a given environment of material production with the "fortuitous" gathering
   of disparate social elements within that same environment'.[26] This is a very
   vivid image of the concrete development of a socio-economic formation and
   of the ideologies of the subaltern strata gathered within it. And, therefore,
   of concrete processes of the production of subjectivity. The 'spontaneity' of
   'movements' has deficiencies that are in some measure *inevitable* on account
   of the very formation of 'common sense' as a subaltern 'worldview' within a
   given socio-economic order.
b) 'This element of "spontaneity"', Gramsci writes, 'was not neglected, much
   less disdained: it was *educated*, it was given a direction, it was cleansed
   of everything extraneous that could contaminate it, in order to unify it
   by means of modern theory but in a living, historically effective manner',
   the modern theory in question being Leninist Marxism.[27] *Educating* the
   spontaneous movement of the masses in the light of Marxism in order to
   'unify it' at the level reached by the conscious political leadership: the *Ordine
   Nuovo* group, a surrogate for the revolutionary party which did not yet exist,
   sought to play a *pedagogical function*. While learning from the workers, in its

---

24   Gramsci 1975, pp. 329–30; Gramsci 1996b, p. 50.
25   See, above all, Gramsci 1975, pp. 330–2; Gramsci 1996b, pp. 50–2.
26   Gramsci 1975, p. 330; Gramsci 1996b, p. 50.
27   Ibid.

relationship with the movement this group represented the 'active' moment – but not in a doctrinaire, bookish manner, but in a 'living manner', that is, in a manner able to enter into harmony with the workers' real condition at a certain moment of the historical development of their subjectivity. This, without any bookish pedantry, without intellectual arrogance.

c) A little further on Gramsci offers us an important clarification of the term 'spontaneous', writing: '"spontaneous" in the sense that they are not due to the systematic educational activity of an already conscious leadership but have been formed through everyday experience in the light of "common sense"'.[28] He reiterates that a conscious leadership *must* educate the masses, or otherwise these latter will remain stuck at the spontaneous level of common sense: a level which he judges limited, insufficient, intrinsically subaltern, even if at times it contains precious embryonic elements of an *autonomous* worldview.

d) For Gramsci, indeed, the element of conscious leadership – that of the party – and the '"spontaneous" sentiments of the masses' cannot 'be in opposition',[29] because, he argues 'there is, between the two, a "quantitative difference" – of degree, not of quality'. Of course, only if the 'spontaneous' element has a certain *necessity*, being structurally rooted, will the 'conscious leadership' not be something *arbitrary* and have real hegemonic potential, as it will be *rooted* in an objective possibility of change. Gramsci himself says as much in posing the distinction between an unrealistic wish without structural roots, and, on the contrary, 'a rational, not an arbitrary will, which is realised insofar as it corresponds to objective historical necessities'.[30]

e) From all this emerges the following conclusion (of Gramsci's): 'Ignoring and, even worse, disdaining so-called "spontaneous" movements – that is, declining to give them a conscious leadership and raise them to a higher level by inserting them into politics – may often have very bad and serious consequences'.[31] It would mean opening the way to reaction, to Fascism: as, indeed, happened after the *biennio rosso*, when the Socialist Party and the reformist union left the small *Ordine Nuovo* group alone to perform a leadership role that it could not exercise on a wide, national scale. It was thus destined to ultimate defeat in Turin, too.

---

28   Gramsci 1975, pp. 330–1; Gramsci 1996b, p. 51.

29   Gramsci 1975, p. 331; Gramsci 1996b, p. 51.

30   Q11, §59: Gramsci 1975, p. 1485; Gramsci 1971, p. 345.

31   Q3, §48: Gramsci 1975, p. 331; Gramsci 1996b, p. 51.

I believe that Gramsci's arguments can be summarised as follows: a) a strong social movement is a necessary but not sufficient condition for the beginning of a conscious revolutionary process; b) a political leadership worthy of the name 'revolutionary' is nothing if it does not take its cue from the class's movement and make it grow; c) there cannot and must not be a counterposition between the party and the masses, because between them there cannot and must not be a qualitative distinction, but only a quantitative one.

When Gramsci distanced himself from Bordiga in the years 1922–4, and moved forward with the project of forming a new leadership group and refounding the Communist Party born in 1921 – a process which would culminate with the Lyon Congress and *Lyon Theses* of 1926 – he did so in polemic against a conception of the party that understood it as the *organ* of the class, in the name of a party that was, instead, *part* of the class.[32] This was a consideration of decisive importance; and it was a position that had its roots precisely in Gramsci's leadership of the Turin struggles of the 1919–20 *biennio rosso*. For the party to be the 'organ' of the class, as in Bordiga's conception, meant seeing it as something external to the class, on account of its being endowed with the historical consciousness that 'spontaneity' could not produce. The difference, here, appears as a qualitative, not quantitative one. For the party to be 'part' of the class meant to say that there was a *continuum* between 'spontaneity' and 'conscious leadership', between movement and party. The only possible course, therefore, was for the party to be connected to the movements, notwithstanding their weaknesses, in order to make them grow. That is, the party should be particularly committed – devoting all its strength – to being 'part' of the working-class movement in the factories and, more generally, of the social movements of the 'subalterns' as a whole. The party could not be external to the class. It started from the existing level of consciousness of the masses, in order to raise it. It could not be an *organ* in possession of some illusory theoretical-political knowledge, a vanguard with the illusion of being 'ahead' but in fact detached from movements, the class, those people endowed with 'common sense' alone.

---

32   See Spriano 1967, pp. 482 et sqq.

CHAPTER 5

Ideologies and Conceptions of the World

1   From Marx to Gramsci

Taking his lead from an article in *Marzocco*, Gramsci himself turned to 'the origin of the concept of "ideology"',[1] whose genesis can be traced back to sensationalism. In Gramsci's text, the alternating use of the capitalised or lower-case versions of 'ideology' serves to mark a distinction between the ideologues' conception ('Ideology' as the 'science of ideas') from the subsequent use of the term ('ideology' as a 'system of ideas'). Gramsci demonstrated the vulgar-materialist imprint that distinguished the capital I 'Ideology' of the philosophical movement of a sensationalist stamp – not for nothing compared with Bukharin[2] – while emphasising its separateness from 'historical materialism'. For Marx, Gramsci contended, the origin of ideas was not to be sought in sensation – in 'physiology'. And it was precisely this root, subjected to critique and rejected, that led to the implicit 'value judgment' (a 'negative value judgment', the text C clarifies)[3] implied by this term in the works of the 'founders of the philosophy of praxis'.

In reality, matters were more complicated than Gramsci here portrays them. Looking at the genesis of this concept, he did not note its negative branding at the hands of Napoleon I, who likewise imputed it strongly political connotations (ideologies as ideas with the pretense of directing politics), when he 'dismissively defined Destutt de Tracy and Volney as ideologues who had sought to oppose his imperial ambitions', letting it be understood that as intellectuals they substituted 'abstract considerations for real politics'.[4]

In the second place, and above all, we do not know whether Gramsci was acquainted with the *German Ideology*. The book was written by Marx and Engels in 1845–6 but only published in 1932, with its first chapter 'Feuerbach'

---

1   Q4, § 35: Gramsci 1975, pp. 453–4; Gramsci 1996b, p. 174.

2   On the theory of ideology in Bukharin's *Popular Manual* of historical materialism, see Prestipino 2000, p. 36, and Tuccari 2001, pp. 146–7. For Bukharin, ideology is a system of ideas, sentiments and behavioural norms, whose importance he reaffirmed in his polemics against deterministic conceptions.

3   Q11, § 63: Gramsci 1975, p. 1491; Gramsci 1971, p. 376.

4   Boudon 1991, p. 36.

having been 'published for the first time in Russian in 1924 and subsequently (1926) in German'.[5] Could Gramsci have read it, or a review of it? According to Francesca Izzo,[6] he could have read some pages from it in an 'anthology of Marx and Engels on historical materialism' that had come out in Russia, which he mentions in a letter to Zino Zini sent from Vienna on 10 January 1924. Yet there remains the fact that there is no trace of this in his works. That is, he did not know or did not use a text that we today habitually consider the birthplace of Marx's negatively-connoted concept of ideology. It is in this text by Marx and Engels, indeed, that we read: 'If in all ideology men and their circumstances appear upside-down as in a *camera obscura*, this phenomenon arises just as much from their historical life-process as the inversion of objects on the retina does from their physical life-process.'[7]

As we can see, here, the *coupure* between Marx and the ideologues was not as total as it seemed to Gramsci. Certainly, Marx and Engels – reprising the term inasmuch as they, too, wanted to investigate the genesis of ideas – did shift research onto the historical-social plane. But their language still leaves room for a way of reasoning modelled on the *physiological* framework (with the retina metaphor) considered unacceptable by Gramsci.[8] If Gramsci was perhaps not acquainted with the *German Ideology*, he did know well – and utilised – Marx's 1859 'Preface', where we read:

> The changes in the economic foundation lead sooner or later to the transformation of the whole immense superstructure. In studying such transformations it is always necessary to distinguish between the material transformation of the economic conditions of production, which can be determined with the precision of natural science, and the legal, political, religious, artistic or philosophic – in short, ideological forms in which men become conscious of this conflict and fight it out. Just as one does not judge an individual by what he thinks about himself, so one cannot judge such a period of transformation by its consciousness.[9]

---

5 Luporini 1967, p. xc.

6 See Izzo 2009, pp. 45–6 n.

7 *MECW*, Vol. 5, p. 36.

8 Eagleton 1991 has argued that a different conception of ideology is implicitly present in the *German Ideology*: if 'The ideas of the ruling class are in every epoch the ruling ideas', then ideology is a 'weapon' consciously used in service of a particular class.

9 *MECW*, Vol. 29, p. 263.

Fabio Frosini has highlighted[10] how Marx here wanted to warn scholars against confusing the scientific study of the 'economic conditions of production' with their ideological representation. It is also true, however, that Marx's statement according to which 'ideological forms' allow men to 'become conscious of' and 'fight out' the struggle between classes is something rather different to his blunt 1845–6 portrayal of ideology in *solely* negative terms. Here, 'there is a notable correction with regard to 1845–6 and the ideologies that he simply equated to distorted consciousness, an "upside-down" consciousness of the real world. He does not say that they are always upside-down images of that kind'.[11] Alongside his science/ideology dichotomy, that is, Marx seems to have (sincerely) laid out a conception of 'ideological forms' that did not have negative connotations, but rather appear as useful and necessary. Is this reason enough to say that there were in Marx at least[12] two theories of ideology, or at least two faces of one same theory? In my view, yes. It is no chance thing, then, that it was precisely from this text that Gramsci took his cue for his positive conception of the theory of ideologies, even if thanks to a *dilated* interpretation of the passage in question.

In a letter from the elderly Engels to Franz Mehring dated 14 July 1893, we find a very interesting 'appendix' to this suggestion that ideology had *two faces* in the works of the 'founders of the philosophy of praxis'. Here we find reference – which later became canonical – to ideology as 'false consciousness', whose wide publicisation owes precisely to Mehring and his successful *History of the German Social Democracy*,[13] which Gramsci, too, may well have read. Engels writes: 'Ideology is a process accomplished by the so-called thinker consciously, indeed, but with a false consciousness. The real motives impelling him remain unknown to him, otherwise it would not be an ideological process at all'.[14]

We are here continuing in line with the *German Ideology*, slightly seasoned with a proto-Freudian spice, which does not resolve the problems opened up

---

10   Frosini 2003, p. 90. On the theme of ideology in Gramsci, see also Frosini's *La religione dell'uomo moderno. Politica e verità nei 'Quaderni del carcere'* (Frosini 2010).

11   Merker 1986, p. 21.

12   In Marx there is also a conception of ideology posed in terms of a mistaken vision of reality dependent on the author's particular point of view (see Boudon 1991, p. 62). Finelli 1997, pp. xv–xvi, argues that in *Capital* Marx suggested a 'different, more coherent conception of ideology', defining this as 'the way in which the social process of capital production and reproduction dissimulates its own existence'.

13   Engels's letter was first published by Mehring, in the 1898 German edition of his *History*.

14   MECW, Vol. 50, p. 162.

by the 1845–6 definition. For example, we cannot but ask: if we speak of 'false consciousness', does that presuppose the possibility of a 'true consciousness' that is not straightforwardly 'science'? In Engels's letter – in line with his effort in these years to correct the economistic determinism of Marxian and Marxist thought, an activity of which Gramsci was aware and noted and praised in the *Notebooks*[15] – there also appeared the following statement:

> Hanging together with this too is the fatuous notion of the ideologists that because we deny an independent historical development to the various ideological spheres which play a part in history we also deny them any effect upon history. The basis of this is the common undialectical conception of cause and effect as rigidly opposite poles, the total disregarding of interaction; these gentlemen often almost deliberately forget that once an historic element has been brought into the world by other elements, ultimately by economic facts, it also reacts in its turn and may react on its environment and even on its own causes.[16]

For Engels, here, 'ideologists' are those who deny the 'historical efficacy' of ideologies, their relative autonomy, their activity through which it is even possible to change thinkers' 'real motives', the structuring of the socio-economic world. These are concepts that reached Gramsci also by way of Labriola,[17] from as early as the *Grido del popolo* years when the young Sardinian socialist published the third section of the essay 'On Historical Materialism' (in which is discussed precisely the concept of 'in the last instance'), giving it the title 'Le ideologie nel divenire storico' ['Ideologies in the Becoming of History'].[18] But already with Engels we are a step away from Gramsci, right from the beginning of his discourse on ideology. It was through combining a *dilated* reading of the 1859 'Preface' with the fundamental *Theses on Feuerbach* and his reading of the late Engels that Gramsci arrived, in the *Notebooks*, at his *positive* conception of ideology.[19] Yet if Gramsci found in the late Engels a pedestal for his own

---

15   See Chapter 11.

16   MECW, Vol. 50, p. 162.

17   On the concept of 'ideology' in Labriola, see Chapter 12.

18   See Paggi 1970, pp. 18 et sqq.

19   The young Gramsci had a number of influences that contributed to leading him toward an original conception of ideology by way of a complex labour of assimilation/distinction: as well as Marx, Engels and Labriola, authors like Sorel and Croce also played a fundamental role, as well as Barbusse (see Paggi 1970, p. 158) and Pareto.

'rehabilitation' of the concept of ideology, already before him the Marxist tradition had arrived at the use – albeit without an adequate thematisation – of a concept of ideology different from that of 1845–6. Some hint of this was already apparent in the work of Eduard Bernstein.[20] The best-known example appears in Lenin's *What Is To Be Done?*:

> the only choice is – either bourgeois or socialist ideology. There is no middle course (for mankind has not created a 'third' ideology, and, moreover, in a society torn by class antagonisms there can never be a non-class or an above-class ideology). Hence, to belittle the socialist ideology *in any way, to turn aside from it in the slightest degree* means to strengthen bourgeois ideology ... bourgeois ideology is far older in origin than socialist ideology, that it is more fully developed, and that it has at its disposal *immeasurably* more means of dissemination.[21]

Ideology against ideology, even with a hint of the theory of 'ideological apparatuses', with the stamp of an absolute and total Sorelian 'spirit of cleavage'. Strange though it may seem to compare Lenin and Sorel, these were two very different authors who contributed to forming Gramsci's specific attention to revolutionary subjectivity, which became one of his distinctive traits. No surprise, then, that together with a more traditional, pejorative use of the term, in the young Gramsci there are formulations similar to Lenin's,[22] such as in March 1918 when he defined 'President Wilson and the Russian maximalists' as 'the furthest logical extremes of bourgeois and of proletarian ideology'.[23]

For the young Gramsci, Marx's conception of ideology (that today considered *classic*: ideology in the sense of a distorted view of reality) was inadmissible: Marx himself was an ideologue, because though on the one hand he 'derided ideologies', on the other hand 'he was an ideologue inasmuch as he

---

20   Eagleton 1991 also makes this point, though without delving deeper into this argument.

21   Lenin 1987, p. 82.

22   I am thinking of a use that had become commonplace among socialists internationally, rather than his direct parentage of this idea.

23   Gramsci, 'Wilson e i massimalisti russi', 2 March 1918, reproduced in Gramsci 1982, p. 691. In the same article he demonstrates his attention toward 'the new relations between ideologies and economics' (p. 690). As concerns the use of the term in the sense of 'political theory', Gramsci wrote – in his 24 December 1917 'La rivoluzione contro il *Capitale*' – that 'events overcame ideology', referring to the Russian Revolution and Marxian thought.

was a modern-day politician, a revolutionary'.[24] Here, there appears a distinction, one that would again be posed in the *Notebooks*, between *two different* semantics of the term: 'ideologies are risible when they are pure chatter, when they are devoted to creating confusion, to sowing illusions and subduing potentially antagonistic social forces': and it was these that Gramsci saw Marx pouncing upon. Who, however, 'as a revolutionary, as a modern-day man of action, could not disregard ideologies and practical schemes, which are potential historical forces in formation'?[25]

2   Gramsci and Marx (and Croce)

If we leaf through the first three of Gramsci's *Notebooks*, we find a variegated and diffuse use of the term 'ideology'. However, this is not of great significance, insofar as the term appears without yet having been conceptualised. It is worth going onward to *Notebook* 4 (from the same time as the first three) where Gramsci deals with Marx's theory of ideology (and that of Croce). Not before noting, though, that a brief passage from the 1859 'Preface' appears already in Q1, §113, with reference to the history of criminal law. Gramsci quotes from memory, translating in an approximate manner, which he would later correct after translating part of Marx's text in *Notebook* 7.[26] What remains true, though, is that the piece in question was very much in his mind, and alongside the *Theses on Feuerbach* was the Marx text to which he most often returned in the *Notebooks*.

It was in his 'Notes on philosophy. Materialism and idealism. First series' that Gramsci began to delve into Marxism and its clash with Croce. One of the stakes of this opposition was the theme of ideology, which, indeed, he indicated as being of primary importance:

> For the idealists, see which elements of Marxism have been absorbed 'explicitly', that is, avowedly. For example, historical materialism as an empirical canon of historical research by Croce ... the value of ideologies, etc.[27]

---

24   Gramsci, *'Astrattismo e intransigenza'*, 11 May 1918, reproduced in Gramsci 1984, p. 17.

25   Ibid. I cannot dwell, here, on the young Gramsci's reception of Croce's concept of religion or faith, fundamental to his future development. See, for example, 'Il Sillabo ed Hegel', 15 January 1916, in Gramsci 1980, p. 71: 'every man has his own religion, his own faith'.

26   See Gramsci 1975, p. 2523.

27   Q4, §3: Gramsci 1975, p. 422; Gramsci 1996b, p. 140. Continuing this text, Gramsci goes

Gramsci was attempting, in the first place, to *defend* Marx from Croce's distorted and self-interested reading, which on the one hand asserted in the *Elementi di politica* that 'the founder of the philosophy of praxis' had reduced superstructures to 'appearances and illusions', and on the other hand, Gramsci wrote, appropriated part of the Marxian-imprinted theory of ideology:

> The most interesting point to examine concerns 'ideologies' and their value: point out the contradictions Croce falls into with respect to this matter. In his booklet *Elementi di politica*, Croce writes that for Marx the 'superstructures' were an appearance or an illusion, and he wrongly faults Marx for this ... The source of Croce's theory on ideologies – recently repeated in his review of Malagodi's book in *La Critica* – is obviously Marxist: ideologies are practical constructs, they are instruments of political leadership. Croce's theory, however, reproduces only one part, the critical-destructive part, of Marxist theory. For Marx, 'ideologies' are anything but appearances and illusions: they are an objective and operative reality; they just are not the mainspring of history, that's all. It is not ideologies that create social reality but social reality, in its productive structure, that creates ideologies. How could Marx have thought that superstructures are appearance and illusion? Even his theories are a superstructure. Marx explicitly states that humans become conscious of their tasks on the ideological terrain of the superstructures, which is hardly a minor affirmation of 'reality', and the aim of his theory is also, precisely, to make a specific social group 'become conscious' of its own tasks, its own power, its own coming-into-being. But he destroys the 'ideologies' of the hostile social groups, those 'ideologies' are in fact practical instruments of political domination over the rest of society, and Marx shows how they are meaningless because they are in contradiction with actual reality.[28]

The note is of decisive importance, for the purposes of our study. Gramsci, indeed, here states that:

a) Croce takes from Marxism only a part of its theory of ideologies, the 'critical-destructive' part, holding that these are 'practical constructs' and 'instru-

---

on to write 'Marxism had two tasks: to combat modern ideologies in their most refined form; and to enlighten the minds of the popular masses'. This had proven inadequate for combating 'the other ideologies of the educated classes' (Gramsci 1996b, p. 141).

28   Q4, §15: Gramsci 1975, pp. 436–7; Gramsci 1996b, p. 157.

ments of political leadership'; This is a restricted vision, but one that Gramsci
does not rebut. So for Marxism also, ideologies are 'practical constructs' and
'instruments of political leadership';

b) The expression that Gramsci here uses – 'It is not ideologies that create social
reality but social reality, in its productive structure, that creates ideologies' –
sounds rather similar to where the *German Ideology* declaims: 'it is not consciousness that determines life, but life that determines consciousness':[29]
what is in question, here, is not his basic adherence to the Marx-Engels
worldview, but rather its *interpretation*;

c) For Marx, Gramsci says, '"ideologies" are anything but appearances and
illusions: they are an objective and operative reality', even if they are not
'the mainspring of history': Engels's 1893 letter rejected the thesis as to
ideologies' lack of historical efficacy; Gramsci supports the late Engels's
anti-deterministic correction to Marxism with his own interpretation;

d) Gramsci invokes the Marx of 1859 and considerably *expands upon* it, founding on this the possibility of a *positive* conception of ideology. Marxism, then,
becomes one ideology among others, with the scope of making a class, the
proletariat, 'become conscious';

e) The critical part of Marx's theory of ideologies is, for Gramsci, to be reserved
for rival theories, 'practical instruments of political domination over the rest
of society' and 'meaningless because they are in contradiction with actual
reality'. If we compare this to the corresponding text c[30] of the passage
in question, the difference between Marxism and 'the other ideologies' is
drawn even more sharply into relief, given the fact that these are 'inorganic
because they are contradictory, because they are directed at conciliating
opposed and contradictory interests', whereas Marxism 'is not inclined to
resolving contradictions peacefully ... but rather is the very theory of such
contradictions'.

Ideology is not negative *per se*, but neither are all ideologies equal. They constitute the necessary common ground of consciousness and also of knowledge,[31]
but the superiority of Marxist ideology is due to its consciousness of its own
non-absolute and non-eternal character: its consciousness of its partiality, as
it is linked to a given class and historical moment. Marxism is one ideology

---

29   *MECW*, Vol. 5, p. 37.

30   Q10ii, § 41xii: Gramsci 1975, p. 1318.

31   On the gnoseological value of Gramsci's theory of ideology and its overcoming of the
rationalist science/ideology dichotomy, see Frosini 2010.

among others, but unlike the others it does not deny contradictions but rather unveils and analyses them. In common with other ideologies, it performs a certain *utility* for a given social group. But it does not pass itself off as something above or beyond history. Re-elaborating another text from this *Notebook*,[32] in the second draft Gramsci wrote: 'The philosophy of praxis not only claimed to explain and to justify all the past, but to explain and justify historically itself as well. That is, it was the greatest form of "historicism", total liberation from any form of abstract "ideologism"'.[33]

Whenever Marxism forgets its specificity (as in the case of Bukharin's *Popular Manual*) it ends up becoming 'an ideology in the pejorative sense: that is, an absolute and eternal truth'.[34] Historically, ideologies have been quite different things depending on how far they were 'necessary' and 'organic'. And this is not only a question that concerns Marxism. In fact, Gramsci makes clear, 'the name ideology' is mistakenly given 'both to the necessary superstructure of a particular structure and to the arbitrary elucubrations of particular individuals. The bad sense of the word has become widespread, with the effect that the theoretical analysis of the concept of ideology has been modified and denatured'.[35]

It was 'necessary to distinguish between historically organic ideologies, those, that is, which are necessary to a given structure, and ideologies that are arbitrary, rationalistic, or "willed"'. This is not only a question of Marxism or historically 'progressive' ideologies. That is because, Gramsci adds, 'To the extent that ideologies are historically necessary they have a validity which is "psychological"; they "organise" human masses, and create the terrain on which men move, acquire consciousness of their position, struggle, etc.'[36] Here, we are back with the 1859 'Preface', which Gramsci here paraphrases and interprets in the light of his own convictions. Ideologies 'organise' the masses: they even become a *subject*, albeit only in this passage. In the *battle* to restate the 'validity of ideologies', Gramsci also calls upon other parts of Marx's *oeuvre*, namely from *Capital* and from the 'Introduction' to the *Critique of Hegel's Philosophy of Right*:[37]

---

32   Q4, §24.

33   Q16, §9: Gramsci 1975, p. 1864; Gramsci 1971, p. 399.

34   Q4, §40: Gramsci 1975, p. 466; Gramsci 1996b, p. 189.

35   Q7, §19: Gramsci 1975, p. 868; Gramsci 1971, p. 376.

36   Q7, §19: Gramsci 1975, p. 869; Gramsci 1971, pp. 376–7.

37   See Gramsci 1975, p. 2755.

It is worth recalling the frequent affirmation made by Marx on the 'solidity of popular beliefs' as a necessary element of a specific situation ... Another proposition of Marx is that a popular conviction often has the same energy as a material force or something of the kind, which is extremely significant. The analysis of these propositions tends, I think, to reinforce the conception of historical bloc in which precisely material forces are the content and ideologies are the form, though this distinction between form and content has purely didactic value, since the material forces would be inconceivable historically without form and the ideologies would be individual fancies without the material forces.[38]

Here, we have an anti-deterministic and anti-economistic reading of Marx, to which is added the 'solidity of popular beliefs', Gramsci did not fail to see the *dangerous* implications of these latter, even if they could be useful in periods of defeat and retreat. His objective was to free Marxism of its economistic 'encrustations': 'Economy and Ideology: The claim, presented as an essential postulate of historical materialism, that every fluctuation of politics and ideology can be presented and expounded as an immediate expression of the structure, must be contested in theory as primitive infantilism'.[39]

This is in polemic against Bukharin and the 'orthodox Marxism' of the Third International, one among the causes of the bankrupt political 'turns' of those years. In his re-evaluation of ideologies, Gramsci was however always attentive to conducting a 'struggle on two fronts', against 'economism', on the one hand, and 'ideologism' on the other, that is, against the tendency to place exaggerated stress on either 'mechanical causes' or the '"voluntary" and individual element'.[40] Still, his attempt to elaborate an innovative theory but without breaking his bridges with Marx could not hide Gramsci's substantial rejection of the German thinker, here. With this – without knowing it (as he did not know the *German Ideology*) – he brought to light a contradiction: one cannot claim that ideology means a distorted vision of reality (1845–6) and also make it the terrain of a fundamental 'becoming consciousness' (in 1859). Gramsci did not note such a contradiction, since he was unaware of the manuscript abandoned to the 'gnawing criticism of the mice',[41] but also because he reclassifies the *negative* theory of ideology as being only the responsibility of 'adversarial' groups.

---

38   Q7, § 21: Gramsci 1975, p. 869; Gramsci 1971, p. 377.

39   Q7, § 24: Gramsci 1975, p. 871; Gramsci 1971, p. 407.

40   Q4, § 38: Gramsci 1975, p. 456; Gramsci 1971, pp. 177–8.

41   As Marx himself puts it in the 1859 'Preface'.

The *positive* theory of ideology that we see in the *Notebooks*, namely as a conception of the world and site of constitution of collective subjectivity, in reality concerns all 'social groups', because around this revolves the 'war of position' and struggle for hegemony with which all society is permeated.

3   The Term 'Ideology'

The term 'ideological' has an accentuated polysemy. Terry Eagleton[42] has enumerated six different ways of using the term, and Ferruccio Rossi-Landi[43] eleven. Seeking to study how our author used the term and its derivations, I will not imitate any of the existing interpretative *cages*. I will point out, however, many scholars of ideology seem to accept that the basic distinction is between ideology as false consciousness and ideology as a vision or conception of the world. Gramsci situates himself mainly, even if not exclusively, in the second version.

In order to reconstruct the use of the term in the *Notebooks*, I will firstly examine the different meanings in which the term appears, and thus the family of terms and concepts into which it is inserted. So let us return to the first *Notebook*. We have said that the term in question and its derivations often appear in a seemingly unimportant manner. That is to say, Gramsci used the term in its *everyday* usage, even if with *flashes* of meaning. For example – and these are almost all A texts – he speaks of the 'ideological attitudes' of Ojetti;[44] of an 'ideology (the myth of America)' determined by the phenomenon of migration;[45] of the fact that in every region of Italy 'there exist groups or small groups characterised by their own ideological or psychological impulses';[46] of the sphere of culture in which 'the ideological currents' enter into 'various combinations';[47] of the 'cities of silence' and their '"urban" ideological unity against the countryside';[48] or else when he observes that 'Once the dominant class has exhausted its function, the ideological bloc tends to disintegrate'[49]

---

42   Eagleton 1991.
43   Rossi-Landi 1982, pp. 33 et sqq.
44   Q1, § 24: Gramsci 1975, p. 18; Gramsci 1992, p. 112.
45   Q1, § 24: Gramsci 1975, p. 18; Gramsci 1992, p. 113.
46   Q1, § 43: Gramsci 1975, p. 33; Gramsci 1992, p. 128.
47   Q1, § 43: Gramsci 1975, p. 34; Gramsci 1992, p. 129.
48   Q1, § 43: Gramsci 1975, p. 35; Gramsci 1992, p. 130.
49   Q1, § 44: Gramsci 1975, p. 42; Gramsci 1992, p. 138.

and that 'the Action Party was implicitly anti-French because of its Mazzinian ideology'.[50] And this is just in the first 43 pages of Gerratana's critical edition: I could continue. In the first *Notebook*, therefore, the term recurs frequently, in contexts and in ways that are more or less a matter of chance, and of greater and lesser degrees of interest (the last two examples have much greater depth than the others). We will seek, here, to carry forward a process of classification in order to understand what 'ideology' meant not only in the philosophical language of Gramsci and his era, but also in the everyday language of the time, in which – as Gramscians, we know it – a 'conception of the world' is being expressed.

First of all, we should note that in Gramsci, too, there is a pejorative use of the term, one which I would define as 'Napoleonic'. We find him saying: 'All the rest is an ideological serial novel';[51] 'Boullier, who adopts a purely ideological point of view, does not understand anything about this issue';[52] 'What is strange is how some Marxists believe "rationality" to be superior to "politics", ideological abstraction to economic concreteness';[53] 'as if what has been and was destroyed were not "ideological", "abstract", "conventional", etc.';[54] 'Each group can appeal to one of these traditional currents, distinguishing between real facts and ideologies';[55] 'Catholic "social thought" ... should be studied and analysed as an ingredient of an ideological opiate';[56] 'we are dealing here with an "ideology", a unilateral practical-political tendency that cannot serve as the foundation of science';[57] 'ideological fanaticism';[58] 'the greatest defect of all these ideological interpretations of the Risorgimento';[59] 'To understand the positions and the reasoning of the adversary ... means precisely to liberate oneself from the prison of ideologies (in the pejorative sense, that of blind ideological fanaticism)'.[60]

Ideology *in the pejorative sense of the term* appears, then, in a wide range of cases in the early *Notebooks*. But also present, from these early years of his

50   Q1, § 44: Gramsci 1975, p. 43; Gramsci 1992, p. 139.

51   Q1, § 143: Gramsci 1975, p. 129; Gramsci 1992, p. 226.

52   Q1, § 144: Gramsci 1975, p. 129; Gramsci 1992, p. 226.

53   Q1, § 151: Gramsci 1975, p. 134; Gramsci 1992, p. 231.

54   Q2, § 91: Gramsci 1975, p. 249; Gramsci 1992, p. 334.

55   Q3, § 62: Gramsci 1975, p. 342; Gramsci 1996b, p. 61.

56   Q5, § 7: Gramsci 1975, p. 546; Gramsci 1992, p. 274.

57   Q8, § 27: Gramsci 1975, p. 958.

58   Q9, § 104: Gramsci 1975, p. 1167.

59   Q9, § 107: Gramsci 1975, p. 1171.

60   Q10ii, § 24: Gramsci 1975, p. 1263.

prison reflection onwards, is ideology understood to mean a system of political ideas. In Q4, §15, Gramsci's reflection turns to Croce, who had written a review of Giovanni F. Malagodi's 1928 book *Le ideologie politiche*, itself among the titles Gramsci kept in prison.[61]Gramsci also used 'ideology' in the sense of political ideology, speaking of 'Mazzinian ideology' (Q1, §44); of Jacobins who 'followed a certain ideology' (Q1, §48); of novels 'with a markedly ideological character, democratic leanings, linked to the ideologies of 1848' (Q3, §78),[62] and of 'liberal ideology' (Q6, §81).[63] But the reference can also be political in a broader sense: so we get 'masonic ideology' (Q1, §157)[64] and 'puritan ideology' (Q1, §158),[65] 'Southern ideology' (Q1, §44)[66] and 'patriotic ideology' (Q2, §107),[67] and 'the ideology linked to the Roman tradition' (Q4, §67).[68] The term is also used with reference to social groups and strata. Particularly interesting, it seems to me, is Q1, §43, where Gramsci, in his survey of 'types of periodicals', states that

> in every region, especially in Italy, given the very rich variety of local traditions, there exist groups or small groups characterised by their own ideological or psychological impulses: 'every village has or has had its local saint, hence its own cult and its own chapel'. The unitary elaboration of a collective consciousness requires manifold conditions and initiatives. The diffusion from a homogeneous centre of a homogeneous way of thinking and acting is the principle condition, but it must not and cannot be the only one. A very common error is that of thinking that every social stratum elaborates its consciousness and its culture in the same way, with the same methods, that is, with the methods of professional intellectuals.[69]

If we read this passage attentively, it seems to me that we can deduce that:

a) Gramsci makes a link between ideology, (popular) religion, folklore and (later in the note) common sense;

61   Gramsci 1975, p. 2631.
62   Gramsci 1975, p. 378; Gramsci 1996b, pp. 76–7.
63   Gramsci 1975, p. 752.
64   Gramsci 1975, p. 138.
65   Gramsci 1975, p. 138.
66   Gramsci 1975, p. 46.
67   Gramsci 1975, p. 254.
68   Gramsci 1975, p. 512.
69   Gramsci 1975, p. 33; Gramsci 1992, p. 128.

b) He foresees a 'collective consciousness' that could overcome and replace the dominant ideology, and holds that to this end there needs to be an organised activity that is able to engage with 'common sense' dialectically, albeit with the objective of overcoming it;

c) 'every social stratum' has 'its consciousness and its culture', that is, its ideology.

Ideology, therefore, is not only narrowly political. It identifies a group or a social stratum. Other traces of this way of understanding the term (as 'social ideology') are, moreover, present both in the notebooks on which we have concentrated our analysis and elsewhere. In Q1, §107, speaking of Latin America, it is stated that 'Freemasonry and the positivist Church are the ideologies and the lay religions of the urban petty bourgeoisie';[70] in Q3, §153, that *The Count of Monte Cristo* encapsulates 'the popular ideology surrounding the administration of justice'.[71] Later on, we will find a Lenin-hued reference to 'proletarian ideology'.[72]

His initial investigation of the role of ideology is closely linked to religion. Still, and not by chance, in his 'Points on philosophy I', we read: 'that science is a superstructure is demonstrated by the fact that it has been eclipsed for entire periods, driven out by the dominant ideology and above all by religion'.[73]

The expression 'dominant ideology' had already appeared in Q3, §34. But what is particularly worth pointing out, here, is that right from the outset of Gramsci's reasoning, alongside ideology in the pejorative sense and political ideology, there is also a conception of ideology as a system of ideas that is not immediately political, but a *vision or conception of the world* in a much broader sense. Reflecting on religion and the serial novel, on Southern Italy and South America, the *Notebooks* sought to bring to light how a *diffuse* and not always 'political' ideology is formed – and this is essential to the conquest and maintenance of power, given that 'Once the dominant class has exhausted its function, the ideological bloc tends to disintegrate'.[74]

---

70   Gramsci 1975, p. 98; Gramsci 1992, p. 195.

71   Gramsci 1975, p. 405; Gramsci 1996b, p. 123.

72   Q6, §168: Gramsci 1975, p. 820.

73   Q4, §7: Gramsci 1975, p. 430; Gramsci 1996b, p. 150. I will not dwell here on the question of the science/ideology relationship in Gramsci, nor on that concerning the ideology *of* science. As well as referring the reader once again to the work of Frosini, I recommend Boothman 2003.

74   Q1, §44: Gramsci 1975, p. 42; Gramsci 1992, p. 138.

The 'ideological bloc' is a concept that Gramsci deepens and articulates in the third *Notebook*, asking himself how the 'ideological structure'[75] of a ruling class is articulated:

> A study of how the ideological structure of a ruling class is actually organised: that is, the material organisation meant to preserve, defend, and develop the theoretical or ideological 'front' … The press is the most dynamic part of the ideological structure, but not the only one. Everything that directly or indirectly influences or could influence public opinion belongs to it: libraries, schools, associations and clubs of various kinds, even architecture, the layout of streets and their names … What can an innovative class set against the formidable complex of trenches and fortifications of the ruling class? The spirit of cleavage – that is, the progressive acquisition of the consciousness of one's historical identity – a spirit of cleavage that must aim to extend itself from the protagonist class to the classes that are its potential allies: all of this requires complex ideological work.[76]

It would be difficult to exaggerate the importance of this passage. The struggle for hegemony is a struggle between ideologies. On the one hand, the 'material structure of the ideology' of the class in power: the ideological struggle is not only a 'battle of ideas', as these ideas have a 'material structure' articulated in 'apparatuses'.[77] And, therefore, contrary to what one might think if one did not correctly frame one's reading of the state/civil society relation in Gramsci in terms of a dialectical relation, ideology does not inhabit civil society but rather the ('enlarged' or 'integral') state, also because – as Gramsci clarifies in Q10ii, §41iv – ideology 'provides civil society and thus the state with its most intimate cement'.[78] On the other hand, Gramsci evokes the Sorelian 'spirit of cleavage', which is, however, interpreted as 'the progressive acquisition of the

---

75   In the *Notebooks*, there appear various terms similar to 'ideological structure', from 'ideological front' (Q7, §26: Gramsci 1975, p. 875) to 'ideological sphere' and 'ideological terrain' (Q11, §16: p. 1407), from 'ideological community' and 'ideological panorama' (Q11, §12: p. 1392) to 'ideological world' (p. 1394). 'Ideological apparatus' does not appear, but Gramsci does write: 'the realisation of a hegemonic apparatus … creates a new ideological terrain' (Q10ii, §12: p. 1250).

76   Q3, §49: Gramsci 1975, pp. 332–3; Gramsci 1996b, pp. 52–3.

77   See Mancina 1980 and Ragazzini 2002. Here we can also look to Althusser, for whom 'an ideology always exists in an apparatus and in its practice'.

78   Gramsci 1975, p. 1306; Gramsci 1995, p. 469.

consciousness of one's historical identity'. It is thanks to ideology that a collective subject becomes conscious of itself *and therefore* able to oppose itself
to the rival hegemony: this is ideology as the site of the constitution of subjectivity. But if it is not then understood that this subject, having become conscious of itself and capable of mounting its own struggle for hegemony, must
fit itself out with its own 'hegemonic' or 'ideological apparatuses', or, better,
that it must wage its struggle within the concrete 'fortresses and earthworks'
of the 'integral state' – then we remain stuck at an idealistic and simultaneously rationalist-enlightenment conception. Thought, rather, *provides force*
and is an *organiser* at the moment that *it organises itself* – or, better, *is organised* – and this is also the case for the subaltern classes who want to become
hegemonic, starting from the basis of the 'homogeneous centre of a homogeneous way of thinking and acting'.[79] And for Gramsci this means the party.[80] And
this is why we can say that there is a *materialist* theory of ideology in the *Notebooks*.

4   The Family of Concepts

To understand fully the concept of ideology in the *Notebooks*, it is necessary to
bear in mind that this concept is articulated amongst a *family of terms* which
is also a *family of concepts*: ideology, philosophy, visions or conceptions of the
world, religion, conformism, common sense,[81] folklore, and language. Each of
these indicates a concept that cannot entirely be mapped onto any of the others. But, at the same time, all of these terms are related amongst themselves and
appear contextually. They make up a *conceptual network* that, taken as a whole,
marks out Gramsci's conception of ideology. Ideology, philosophy, conception
of the world, religion, common sense, and so on can differ according to the
given degree of consciousness and functionality, being more or less mediated
with respect to praxis and politics. I will try to give account of some of Gramsci's
definitions and 'equations', remembering that the *Notebooks* are a research project, an ongoing (and only apparently incomplete) reflection, which *as a whole*
expresses a theory that is coherent and explicit enough.

---

79   Gramsci 1975, p. 33; Gramsci 1992, p. 128.
80   'One should stress the importance and significance which, in the modern world, political
      parties have in the elaboration and diffusion of conceptions of the world': Q11, § 12: Gramsci
      1975, p. 1387; Gramsci 1971, p. 335.
81   See the next chapter on 'common sense'.

For clarity's sake, I shall begin with a text C, one of the richest and most important for the purposes of the present discussion: Q11, § 12, where among other things we read:

> But at this point we reach the fundamental problem facing any conception of the world, any philosophy that has become a cultural movement, a 'religion', a 'faith', any that has produced a form of practical activity or will in which the philosophy is contained as an implicit theoretical 'premise'. One might say 'ideology', here, but on condition that the word is used in its highest sense of a conception of the world that is implicitly manifest in art, in law, in economic activity and in all manifestations of individual and collective life. This problem is that of preserving the ideological unity of the entire social bloc which that ideology serves to cement and to unify.[82]

Thus, a conception of the world and a philosophy that have become a 'cultural movement' – a 'religion' or 'faith' in the Crocean sense, but a Croce whom Gramsci criticises for his pretense of holding philosophy and ideology, cognitive activity and political activity in separation[83] – can be defined as 'ideology' in its 'highest sense'. It is precisely as a 'conception of the world' that ideology 'is implicitly manifest ... in all manifestations of individual and collective life', thus pervading all social being, from language to art and culture in the anthropological sense ('all manifestations of individual and collective life'), up to the most rarefied and complex philosophical system. After all, this, too, sometimes 'implicitly', expresses a conception of the world that ultimately does make its presence felt on the stage of the struggle for hegemony (and because a depiction embracing the entirety of 'individual and collective life' does not seem to leave anything out). Namely, a conception of the world, a philosophy, an ideology that have the scope of *cementing* a social bloc, and thus constituting it into a subjectivity, if only because it is precisely by such an ideology that such a bloc is 'unified'.

To repeat, each of the terms of this *family* indicates a concept that cannot entirely be mapped onto another. Let us start looking at what this means for the relation between ideology and philosophy. Gramsci notes that Croce does not succeed even from his point of view.[84] The distinction is 'only one of degree'

---

82   Gramsci 1975, p. 1380; Gramsci 1971, p. 328. Translation altered.
83   See Q10ii, § 2: Gramsci 1975, pp. 1241–2; Gramsci 1995, pp. 382–3.
84   Q10i: Gramsci 1975, p. 1231.

(a consideration that could be extended to this whole *family*): 'philosophy' is the general conception of a class, 'ideology' (especially if it is 'political') the particular conception of the world of certain groups that act organically within that class. But this acquisition is more problematic and relativised in another note, Q10ii, § 31, where Gramsci asks himself whether 'philosophy without a conformant moral will' exists,[85] whether there can be a difference 'between ideology and philosophy'. These seeds also appear in Q11, § 12.[86] These reflections arose from his *one-on-one* engagement with Croce. Gramsci – with the method to which he was accustomed, not thinking *in the abstract*, but with polemical reference to another author or text – thus arrived at his own mature definition of ideology and the relation between ideology and philosophy, as well as *framing* religion within the system of terms in which he portrayed the concept of ideology. And if 'lay' religion is more or less equivalent to 'ideology', as a 'conception of the world', then religion as traditionally understood *is an ideology*, indeed 'the most widespread and deeply rooted ideology'.[87] All men are philosophers ('every individual ... is a philosopher, he shares in a conception of the world'),[88] Gramsci repeats in Q10ii, § 17. But this true because, *if nothing else*, their 'practical activity' (and also, of course, their language: see, for example, Q10ii, § 44) implicitly contains 'a conception of the world, a philosophy ... the history of philosophers' philosophies is the history of attempts made and ideological initiatives ... to change, correct and perfect the conceptions of the world that exist in any particular age'.[89]

The 'traditional' sense of philosophy is, therefore, the more advanced part of the ideological continuum, equivalent to 'conceptions of the world' (or 'conceptions of life' or 'visions of the world'). But there is a vast range of terms equated to 'conception of the world' (and thus to ideology) and a vast range of contexts and modalities in which the term is used. Though not insisting on the category 'common sense' – to which the following chapter is dedicated – I will point out the following: 'folklore ... ought to be studied as a "conception of the world" of particular social strata';[90] school must struggle 'in opposition to the conception of the world conveyed by the traditional environment (folklore in its full scope)';[91] 'does [religion in Japan] still have the importance of a

---

85   Gramsci 1975, p. 1269; Gramsci 1995, p. 383.
86   Gramsci 1975, p. 1378; Gramsci 1971, p. 326.
87   Q4, § 41: Gramsci 1975, p. 466; Gramsci 1996b, p. 189.
88   Q4, § 51: Gramsci 1975, p. 488; Gramsci 1996b, p. 215.
89   Gramsci 1975, p. 1255; Gramsci 1971, p. 344.
90   Q1, § 89: Gramsci 1975, p. 89; Gramsci 1992, p. 186.
91   Q4, § 50: Gramsci 1975, p. 485; Gramsci 1996b, p. 211.

living and functioning conception of the world?';[92] 'America ... has not yet created a conception of the world'.[93] And, furthermore, 'The state has its own conception of life and it strives to disseminate it';[94] 'Tolstoy's conception of the world and Manzoni's';[95] 'If one wants to study a conception of the world that has never been systematically expounded by its author-thinker'[96] (as is well-known, Gramsci is here speaking of Marx, who, Q7, § 33 tells us, 'produced an original and integral conception of the world').[97]

We could go on. But it is better to emphasise one further point. For Gramsci, there is no-one who does not share in some conception of the world 'even if unconsciously so'.[98] But is it preferable 'to share in a conception of the world "imposed" from the outside, by a social group ... or is it preferable to elaborate one's own conception of the world consciously and critically?' The question seems a little pie in the sky, since it suggests a choice that could never exist. The degree of consciousness and the contribution made to a conception of the world varies, on a scale reaching from the 'simple people' to the most refined intellectuals. But even they think 'consciously and critically' on the basis of the conception of the world within which they are inserted, contributing to enriching and changing it. And, indeed, in the relevant text c, Gramsci makes a fundamentally-important addition:

> In acquiring one's conception of the world one always belongs to a partic-
> ular grouping which is that of all the social elements which share the same
> mode of thinking and acting. We are all conformists of one conformism
> or other.[99]

He makes this assertion, before adding 'When one's conception of the world is not critical and coherent but disjointed and episodic, one belongs simultaneously to a multiplicity of mass human groups. The personality is strangely composite ...'. In any case, 'conformism has always existed: today it is a matter of two conformisms, that is, a struggle for hegemony'.

---

92   Q5, § 50: Gramsci 1975, p. 580; Gramsci 1996b, p. 306.
93   Q6, § 10: Gramsci 1975, p. 692; Gramsci 1971, p. 272.
94   Q1, § 89: Gramsci 1975, p. 90; Gramsci 1992, p. 187.
95   Q3, § 148: Gramsci 1975, p. 402; Gramsci 1996b, p. 120.
96   Q4, § 1: Gramsci 1975, p. 419; Gramsci 1996b, p. 137.
97   Gramsci 1975, p. 882; Gramsci 1971, p. 382.
98   Q8, § 204: Gramsci 1975, p. 1063.
99   Q11, § 12: Gramsci 1975, p. 1376; Gramsci 1971, p. 324.

5   Ideology and Will

Let's take stock. Ideology, in Gramsci, is the representation of reality proper to a social group. The individual subject has a vision of the world that is not only hers, but belongs to the group of which she is part, or else she shares in several visions of the world, often in a syncretic manner. Ideologies are 'the terrain on which men move'. Collective subjects are defined precisely by ideologies. Without ideologies, there are no subjects. Ideology is the site of the constitution of collective subjectivity, but also – in a more contradictory manner – of individual subjectivity, within the ambit of the struggle for hegemony.

Ideology, being something that one cannot but have, seems to come before political choices pondered over by individuals[100] and behaviour that is more attached to will. It conditions such choices and behaviours, although sometimes *silently* so. It has a dialectical relationship with them, though it does seem to play a determining role. It is explicated in the forms of everyday life. We are, therefore, here outside of any rationalist-enlightenment conception. Ideologies exist in abstraction from the will and behaviour of individuals. They change, but cannot be totally redirected, since no subject has the capacity to control their whole process and outcome. They are the result of the struggle for hegemony and the struggle between classes, but also the partiality of the viewpoint of the societal actor and her inherent need for identity. At the same time, they are organised and spread; they imbue apparatuses, 'trenches and earthworks'; they are re-elaborated, adapted, and propagated – not only, as Gramsci notes, by the press, publishing houses, schools and various types of 'clubs and circles', but also by what we would today call the culture industry, the *mass media*, the enormous expansion of the new, internationalised dimension of music, the mores and consumption of sex; and, still, by religion and faith, and not only in the *secular* sense. It is obvious how this relates to the importance of the *Notebooks*' extended conception of intellectuals and their social role.

Though Gramsci was sometimes the philosopher of *will*, he maintained that will cannot do everything: the subject is *the outcome* of a complex and intangible but nonetheless real combination. The individual and collective revolutionary break takes place on the basis of a complex and in many ways unintentional process.

---

100   'It is the fantasy of fossilised intellectuals to believe that a conception of the world can be destroyed by critiques of a rational character' (Q 10ii, 41i: Gramsci 1975, p. 1292).

CHAPTER 6

Good Sense and Common Sense

1 Two Meanings

The first time that the phrase 'common sense' appears in the *Notebooks* is the beginning of the first notebook, in the list of 'main topics' that Gramsci laid out on 8 February 1929. It is entry number 13 in a list of 16, and includes a bracketed reference (the only such case in this list) to another entry, point 7, which concerns 'the concept of folklore'.[1] In the second list that we find in the *Notebooks*, at the beginning of the eighth notebook – an unnumbered list, composed of 21 'main essays' – we read, in the third entry, 'Folklore and common sense'.[2] Gramsci has thus brought together two points that, in the first list, were only connected by a reference.

Attention toward the concept of 'common sense' thus appears right from the beginning of Gramsci's prison work plans, and he speaks of 'common sense' even in the early notes of the first notebook. Among his first nine miscellaneous notebooks, 'common sense' appears repeatedly in notebooks 1, 3 and 4, in a series of A and B texts. It then appears in numerous A and B texts in notebooks 5, 6, 7, 8 and 9, above all in the eighth notebook, in the third series of 'Points on philosophy'. Numerous of these B texts also appear in notebook 10ii, and then in 14, 15 and 17, the last miscellaneous notebooks that Gramsci began in prison.[3] Starting with notebook 10, the entry 'common sense' recurs in a number of C texts. The term is altogether absent only from notebooks 2, 12, 18–22, 25–6 and 29.

Apart from its appearance in his initial list, we see the phrase 'common sense' for the first time in a B text of the first notebook, Q1, §16, in a note on a section of the *Domenica del Corriere* entitled 'readers' postcards'. Gramsci writes that 'the "reader's postcards" are one of the most typical documents of Italian popular common sense. Barilli belongs to an even lower level than this common sense: philistine for the classical philistines of the *Domenica del Corriere*'.[4]

---

1 Q1: Gramsci 1975, p. 5; Gramsci 1992, p. 99.
2 Q8: Gramsci 1975, p. 38.
3 Frosini 2003, p. 26.
4 Gramsci 1975, p. 14; Gramsci 1992, pp. 107–8.

We can note that in this passage: a) 'common sense' takes the epithet 'Italian popular', suggesting that Gramsci is implicitly claiming that there are various different common senses, which it is possible to distinguish between and which are geographically and socially connoted; b) 'common sense' is not appraised positively, because one can be at an *'even* lower level' (my italics) than it: evidently a harsh comparison precisely due to the qualitatively very low level of common sense. Immediately, we can ask ourselves if this stands in contrast with point a). That is, if there are various different forms of common sense, articulated according to geographical area and above all by social group, how can it be said that *all* of them are of a *very low* level? As such, there are already in this first passage, *in nuce,* two partially different ways (which could at times also converge) of understanding common sense: a) as the widespread and often implicit 'conception of the world' of a social or territorial group; b) as being opposed to a developed and congruous 'conception of the world'. I would at once advance that it was in the first sense that Gramsci contented, for example, that even intellectuals have their own common sense; and in the second sense that he used the phrase with a manifestly negative connotation, or even pejoratively.

The second note in which we come across 'common sense' can be ascribed to this second meaning. It is an A text, also in notebook 1, with the section heading 'types of periodicals'. This is Q1, § 43, a long and important passage that later flowed into the 'special' – monographic – note 3 of notebook 24, entitled 'Journalism'. The study of 'types of periodicals' is also important to the *Notebooks* because it is with this that Gramsci enters onto the terrain of the organisation of hegemony, and thus of the consciously sought spread of an ideology, a true and proper 'educational-formative work that a homogeneous cultural centre performs'.[5] To me, it seems that we can say that in writing this, in a somewhat coded manner, Gramsci was also thinking of what the activity of the Communist Party ought to be. Gramsci guards against committing an '"enlightenment" error', namely 'to think that a well propagated "clear idea" enters diverse consciousness with the same "organising" effects of widespread clarity'. He adds:

> The ability of the professional intellectual skillfully to combine induction and deduction, to generalise, to infer, to transport from one sphere to another a criterion of discrimination, adapting it to new conditions etc. is a 'specialty', it is not endowed by 'common sense'. Therefore, the premise

---

5   Q1, § 43: Gramsci 1975, p. 34; Gramsci 1992, p. 129.

of an 'organic diffusion from a homogeneous centre of a homogeneous way of thinking and acting' is not sufficient.[6]

The 'enlightenment' error, therefore, is to hold that all men *are* equal. Much as one may wish that this should tend to *become* the case, it is necessary to start out by realistically recognising the disparities that do exist – including *cultural* or *intellectual* disparities. Here, a sharp division is drawn between what we could call the 'professional intellectual' and those whose cultural development remains at the level of 'common sense'. If all men are intellectuals, as Gramsci says elsewhere, this is not to say that all are intellectuals in the same way: there are evidently those who have had the privilege of being able to develop their personal intellectual capacities. 'Common sense' (in its largely negative meaning) seems to be situated beyond and outside this citadel of privilege.

The third text in the *Notebooks* in which we find 'common sense' is Q1, § 65, again entitled 'types of periodicals'. It is important in at least two aspects: a) it is the first time that we come across 'common sense' appearing together with 'good sense'; b) the two concepts are deeply thematised and the phrases in question appear together repeatedly, as Gramsci tried to bring into focus for the first time what he meant by 'common sense'. In the first place, speaking of various periodicals, he states that 'this general type' of periodicals

> belongs to the sphere of 'good sense' or 'common sense': it tries to modify the average opinion of a particular society, criticising, suggesting, admonishing, modernising, introducing new 'clichés' … they must not appear to be fanatical or excessively partisan: they must position themselves within the field of 'common sense', distancing themselves from it just enough to permit a mocking smile, but not contempt or arrogant superiority.[7]

Apart from noting that here 'good sense' and 'common sense' appear as equivalents, from this paragraph we get a few *tactical* warnings (evidently directed at that 'homogeneous centre' carrying out 'educational-formative work', as mentioned above). These already express, however, a certain conception of 'common sense': in order to have an impact on it, 'they must position themselves within the field of "common sense"'. Common sense is not, *in toto*, 'an enemy to be fought': a dialectical and maieutic relation with common sense must be established in order that it be transformed and, indeed, transform itself, up

---

6   Gramsci 1975, p. 33; Gramsci 1992, p. 128.
7   Q1, § 65: Gramsci 1975, p. 76; Gramsci 1992, p. 173.

until the conquest – as we will see – of 'a new common sense', which must be arrived at within the terms of the struggle for hegemony.

Richer and more complex still is the following paragraph, where Gramsci advances his reflection with a real logical-argumentative leap, revealing to the reader the level at which his elaboration had now arrived:

> Every social stratum has its own 'common sense' which is ultimately the most widespread conception of life and morals. Every philosophical current leaves a sedimentation of 'common sense': this is the document of its historical reality. Common sense is not something rigid and static; rather, it changes continuously, enriched by scientific notions and philosophical opinions which have entered into common usage. 'Common sense' is the folklore of 'philosophy' and stands midway between real 'folklore' (that is, as it is understood) and the philosophy, the science, the economics of the scholars. 'Common sense' creates the folklore of the future, that is a more or less rigified phase of a certain time and place.[8]

We can find many signposts in this text; to emphasise just the most relevant: a) 'Every social stratum has its own common sense', meaning that the notion is relativised synchronically;[9] b) 'common sense' can be defined as 'the most widespread conception of life and morals' (among a given social stratum); c) 'common sense' derives from the 'sedimentation left by prior philosophical currents' and is the 'folklore of philosophy'; d) 'common sense' is constantly changing (the notion is also diachronically relativised, that is, historicised),[10] incorporating ever new fragments of science and philosophy and evolving with the evolution of society.

To me, it seems that here we have a general conception of 'common sense' that makes it a fully-fledged variant of the concept of ideology, a 'conception of the world' in Gramsci's terms. Another 'conceptual link' of this chain, particularly close to the concept of 'common sense', is that of 'conformism'. Common sense, in the light of this passage from the first notebook, is a given social stratum's conception of the world, largely to be characterised as a passive moment of reception of the active elaboration carried out by that same social group's 'intellectual' or 'leadership' stratum. As a passive moment, common sense shows the signs of lag, and even very weak elaborations. But the accent

---

8   Ibid.
9   See Luporini 1987, pp. 132–3.
10   See Luporini 1987, p. 132.

placed on the fact that 'every social stratum has its own "common sense"'
excludes the possibility of common sense being defined only as the qualitatively lower level of a conception of the world. It concerns, in general, the most
widespread and often implicit ideology of a social group, at a minimal level,
even in the commonplace sense of the word minimal. For this reason, it moves
in dialectical relationship with philosophy, that is, with the advanced level of
ideology, proper to the leadership strata of the various social groups.

Here, however, we are largely – as in Gramsci's whole conception of the *continuum* describing ideology at its various different levels of elaboration – on
the terrain of the *pre-intentional*, where the greater part of subjects are not
mobilised, but *defined* (in their subjectivity, in their individual and collective
way of being) by ideology and, therefore, also by common sense. A problem
this poses – one we are not able to address here – is how to marry this largely
pre-intentional character of common sense with the activity of the 'homogenous centre' carrying out 'educational-formative work' to change it, creating a
new common sense. To me it seems obvious that the 'homogeneous centre'
must not delude itself as to the possibility of forming an entirely new common
sense. Indeed, common sense derives also from the influence of many other
uncontrollable factors – and this is itself linked to the open and impossible-to-
predefine character of the process of history. It is difficult to say to what extent
Gramsci was conscious of this, but we must not forget the role that the concepts
of will and 'collective will' – appearing in the text alongside these considerations on the pre-intentional – played in the thinking of the Sardinian Marxist,
indicating the complexity of the anthropological conceptions that we can find
in the *Notebooks*.[11]

2   Spontaneity and Backwardness

What is the connotation of 'common sense' in these early notebooks? It is
defined in Q3, § 48[12] as a given social stratum's '[traditional] conception of the
world', and to me it seems that the stress falls on the word 'traditional', an adjective which Gramsci *added* either between the lines or in the margins. This note
is dedicated to examining the bond between spontaneity and leadership, with
explicit reference to *L'Ordine Nuovo*. Gramsci here at least partially picks up on

---

11   On the whole problematic field connected to the construction of a new common sense, it
         is worth looking at Forenza 2012.
12   Gramsci 1975, p. 1380; Gramsci 1971, p. 328.

the importance of the element of popular 'spontaneity', albeit as something to be educated. He writes that in the *L'Ordine Nuovo* experience 'This element of "spontaneity" was not neglected, much less disdained: it was *educated*, it was given a direction, it was cleansed of everything extraneous that could contaminate it, in order to unify it by means of modern theory'.[13] As such it was not an 'enlightenment' action making the errors outlined in Q1, § 43 and Q1, § 65. Within this ambit, there is undoubtedly a re-evaluation of common sense. In the first place, it is set in relation with 'the "spontaneous" sentiments of the masses', 'formed through everyday experience in the light of "common sense", that is, the traditional popular conception of the world'.[14] But, above all, Gramsci establishes a 'quantitative' – and thus not 'qualitative' – difference between philosophy and common sense, since he recalled that 'I. Kant considered it important for his philosophical theories to be in agreement with common sense; the same is true of Croce'.[15]

Let us leave aside for now this mention of Croce, to whom we shall return. As for the rest, it must be said that this positive evaluation of common sense is, however, substantially an isolated case among Gramsci's near-contemporaneous early notebooks. We can, though, glean some other implicitly positive evaluations of 'common sense' in Gramsci by studying how he *used* this phrase. In Q5, § 39, for example, we read

> Scepticism: The common-sense objection that one can make against scepticism is this: that to be consistent with himself the sceptic should do nothing else but live like a vegetable, without involving himself in the business of ordinary life.[16]

Here, common sense is not considered in a wholly negative manner: it is a *good-sense* position, one that Gramsci appears to make his own. And in Q8, § 151, we read:

> We speak of 'second nature'; a certain habit has become second nature; but does 'first nature' really come 'first', right at the beginning? Is there not, in this way of talking about common sense, a hint at the historicity of human nature?[17]

---

13   Gramsci 1975, p. 330; Gramsci 1971, p. 50.
14   Gramsci 1975, pp. 330–1; Gramsci 1996b, pp. 50–1.
15   Gramsci 1975, p. 331; Gramsci 1996b, p. 51.
16   Gramsci 1975, p. 571; Gramsci 1971, p. 374.
17   Gramsci 1975, p. 1032.

Here, too, is a glimmer of a common-sense position in which Gramsci is able to share. But – I repeat – this is very little to go on: the fascinating discussion of Q3, § 48 is not taken up again, neither in the third notebook nor in subsequent ones, nor where it was rewritten (being a text A). If we want to adopt Gramsci's well-known call not to cling onto a single quotation, instead seeking to grasp 'the rhythm of the author's thought' in development, it seems to me that we cannot but begin from the notes in which his negative judgements on common sense, both implicit and explicit, are a great deal more numerous and also qualitatively significant. For example, in a text A in the fourth notebook (Q4, § 18), entitled 'The technique of thinking', Gramsci writes:

> The technique of thought will certainly not produce a great philosophy, but it will provide criteria for judgment, and it will correct the deformities of the modes of thinking of common sense. It would be interesting to compare the *technique* of common sense – i.e., of the philosophy of the man in the street – with the technique of the most advanced modern thought. In this respect, it is also worth taking into account Macaulay's observation on the logical weaknesses of a culture formed by oratory and declamation.[18]

Common sense appears here, then, with precise weak points, of a logical type: its deformities, seemingly linked to the 'oratory and declamatory' formation of the 'philosophy of the man in the street', must be corrected. Yet more negative is the judgement on common sense in relation to a theme on which Gramsci long dwelled: that of the 'objective existence of reality' (Q4, § 41), which is, for Gramsci, 'the most important question for science' but 'as far as common sense is concerned, the question does not even exist'.[19] What provides common sense with such certainties 'is essentially religion ... above all Christianity', making it into 'an ideology, the most widespread and deeply rooted ideology'.[20] Here, for Gramsci, common sense is a vision of the world that is backward both because it is conditioned by religious ideology – which is inevitably not monistic – and because it does not take in the new discoveries of science, which even learned Christianity has absorbed:

---

18   Gramsci 1975, p. 439; Gramsci 1996b, p. 160.
19   Gramsci 1975, pp. 466–7; Gramsci 1996b, p. 189.
20   Ibid.

Common sense affirms the objectivity of the real in that this objectivity was created by God; it is therefore an expression of the religious conception of the world ... it is not, in fact, really 'objective' because it cannot conceive of objective 'truth'. For common sense, it is 'true' that the world stands still while the sun and the whole firmament turn around it, etc. Yet it makes the philosophical affirmation of the objectivity of the real.[21]

Here, for Gramsci, 'common sense' is undoubtedly equivalent to a pre-modern vision of the world. Further on, in notebook 6, speaking of Pirandello, Gramsci argues that the Sicilian dramatist's dialectical conception of objectivity 'seems acceptable to the public because it is enacted by exceptional characters; hence it has the romantic quality of a paradoxical struggle against common sense and good sense'.[22] Here, too, common sense is seen as stuck at the Aristotelian-Catholic 'objectivity of the real'.[23] Again in this same notebook, Gramsci connotes common sense with an undoubtedly conservative and traditional character: 'common sense is led to believe that what today exists has always existed'.[24] Q6, § 207 repeats the equation between common sense and folklore that we saw even on the first page of the *Notebooks*.

In the course of the *Notebooks*, the negative entries and judgements on common sense – which very often takes the adjective 'vulgar' – seem to prevail clearly over the positive ones. And it is superfluous to insist on this point – having been made aware of this, the reader can easily see it for herself in following Gramsci's discourse. I only want to add – somewhat anticipating the set of polemical notes on this question and how Bukharin dealt with it – something on Q7, § 29:

One gets the sense that the dialectic is something very arduous and difficult insofar as it goes against vulgar common sense that expresses itself through formal logic, is dogmatic, and eagerly seeks absolute certainties ... the author of the *Popular Manual* ... really capitulated before common

---

21   Gramsci 1975, p. 467; Gramsci 1996b, p. 190.

22   Gramsci 1975, p. 706; Gramsci 2011, p. 22.

23   Polemicising later on against both idealism and – above all – Bukharin, Gramsci again sets his focus on common sense and 'the reality of the external world', remarking on the religious origin of the *realist* conception and posing Marxism as the alternative both to 'religious "transcendence"' and to common sense: see Q8, § 215 and § 217 (and the text C recapitulating it: Q11, § 17). On this question, see Jaulin 1991.

24   Q6, § 78: Gramsci 1975, p. 745.

sense and vulgar thought, for he did not pose the issue in correct theoretical terms and was therefore practically disarmed and impotent. The uneducated and crude environment has exercised control over the educator; vulgar common sense has imposed itself on science instead of the other way round. If the environment is the educator, it must in turn be educated, as Marx wrote, but the *Popular Manual* does not comprehend this revolutionary dialectic.[25]

This text depicts common sense (defined as 'vulgar') as backward both in terms of its content (stuck at the level of 'formal logic') and in light of its form (it is 'dogmatic and eagerly seeks absolute certainties'). Bukharin is even accused of 'capitulat[ing] before common sense'. Gramsci refers back to the third of Marx's *Theses on Feuerbach*, with its well-known passage on the reciprocal relation between subject and environment and the educator who must be educated; though he adds a little confusion in his use of the metaphor, the sense of Gramsci's reasoning is clear. He puts 'vulgar common sense' side-by-side with 'the uneducated and crude environment', which overcomes the 'educator' – and this is his accusation against Bukharin –; it overcomes science and the party as a theoretical and political vanguard.

Gramsci insists, therefore, on the counterposition between common sense, on the one hand, and science (Marxism) and consciousness on the other. Why? Why, given the 'Janus face' of common sense (like that of folklore) – reactionary but at the same time necessary, conservative but potentially susceptible to insertion within a new hegemonic project – does Gramsci insist above all on the negative 'face' of this lower segment of the ideological *continuum*? In my view, we should seek the answer in terms of the theoretical-practical character of the *Notebooks*. Gramsci was here dealing not only with a fact-finding survey of the real, but also with the task of elaborating a line of political activity that could shift the relations of force and again open up the struggle for hegemony, thus transforming common sense. In order to achieve this, his first step could not but be the critique of what exists and the rejection of any populist temptation.

Before addressing the discourse on common sense that Gramsci elaborated through his polemic with Bukharin, however, let us first examine his considerations on this same theme in relation to Croce.

---

25   Gramsci 1975, p. 877; Gramsci 2011, p. 179.

3   Common Sense, Neoidealism, Misoneism

Focusing on Croce's philosophy at the beginning of the second series of 'Points of philosophy' in the seventh notebook – including with regard to 'religion' – Gramsci cites a passage from Mario Missiroli, taken from his article 'Religione e filosofia'. Missiroli here focuses on the difficulty idealism has in making itself understood by both 'common sense' (of students) and 'good sense' (of teachers of subjects other than philosophy) insofar as 'humanity is still wholly Aristotelian, and the common view remains attached to the dualism that is characteristic of Greco-Christian realism'.[26] Continuing, Gramsci states that 'Croce is continuously flirting with the "common sense" and "good sense" of the people (all Croce's pieces on the relation between philosophy and "common sense" need to be collected)'.[27] Let us put off, for now, our study of the implications of this mention of 'good sense' and focus on one important fact: Gramsci has posed the question of 'Croce and common sense'. This theme is an important one because it leads us to contextualise Gramsci's reflections on common sense within the philosophical discussion (in Italy and elsewhere)[28] at the turn of the 1920s–30s, and above all in that it identifies Croce as one of the fundamental sources of Gramsci's discourse, in a complex relation of adoption and rejection. Which, obviously, confirms the fact that in this reflection also – as throughout the *Notebooks* – 'engagement with the philosophical tradition remains an essential constant of Gramsci's observations in this regard, but not with a view to following it, but rather to transform the notion of "common sense" profoundly by inserting it into political discourse; that is, by making it into a category of political science, an interpretative category of social reality, and at the same time an operative one'.[29]

As is well known, Croce himself had begun the 'discussion' (if understood in the broad sense) in which, among others, Giovanni Gentile,[30] Mario Missiroli (with the article Gramsci cites),[31] and Santino Caramella[32] participated,

---

26   Quoted in Q7, § 1: Gramsci 1975, p. 853; Gramsci 2011, p. 155.

27   Ibid. The relevant text c misses out the phrase 'Croce is continuously flirting ...', but we find an added mention of 'The dualistic conception, that of the "objectivity of the external world", as it has taken root among the people through the traditional philosophies and religions that have become "common sense"' (Q10ii, § 41i: Gramsci 1975, p. 1295).

28   See Sobrero 1976; 1979, pp. 623 et sqq.

29   Luporini 1987, p. 132.

30   Gentile 1931.

31   Missiroli 1930.

32   Caramella 1932. In 1933's Q15, § 65, (Gramsci 1975, p. 1829) Gramsci notes: 'Introduction

with his essay *Filosofia come vita morale e vita morale come filosofia*.[33] In this essay, Croce upheld the need to 'abandon the traditional distinction between ordinary and extraordinary thought', between common sense and philosophy, because 'each thought is always ordinary and always linked to experience'.[34] The distinction between philosophical and non-philosophical thought was, for the neo-idealist philosopher, not 'a logical distinction, but only a psychological one': the philosopher in the full sense of the word is called upon to overcome incoherency and incompleteness, whereas the non-philosopher is content to live with these. But – Croce admonished – 'no man is entirely not a philosopher, and no philosopher is a perfect one'.[35]

Adding that even he 'who does not write of philosophy and is even unaware of the name of this discipline' can also be a philosopher, even 'modest men', and that 'even ... plebeians and peasants' can think and speak wisely and 'are secure in possessing the substantial truths'.[36] It is not difficult to see the paternalistic character of Croce's discourse. But also that such statements are close to Gramsci's – though connoted by a quite different spirit – which we see in his 'The study of philosophy. Some preliminary points of reference' (Q11, §12) and which appear already in the eighth notebook in the form of an A text. It is in this same eighth notebook that Gramsci's prison-era reflection on common sense was at its most extensive, taking its cue from engagement with both Bukharin's theses and those of Croce and Gentile. In the highly important Q8, §173, entitled 'On the *Popular Manual*' (an A text that was revisited – together with other notes including Q8, §175 – in Q11, §13), Gramsci resumes and deepens his engagement with neo-idealism on the theme of the relation between philosophers' philosophy and the philosophy of common sense, writing:

> Croce's attitude toward 'common sense': does not seem clear to me. For Croce, the thesis that 'every man is a philosopher' has thus far weighed too heavily on his judgment with regard to 'common sense'; Croce often

---

to the study of philosophy. See Santino Caramella's book *Senso comune, Teoria e Pratica*, pp. 176, Bari, Laterza, 1933. Contains three essays: 1) The critique of "common sense"; 2) The relations between theory and practice; 3) Universality and nationality in the history of Italian philosophy'. Gramsci requested that Tania send him this book, in a letter of 23 August 1933 (Gramsci 1996a, pp. 738–9) and it is among the books in the Fondo Gramsci (Gramsci 1975, p. 3042), though this copy is not today held at the Fondazione Gramsci.

33   Croce 1928.
34   Croce 1928, p. 77.
35   Ibid.
36   Croce 1928, p. 78.

seems gratified that certain propositions of philosophy are shared by
common sense, but what concrete meaning can this have? The fact that
'every man is a philosopher' does not make it necessary to hark back, in
this sense, to common sense. Common sense is an unformed aggregate
of philosophical conceptions, within which can be found whatever one
wants to find.[37] After all, in Croce this attitude towards common sense
has not led to a cultural attitude that is fruitful from the 'national-popular'
point of view, that is, to a more concretely historicist conception of philosophy, which can, moreover, be found only in historical materialism.[38]

Notwithstanding the evident debt of some of Gramsci's fundamental ideas to
this Croce, his critique puts pressure on the neo-idealist philosopher precisely
at the point where he derives a certain paternalistic *condescension* toward common sense from their shared assumption that 'every man is a philosopher'.
Gramsci's critique of common sense (insisted upon and deepened in the rewritten version: Q11, §13) surpasses Croce's because – precisely in virtue of the fact
that the communist thinker was working with the objective of the people emerging from its subalternity – he dramatically highlights the full inadequacy of
the *existing* common sense. That is, on the basis of common sense, the subaltern classes cannot mount a real challenge for hegemony and are condemned
to remain subaltern (hence Croce's condescension, since he obviously looks
favourably upon this *political* outcome).[39] In the subsequent note Q8, §175,
Gramsci goes on to address Gentile's position on this question:

> *Gentile.* See his article *La concezione umanistica del mondo* ... It seems to
> me another example of the unabashed crudeness of Gentile's thought,
> 'ingenuously' derived from some of Croce's statements using the people's
> way of thinking as a proof of certain philosophical propositions. The cita-
> tion can be used for the section on 'common sense' ... Gentile speaks of
> an ahistorical 'human nature', and of 'the truth of common sense' as if one
> could not find all sorts within 'common sense' and as if there existed a

---

37   The text c is more radically negative: 'common sense is a chaotic aggregate of disparate
     conceptions, within which can be found whatever one wants to find': Q11, §13: Gramsci
     1975, pp. 1398–9.
38   Q8, §173: Gramsci 1975, pp. 1045–6.
39   On Croce, see also Q8, §225, Gramsci 1975, pp. 1082–3: 'Points for an essay on B. Croce
     ... Croce is popular among the Anglo-Saxons, who have always preferred a conception of
     the world that is not about great systems, as with the Germans, but that seems to be an
     expression of common sense, as a solution of moral and practical problems'.

'single common sense', eternal and immutable. The expression 'common sense' is used in a variety of ways: for example against the abstruseness, the ingenuities and the obscurities of scientific and philosophical exposition that is, as a 'style', etc. Gentile's article offers other gems: a little later, he says 'The healthy man believes in God and in the freedom of his spirit', so we thus find ourselves faced with two 'common senses', one for the healthy man and one for an ill one.[40]

Gentile, therefore, *tactically* bases himself on common sense, even though his philosophy is 'utterly contrary to common sense', making it easier still to demonstrate the crudeness and instrumental character of the actualist position. But above all, recomposing this piece in its C text version, Gramsci adds another consideration that represents a balance-sheet of his reasoning, starting from the recognition that

What was said above does not mean that there are no truths in common sense. It means rather that common sense is an ambiguous, contradictory and multiform concept, and that to refer to common sense as a confirmation of truth is a nonsense. It is possible to state correctly that a certain truth has become part of common sense in order to indicate that it has spread beyond the confines of intellectual groups, but all one is doing in that case is making a historical observation and an assertion of the rationality of history. In this sense, and used with restraint, the argument has a certain validity, precisely because common sense is crudely neophobe and conservative so that to have succeeded in forcing the introduction of

---

40   Gramsci 1975, p. 1047. The text C version of this passage is richer still: 'Gentile writes: "The healthy man believes in God and in the freedom of his spirit". Thus just in these two propositions of Gentile's we find: 1. an extra-historical "human nature" which one can't see quite what it is: 2. the human nature of the healthy man; 3. the common sense of the healthy man and therefore also a common sense of the non-healthy. But what is meant by healthy [*sano*] man? Physically healthy? Or not mad? Or someone who thinks in a healthy way, right-thinking, philistine, etc.? And what does a "truth of common sense" mean? Gentile's philosophy, for example, is utterly contrary to common sense, whether one understands thereby the naive philosophy of the people, which revolts against any form of subjectivist idealism, or whether one understands it to be good sense and a contemptuous attitude to the abstruseness, ingenuities and obscurity of certain forms of scientific and philosophical exposition. This flirtation of Gentile with common sense is quite comical'. Q11, §13: Gramsci 1975, p. 1399; Gramsci 1971, pp. 422–3. See also the 'Note 1' on Gentile, which Gramsci adds at the bottom of this same note.

a new truth is a proof that the truth in question has exceptional evidence and capacity for expansion.[41]

This statement should not be bent out of shape such as to force it to say that Gramsci took a positive view of common sense. He is only saying that even within common sense, within which all sorts of things can be found, there are also elements of truth. It is, certainly, important to note when a given idea has become 'common sense', most of all for those who want to create a *new* common sense. There remains the fact that common sense is here linked to a 'misoneist' view of ideology, a conservative one with a prejudice against the new. It is, therefore, *above all* a major obstacle to revolutionary strategy, in the given historical situation: but also an inevitable *hic Rhodus, hic salta!*

4   Marxism and Common Sense

In the eighth notebook, Gramsci engages in a very sharp polemic with Bukharin, including on the terrain of how 'common sense' is to be appraised. This was already mentioned, with regard to Croce, in Q8, §173. It is a long passage, in which 'common sense' appears some 18 times. Let us examine this passage by breaking it down into its constituent parts (except that on Croce, which we have studied already). Gramsci writes:

> A work like the *Popular Manual* that is aimed at a community of readers who are not professional intellectuals, should have as its point of departure an analysis and a critique of the philosophy of common sense, which is the 'philosophy of nonphilosophers' – in other words, the conception of the world *acritically* absorbed from the various social environments in which the moral individuality of the average person is developed. Common sense is not a single conception, identical in time and place. It is the 'folklore' of philosophy, and, like folklore, it appears in countless forms. The fundamental characteristic of common sense consists in its being a disjointed, incoherent and inconsequential conception of the world[42] that matches the character of the multitudes whose philosophy it is.[43]

---

41   Q11, §13: Gramsci 1975, p. 1399; Gramsci 1971, p. 423.

42   In the relevant text C, instead of 'of the world', Gramsci puts in brackets '(even in the brain of one individual)': Q11, §13: Gramsci 1975, p. 1396; Gramsci 1971, p. 419.

43   Q8, §173: Gramsci 1975, p. 1045; Gramsci 2011, p. 333.

Polemicising against Bukharin's book, then, Gramsci first reaffirms and extends his own definition of 'common sense'. It is 'philosophy' (even if a 'philosophy of nonphilosophers'), a 'conception of the world', 'the "folklore" of philosophy': the umpteenth confirmation of the 'conceptual family' – of which we have spoken already[44] – in which Gramsci's concept of ideology is articulated. But Gramsci again adds extremely critical epithets to 'common sense' and the links in the conceptual chain of reference on which he now focuses: the common-sense conception is 'acritically absorbed', syncretic ('in countless different forms', he specifies in the text C, 'even in the brain of one individual'), 'incoherent' and 'inconsequential'. It is the philosophy of the *multitudes*. And these *multitudes* here appear as a social subject of less determinacy than a 'class' or 'social group', and with a negative connotation. Let's continue reading of the note in question:

> Historically, the formation of a homogeneous social group is accompanied by the development of a 'homogeneous' – that is, 'systematic' – philosophy, in opposition to common sense.[45]

The new revolutionary class in formation, Gramsci says, elaborates its own 'homogeneous' and 'systematic' philosophy, one that is even 'in opposition to common sense'. It would be mistaken to underestimate the importance of this passage (reaffirmed in the relevant C text) in understanding the 'vanguard/masses' relationship. Revolutionary theory emerges *in opposition to* the *existing* common sense. What is at stake is the subalterns' 'conception of the world', which must be transformed or replaced. The *Popular Manual* is mistaken not to start out from common sense; but here, 'starting out from common sense' means the *critique* of common sense. Let us continue:

> The main components of common sense are provided by religions – not only by the religion that happens to be dominant at a given time but also by previous religions, popular heretical movements, scientific concepts from the past, etc. 'Realistic, materialist elements' predominate in common sense, but this does not in any way contradict the religious element. These elements are 'acritical' and 'superstitious'. Herein lies one of the 'dangers' presented by the *Popular Manual*: it often reinforces these acritical elements that are grounded in mere direct perception: which

---

44 See Chapter 4.

45 Q8, § 173: Gramsci 1975, p. 1045; Gramsci 2011, p. 333.

is why common sense has remained 'Ptolemaic', anthropomorphic and anthropocentric.[46]

In the relevant text c, this discourse on the influence of religious conceptions of the world, in particular Catholic ones, is widened and articulated.[47] Gramsci's note from the eighth notebook continues by referring to French philosophical culture's widespread interest in common sense. I will limit myself, here, to pointing out that its national-popular character is read *in a negative sense*, as the hegemony of a social group that hegemonises the subaltern masses by way of the intellectuals and their concern for common sense:

> Common sense has been treated more extensively in French philosoph-
> ical culture than in other cultures. This is due to the 'national-popular'
> character of French culture. In France, more than elsewhere, and because
> of specific historical conditions, the intellectuals tend to approach the
> people in order to guide it ideologically and keep it linked with the lead-
> ing group. One should therefore be able to find in French literature a
> lot of useful material on common sense. The attitude of French philo-
> sophical culture toward 'common sense' might even provide a model of
> hegemonic cultural construction. English and American culture might
> also offer many cues, but not in the same complete and organic sense as
> the French.[48]

---

46   Q8, § 173: Gramsci 1975, p. 1045; Gramsci 2011, pp. 333–4. In the relevant text c, the following
      passage is added, here, 'The above remarks about the way in which the *Popular Manual*
      criticises systematic philosophies instead of starting from a critique of common sense,
      should be understood as a methodological point and within certain limits. Certainly they
      do not mean that the critique of the systematic philosophies of the intellectuals is to be
      neglected. When an individual from the masses succeeds in criticising and going beyond
      common sense, he by this very fact accepts a new philosophy. Hence the necessity, in
      an exposition of the philosophy of praxis, of a polemic with traditional philosophies.
      Indeed, because by its nature it tends towards being a mass philosophy, the philosophy
      of praxis can only be conceived in a polemical form and in the form of a perpetual
      struggle. Nonetheless the starting point must always be that common sense which is
      the spontaneous philosophy of the multitude and which has to be made ideologically
      coherent' (Q11, § 13: Gramsci 1975, pp. 1397–8; Gramsci 1971, pp. 420–1).
47   Among others, Tommaso La Rocca has focused on this argument, dedicating to it the
      book/anthology *La religione come senso comune* (Gramsci 1997).
48   Q8, § 173: Gramsci 1975, p. 1045; Gramsci 2011, p. 334.

We know that France offered, for Gramsci, an impossible-to-equal model of (bourgeois) hegemony. There is also his methodological admonition that even if it is true that 'common sense has been treated in two ways: 1) it has been placed at the base of philosophy; 2) it has been criticised from the point of view of another philosophy', in reality what has been done in both cases has been to 'surmount one particular "common sense" in order to create another that is more compliant with the conception of the world of the leading group'.[49] Which means to say, common sense as such cannot be eliminated. It is part of the stakes of the struggle for hegemony: it is a basic and widespread conception of the world, *which can be replaced but not eliminated.* There remains the question of whether it would be possible – upon some tomorrow where the human race is proceeding down the road of self-emancipation from its own economic, social, political and cultural limits – to eliminate common sense as understood in the pejorative sense, as the passive adaptation of *the led* when faced with the *leaders'* elaboration of the necessary conception of the world.

Let us move on to Q8, § 175, which we just saw with regard to Gramsci's polemic against Gentile. In this piece, Gramsci invokes Giusti,[50] and explains why he does so in the relevant text c.[51] But above all, in the text A, he cites Marx:

> When Marx alludes to 'fixed popular opinion', he is making a historical-cultural reference in order to point out the 'solidity of beliefs' and their effectiveness in regulating human behaviour, implicitly, however, he is affirming the need for 'new popular beliefs', that is, for a new 'common sense', and thus for a new culture, a new philosophy.[52]

---

49   Ibid.

50   '(Giusti's epigram: "Good sense that was once the leading light/In our schools is now completely dead/Science, its little child/Killed it to see how it was made". One should consider whether it was not necessary for science to kill traditional "good sense" in order to create a new "good sense".)': Q8, § 175: Gramsci 1975, p. 1047; Gramsci 2011, p. 336.

51   'This quotation can serve to indicate how the terms good sense and common sense are used ambiguously: as "philosophy", as a specific mode of thought with a certain content of beliefs and opinions, and as an attitude of amiable indulgence, though at the same time contemptuous, towards anything abstruse and ingenious. "It was therefore necessary for science to kill a particular form of traditional good sense, in order to create a 'new' good sense"' (Q 11, § 13: Gramsci 1975, p. 1400; Gramsci 1971, p. 423).

52   Q8, § 175: Gramsci 1975, p. 1047; Gramsci 2011, p. 336.

The text, resumed and reinforced in the relevant text c,[53] reaffirms Gramsci's dynamic conception of common sense as something that must be overcome – and in so doing, leans on Marx's authority. Ideology is a material force, in determinate situations. What is necessary is to produce a 'new philosophy', which, in defeating the *existing* common sense, will become a mass ideology, a *new* common sense.

5   Common Sense and Philosophy

Gramsci further concerns himself with common sense in a series of notes under the heading 'Introduction to the study of philosophy'. In Q8, § 204, for example, he sketches out some 'preliminary points' to bear in mind during the drafting of the 'Introduction', which would later join together with other A texts in Q11, § 12, that is, in the 'Study of philosophy: some preliminary points of reference'.

> In preparing an introduction to the study of philosophy', certain prelimin-ary principles need to be kept in mind: 1) One must destroy the prejudice that philosophy is a difficult thing just because it is the specific activity of a particular category of learned people, of professional or systematic philo-sophers. It is therefore necessary to show that all men are philosophers, by defining the characteristics of this ['spontaneous'] philosophy that is 'everyone's', namely, common sense and religion.[54]

Common sense and religion are the ('disjointed') spontaneous philosophy with which everyone is endowed. As against common sense and religion stands philosophy, which is the critique of them, evidently because it possesses the gifts such as coherence, awareness, and so on, that Gramsci so appreciates. Philosophy is a potentially hegemonic conception of the world, but common sense could never be.

---

53   'References to common sense and to the solidity of its beliefs are frequent in Marx. But Marx is referring not to the validity of the content of these beliefs but rather to their formal solidity and to the consequent imperative character they have when they produce norms of conduct. There is, further, implicit in these references an assertion of the necessity for new popular beliefs, that is to say a new common sense and with it a new culture and a new philosophy which will be rooted in the popular consciousness with the same solidity and imperative quality as traditional belief': Q 11, § 13: Gramsci 1975, p. 1400; Gramsci 1971, p. 423.

54   Q8, § 204: Gramsci 1975, p. 1063; Gramsci 2011, pp. 351–2.

It remains true that for Gramsci it is necessary, for precision's sake, always to speak of 'philosophies', that is, of various different visions of the world (in struggle amongst themselves). Progressive philosophy vs. the *existing* or *vulgar* common sense. The various forms of philosophy and of common sense are divided according to a vertical axis which we could define as *political* (Left/Right) and according to a horizontal axis according to the degree of coherence, awareness and originality by which they are characterised. As such, there are philosophies and types of common sense (in sum, ideologies) that are more and less elaborated and more and less progressive.

Noteworthy, in the corresponding text C (Q11, §12), is that Gramsci provides a list of the articulations in which man's conception of the world appears:[55] 1) in language; 2) in 'common sense and good sense' (which are here equivalent, or at least appear without any specific distinction); and 3) in popular religion. It is important to note that language and common sense are separate spheres. That is not to say that this is a hierarchical articulation; but it does, however, manifestly involve a distinction. As such, it does not seem right to read language and common sense as coincidental[56] – nor, more generally, language and ideology, since Gramsci sees language only as one level (a 'basic', implicit, narrow level) of how an ideology presents itself. Gramsci continues:

> 2) Religion, common sense, philosophy. Find out how these three intellectual orders are connected. Note that religion and common sense do not coincide, but religion is composed of disjointed common sense. There is not just one common sense, but it, too, is a product of history and a historical process. Philosophy is the critique of religion and of common sense, and it supersedes them. In this respect, philosophy coincides with 'good sense'. 3) Science and religion–common sense.[57]

In the relevant C text, the 'connection' is partly found, in a negative sense: philosophy is an 'intellectual order', but religion and common sense are not, 'because

---

55   'It must first be shown that all men are "philosophers", by defining the limits and characteristics of the "spontaneous philosophy" which is proper to everybody. This philosophy is contained in: 1. language itself, which is a totality of determined notions and concepts and not just of words grammatically devoid of content; 2. "common sense" and "good sense"; 3. popular religion and, therefore, also in the entire system of beliefs, superstitions, opinions, ways of seeing things and of acting, which are collectively bundled together under the name of "folklore"' (Q 11, §12: Gramsci 1975, p. 1375; Gramsci 1971, p. 323).

56   See Frosini 2003, p. 173. But Jaulin 1991 set up this same framework.

57   Q8, §204: Gramsci 1975, p. 1063; Gramsci 2011, p. 352.

they cannot be reduced to unity and coherence even within an individual consciousness, let alone collective consciousness':

> Philosophy is intellectual order, which neither religion nor common sense
> can be ... Moreover common sense is a collective noun, like religion: there
> is not just one common sense, for that too is a product of history and a
> part of the historical process. Philosophy is criticism and the supersed-
> ing of religion and 'common sense' ... Religion and common sense cannot
> constitute an intellectual order, because they cannot be reduced to unity
> and coherence even within an individual consciousness, let alone collect-
> ive consciousness. Or rather they cannot be so reduced 'freely' – for this
> may be done by 'authoritarian' means, and indeed within limits this has
> been done in the past.[58]

If 'the philosophy of an epoch' is the 'ensemble of all the philosophies of all
individuals and groups (+ scientific opinion) + religion + common sense',[59] for
Gramsci:

> It seems useful to make a 'practical' distinction between philosophy and
> common sense in order to be better able to show what one is trying to
> arrive at. Philosophy means, rather specifically, a conception of the world
> with salient individual traits. Common sense is the conception of the
> world that is most widespread among the popular masses in a historical
> period. One wants to change common sense, and create a 'new common
> sense' – hense the need to take the 'simple' into account.[60]

The objective being indicated, here, is evident: the creation of a new common
sense. Here, common sense is 'the conception of the world that is widespread
among the popular masses in a historical period': and can this be a wholly
negative thing? Clearly not. And not only that. In the corresponding text C, he
adds:

> every philosophy has a tendency to become the common sense of a fairly
> limited environment (that of all the intellectuals). It is a matter therefore
> of starting with a philosophy which already enjoys, or could enjoy, a

---

58   Q11, § 12: Gramsci 1975, p. 1375; Gramsci 1971, pp. 325–6.
59   Q8, § 211: Gramsci 1975, p. 1069; Gramsci 2011, p. 358.
60   Q8, § 213: Gramsci 1975, p. 1071; Gramsci 2011, p. 360.

certain diffusion, because it is connected to and implicit in practical life, and elaborating it so that it becomes a renewed common sense possessing the coherence and the sinew of individual philosophies. But this can only happen if the demands of cultural contact with the 'simple' are continually felt.[61]

Thus we see, here, the affirmation of the need for 'cultural contact with the "simple"' – and this was his political-philosophical programme from *L'Ordine Nuovo* up to the *Notebooks*. Common sense is understood as the conception of the world that is widespread in a certain field, and not as 'spontaneous philosophy': it is also a brake on 'metaphysical abstruseness', and thus has positive implications also on the technical-philosophical front.[62] Still, Gramsci never loses sight of the fact that:

A philosophy of praxis must initially adopt a polemical stance, as super-seding the existing mode of thinking. It must therefore present itself as a critique of 'common sense' (but only after it has based itself on com-mon sense in order to show that 'everyone' is a philosopher and that the point is not to introduce a totally new form of knowledge into 'everyone's' individual life but to revitalize and already existing activity and make it critical). It must also present itself as a critique of the philosophy of the intellectuals, out of which the history of philosophy arises. Insofar as the history of philosophy is the history of 'individuals' ... it can be considered as the history of the 'high points' of the progress of common sense – or, at least, the 'common sense' of the most culturally refined strata of the

---

61   Q11, § 12: Gramsci 1975, p. 1382; Gramsci 1971, p. 330.

62   'In what exactly does the merit of what is normally termed "common sense" or "good sense" consist? Not just in the fact that, if only implicitly, common sense applies the principle of causality, but in the much more limited fact that in a whole range of judgments common sense identifies the exact cause, simple and to hand, and does not let itself be distracted by fancy quibbles and pseudo-profound, pseudo-scientific metaphysical mumbo-jumbo. It was natural that "common sense" should have been exalted in the seventeenth and eighteenth centuries, when there was a reaction against the principle of authority represented by Aristotle and the Bible. It was discovered indeed that in "common sense" there was a certain measure of "experimentalism" and direct observation of reality, though empirical and limited. Even today, when a similar state of affairs exists, we find the same favourable judgment on common sense, although the situation has in fact changed and the "common sense" of today has a much more limited intrinsic merit' (Q10ii, § 48: Gramsci 1975, pp. 1334–5; Gramsci 1971, p. 348).

society.[63] ... The relation between 'high' philosophy and common sense is assured by 'politics' in the same way that politics assure the relationship between the Catholicism of the intellectuals and of the 'simple'.[64]

But note: 'The position of the philosophy of praxis is the antithesis of the Catholic', Gramsci specifies in his second draft, because 'it does not tend to leave the "simple" in their primitive philosophy of common sense, but rather to lead them to a higher conception of life'. Its scope is to 'construct an intellectual-moral bloc which can make politically possible the intellectual progress of the mass and not only of small intellectual groups'.[65] In any case, as late as notebook 11, in a substantial text C and with a statement which did not appear in the first draft of the piece, *Gramsci again reiterates that common sense is only a primitive philosophy which must be superseded.* It is such a supersession that unblocks the way towards the 'political development of the concept of hegemony', which 'represents a great philosophical advance as well as a politico-practical one'.[66] No hegemony without superseding common sense. It does not seem that hegemony rests on common sense, as much that hegemony emerges when the *existing* common sense is superseded.

6   The Re-evaluation of 'Good Sense'

The expression 'good sense' appears starting from the first notebook, together with 'common sense'. It is missing from the list at the start of the notebook (and, indeed, the list in the eighth notebook) but in Q1, § 65 – cited above – Gramsci writes that the 'type' of periodical of which he is speaking 'belongs to the sphere of "good sense" or "common sense"', a usage implicitly rendering the terms equivalent.[67] It would not always be like this. Rather, Gramsci mainly used 'good sense' together with 'common sense', but in distinction from it (even if in a manner that was not always consistent). Moreover, 'good sense' also has

---

63   He adds in the text C: 'and through them also the common sense of the people'. Q11, § 12: Gramsci 1975, p. 1383; Gramsci 1971, p. 331 (translation altered). From the common sense of the cultured strata to the common sense of the people, that is, through a process that always proceeds from the top to the bottom.

64   Q8, § 220: Gramsci 1975, pp. 1080–1; Gramsci 2011, p. 369.

65   Q11, § 12: Gramsci 1975, p. 1384; Gramsci 1971, pp. 332–3.

66   Q11, § 12: Gramsci 1975, pp. 1385–6; Gramsci 1971, p. 333.

67   Q1, § 65: Gramsci 1975, p. 76; Gramsci 1992, p. 173.

its own philosophical tradition, albeit one less extensive than that of 'common sense'. Santino Caramella, for example, in his aforementioned book, writes that 'common sense' cannot be confused with 'good sense' ('though in certain languages, like English, they are confused – given the ambiguity of "common sense"'), insofar as 'philosophy claims for itself "good sense", a synonym of "reason" (both for Descartes, for whom it was "of all things among men, the most equally distributed", and for Manzoni, who represented it as hiding "in fear of common sense")'. After all, Caramella claims – in contrast to Croce, we could say – philosophy is born precisely from the critique of 'common sense'.[68] 'Good sense', that is, as philosophy in the strict sense, in contrast to 'common sense' as 'non-philosophy'. Missiroli, also, in the article that Gramsci himself cites (Q7, §1) distinguishes – faced with 'the logic of the philosophy professor' – between the *common sense of the students*' and the *good sense* of teachers of subjects other than philosophy'. Here, there also seems to be a distinction – even if it is less clear and argued-through, still a qualitative one – between the concepts that the two phrases express.

We said that in Gramsci the use of the term 'good sense' varies, sometimes having a positive connotation and at other points a negative one: in Q1, §79, for example, we read that 'In order to command, good sense alone does not suffice'[69] (a negative evaluation), whereas in Q4, §32 it is explained that 'a man of good sense' could set in crisis a holistic conception of the state (a positive evaluation).[70] Furthermore, while at times the term is placed alongside and coordinated with 'common sense', at other points it is counterposed to it. In Q8, §213, they even coincide: *Philosophy and common sense or good sense*'.[71] In Q6, §26, writing with regard to Pirandello and the 'dialectical conception of objectivity', Gramsci notes in the dramatist's work the representation of a 'paradoxical struggle against common sense and good sense';[72] and in Q7, §1, Gramsci states that 'Croce is continuously flirting with the "common sense" and "good sense" of the people'[73] (coordinated, with a negative connotation).

---

68   Caramella 1932, p. 3.

69   Gramsci 1975, p. 86; Gramsci 1992, p. 183.

70   Gramsci 1975, p. 451; Gramsci 1996b, p. 173. Missing in the text C, *Qn*, §32.

71   Gramsci 1975, p. 1071; Gramsci 2011, p. 360.

72   Gramsci 1975, p. 705; Gramsci 2011, p. 22.

73   Ibid. The relevant text C misses out the phrase 'Croce is continuously flirting ...', but we find an added mention of 'The dualistic conception, that of the "objectivity of the external world", as it has taken root among the people through the traditional philosophies and religions that have become "common sense"' (Q10ii, § 41i: Gramsci 1975, p. 1295).

While in Q8, §28 we read: '"Good sense" has reacted, but "common sense" has embalmed the reaction and made out of it a "theoretical" "doctrinaire" and "idealistic" canon' (counterposed, positive evalutation of 'good sense'). In Q8, §18, appears the reference to Manzoni that we already saw in Caramella. Gramsci writes:

> *Common sense.* Manzoni distinguishes between *common sense* and *good sense* (Cfr *Promessi Sposi, Chpt. XXXII* on the plague and the anointers). He mentions the fact that there were some people who did not believe the stories about the anointed, but they could not say so publicly, for fear of going against widespread public opinion, then he adds: 'This was clearly a secret disclosure of the truth, a family confidence. Good sense was not lacking; but it stayed in hiding, in fear of common sense'.[74]

Manzioni draws an equals-sign – as Caramella notes – between 'good sense' and 'reason', which can do nothing, however, against 'common sense', the crude ideology of the masses. Gramsci does not comment on the passage. 'Good sense and common sense' becomes a section heading in a note not much later on, a brief text B:

> *Good sense and common sense.* The representatives of 'good sense' are 'the man in the street', the 'average Frenchman' who has become the 'common man', 'monsieur Tout-le-monde'. Bourgeois theater, in particular, is where one should look for representatives of good sense.[75]

We find a positive evaluation of 'good sense' in the *philosophical* contexts in which it is used *in a technical sense*:

> Philosophy is the critique of religion and of common sense, and it supersedes them. In this respect, philosophy coincides with 'good sense'.[76]

But above all, it should be noted that from the tenth notebook onward, in some B texts and also in C texts, in paragraphs *not* present in the first drafts, the

---

74   Gramsci 1975, p. 949; Gramsci 2011, pp. 244–5.

75   Q8, §29: Gramsci 1975, p. 959; Gramsci 2011, p. 254.

76   Q8, §204: Gramsci 1975, p. 1063; Gramsci 2011, p. 352. The point is made yet more strongly in the relevant text C (Q11, §12): 'Philosophy is critique and the superseding of religion and "common sense". In this sense it coincides with "good" as opposed to "common" sense': Gramsci 1975, p. 1375; Gramsci 1971, p. 326 (translation altered).

connotation of the phrase 'good sense' is almost always a positive one.[77] In Q10ii, §48, also entitled 'Introduction to the study of philosophy', we read another note in which common sense and good sense appear as equivalents and are positively appraised:

> In what exactly does the merit of what is normally termed 'common sense' or 'good sense' consist? Not just in the fact that, if only implicitly, common sense applies the principle of causality, but in the much more limited fact that in a whole range of judgments common sense identifies the exact cause, simple and to hand, and does not let itself be distracted by fancy quibbles and pseudo-profound, pseudo-scientific metaphysical mumbo-jumbo.[78]

Here, we see the function – one that we have already examined – of common sense or good sense as the critique and rejection of intellectualism for its own sake. In Q16, §21 we find another example of this:

> The peasants, ruminating at length on the things they have heard declaimed and which momentarily impressed them with their glitter, in the end, with the good sense that has regained the upper hand after the emotion stirred up by exciting words, discover the deficiencies and superficiality of what they heard and thus become habitually distrustful.[79]

It should not be surprising that other examples given of this function of 'good sense' – namely, a sentinel on guard against the excesses of vacuous intellectualism – can be 'applied' even in notebook 28, dedicated to Lorianism, (but not in the relevant A texts!) where, for example, we read: 'This article, given the pleasantries that make up its contents, lends itself to becoming the "negative text book" for a school of formal logic and scientific good sense';[80] or, further still, 'good sense, awoken by an opportune pin-prick, wipes out the effects of intellectual opium with almost lightning-fast speed'.[81]

---

77   An exception is Q15, §42, a B text, entitled 'The non-national-popular character of Italian literature'.

78   Gramsci 1975, pp. 1334–5; Gramsci 1971, p. 348.

79   Gramsci 1975, p. 1889. The text A lacks the references to 'good sense': see Q1, §122 and Q1, §153.

80   Q28, §1: Gramsci 1975, p. 2322.

81   Q28, §11: Gramsci 1975, p. 2331.

Yet more positive is the appraisal of good sense where Gramsci radically distinguishes its fate from that of common sense, as in Q11, §12: 'This is the healthy nucleus that exists in "common sense", the part of it which can be called "good sense" and which deserves to be made more unitary and coherent'.[82] In Q11, §59 he speaks of an individual philosophy that – insofar as it is not arbitrary – becomes

> a culture, a form of 'good sense', a conception of the world with an ethic that conforms to its structure ... It seems that the philosophy of praxis alone has been able to take philosophy a step forward, basing itself on classical German philosophy but avoiding any tendency towards solipsism, and historicising thought in that it assumes it in the form of a conception of the world and of 'good sense' diffused among the many[83]

'Good sense' is here equivalent to 'culture', to 'conception of the world', with a meaning that is not necessarily either positive or negative. We knew that it was part of the *conceptual chain* or *family of concepts* that articulates Gramsci's conception of ideology as a conception of the world in the *Notebooks*. But we do not anywhere else find such an explicit equivalence as is drawn in this note.

7   **The Last Notebooks**

Starting from notebook 13, there are some text Bs and text Cs – above all within the context of passages not present in the first draft – in which 'common sense' is used with a positive connotation, even if not within particularly significant thematisations. This is true, for example, of Q13, §18 and §20. In other notebooks of the 'third period',[84] but there are just as many or even more holding to a conception of common sense associated with the 'passivity of the great mass of the people',[85] the 'most crude and banal materialism',[86] which must be transcended in order to arrive at a 'coherent and systematic thought',[87] which is

---

82   Gramsci 1975, p. 1380; Gramsci 1971, p. 328. Text not present in the relevant A text.

83   Gramsci 1975, p. 1945; Gramsci 1971, p. 346.

84   Here I am invoking the sub-division carried out in the first part of Frosini 2003. F. Frosini, *Gramsci e la filosofia*, cit., parte prima.

85   Q15, §13: Gramsci 1975, p. 1770.

86   Q16, §9: Gramsci 1975, p. 1855. Not present in the A text, Q4, §3: Gramsci 1975, pp. 421 et sqq.

87   Q24, §3: Gramsci 1975, p. 2263. Missing from the relevant A text, Q1, §35.

still, in 1935's notebook 27, 'philosophical folklore'.[88] The interesting comments on pragmatism in Q17, § 22 also speak of the attempt – on the part of US philosophy – to create a ' "popular philosophy" superior to common sense'.[89] The need to overcome common sense is a constantly recurring theme. Meanwhile, the mobile character of Gramsci's use of terms and concepts – now descriptive, now prescriptive, and always dynamic – is reaffirmed.

8   Conclusions: The Double 'Return to Marx'

To me, it seems conclusively the case that in the *Notebooks* Gramsci understood 'common sense' in a mostly *negative* sense. Had something changed relative to the *L'Ordine Nuovo* days, or the mention of 'the creative spirit of the people' in his 19 March 1927 letter to Tania?[90] The answer can only be a 'yes'. Not only and not mainly because of the profoundly important interjection of the 'teachings of Lenin' in the 1920s, and the complexity of what is traditionally called the 'vanguard/masses relationship'. But because Gramsci, in light of his prison reflection seeking to respond to the questions that concerned the relation between economics and politics – more central than ever after 'the defeat' – seems to have grasped the whole complexity of the ideological and social structure of 'the West'. With his recce of the *forms* of hegemony and ideology, which he associated – lest we forget – with the state, a complex, articulated, 'integral' state, Gramsci acquired a new theory of collective subjectivity largely founded on pre-intentionality. Perhaps, given that he explicitly 'returned' to the Marx of the *Theses on Feuerbach*, there was also a re-encounter with the 'ontological' teaching of the mature, more anti-subjectivist Marx.

For sure, Gramsci's conviction as to the role expected of the (collective) subject and (collective) will never diminishes, but he now grasped more than ever the inertia, passivity and subalternity with which common sense is impregnated. Common sense appeared to him as a point of departure that in its 'supersession' ought to be more 'removed' than 'conserved'. The choice is always between different conceptions of the world in struggle amongst themselves, not a 'merely intellectual' choice.[91] It is the struggle for hegemony. But the alternative to the hegemonic bourgeois culture cannot come from any philosophy based on common sense: the historical-materialist conception of the

---

88   Q27, § 1: Gramsci 1975, p. 2311. A statement not present in the relevant A text: Q1, § 89.
89   Gramsci 1975, p. 1925.
90   Gramsci 1996a, p. 57.
91   Q11, § 12: Gramsci 1975, p. 1378; Gramsci 1971, p. 326.

world is established, for Gramsci – as we have seen – through clearly superseding the *existing* common sense, in order to create another. If it is not to be
denatured and defeated, this conception of the world must always remain 'in
contact with the "simple"', 'connected to and implicit in practical life'.[92] The
expansive capacity of the new philosophy – obviously with a dialectical outlook, or this would not be Gramsci – is dependent upon the capacities of those
who must 'elaborate a philosophy', that is, a conception of the world. This new
philosophy, starting from material contradictions, from 'practical life', and taking account of common sense, the needs that it expresses, and the level of
consciousness of the masses which it indicates, will allow the subaltern classes
a new awareness of themselves (and in part, insofar as it is possible working
with largely *pre-intentional* materials, a new subjectivity) and thus a new 'spirit
of cleavage'.

----

92   Q11, § 12: Gramsci 1975, p. 1382; Gramsci 1971, p. 330.

CHAPTER 7

Morality and 'Conformism'

1   Marx and Morality

In Marx's theory and a good part of Marxism, there does not seem to be any space for morality. Marx situated himself among those authors who shared in a realistic and 'anti-moralistic' vision of history. 'Communism', he wrote in 1848, '... is not a state of affairs which is to be established, an ideal to which reality [will] have to adjust itself'.[1] And not only that. The mature Marx of the second half of the nineteenth century, 'contaminated by positivist encrustations' (as Gramsci put it),[2] believed and said himself to be a 'scientist', a 'scientist' of society and history. The unequal exchange of capital and labour, which produces surplus-value and is, therefore, for Marx at the base of the entire edifice of capitalist society, is not 'unjust'. Its corollary exploitation does not result from the 'wickedness' of the capitalist, but from the intrinsic characteristics of labour power, which the scientist Marx maintained he could uncover and explicate in a supposedly value-free manner.

Some interpretative currents, then, see no space for ethics in Marx, also because there does not seem to be any room therein for individual subjects and their freedom. Moreover, in a famous passage of the 'Preface' to the *Contribution to the Critique of Political Economy*, Marx writes that 'In the social production of their existence, men inevitably enter into definite relations, which are independent of their will'.[3] This being the case, it is no surprise that the theoretical vista of Marxism has overlooked morality, especially during those historical moments in which Marxism itself was clearly itself in crisis, whether at the end of the nineteenth century or in the 1980s, when the validity of Marx's so-called 'scientific programme'[4] was heavily in doubt.

Think though, for example, of those Anglo-American authors usually called (rather approximately) the 'Analytical Marxists' – for instance Gerry Cohen,

---

1   *MECW*, Vol. 5, p. 49.

2   Gramsci, 'La rivoluzione contro il "Capitale"', *Avanti!*, 24 December 1917, reproduced in Gramsci 1982, p. 514.

3   *MECW*, Vol. 29, p. 263.

4   As encapsulated in the title of Salvatore Veca's 1977 book *Saggio sul programma scientifico di Marx*.

John Roemer and Jon Elster – who, manifestly influenced by Rawls and the success of his work, have turned back to interrogate Marx as to see whether there
is some ethical and normative dimension to his work, some sort of 'theory of
justice'. They have stressed the Trier thinker's use of a non-neutral terminology
(think of terms like 'exploitation', 'extortion', 'slavery') and emphasised its moral
concern, its denunciation of how unjust the distribution of wealth really is.

Thus, it is claimed, they have managed to uncover an 'implicit' Marx, *a moral
philosopher without even knowing it*. Though Marx repeated many times that
the communists do not appeal to either morality or justice, they maintain that
even so Marx seems to have been moved by a desire for justice, by 'an ethical
vision, even if it was not very conscious, not very explicit, or little-inclined to
recognise itself as an ethic'.[5]

In doing so, however, it seems to me that we risk confusing the morality
motivating the author in question with a moral theory, and the concern for
justice that undoubtedly drove Marx being mistaken for a 'theory of justice'.
This is a far from satisfactory answer to this problem, in my view.

2   Gramsci's World

If we move on from Marx and consider the figure and the works of Antonio
Gramsci, it is not difficult to understand how easy it is to fall into analogous
traps. The absolute morality and ethical depth of the individual concerned
are not in question. The *Lettere dal carcere* are probably without equal in
twentieth-century Italian literature in showing a lack of personal self-interest,
a sense of duty and a high-minded conception of the mission of scholarship
and politics. One well-known passage, in this regard, comes from a 1928 letter
from Gramsci to his mother:

> Life is such, very hard, and sons must sometimes cause their mothers
> great sadnesses if they want to uphold their honour and their dignity as
> men ... The sentence and the imprisonment, I wanted myself ... because
> I have never wanted to change my opinions, for which I would be ready
> not only to be imprisoned, but also to give my life.[6]

---

5   Petrucciani 1992, p. 11.
6   Gramsci 1996a, letter to his mother of 10 May 1928.

The world of family affection, though very important for the imprisoned Gramsci, has to come second, meeting an insurmountable limit in the fact that there is a higher duty, concerning the sphere of public ethics. What Gramsci often defined as the 'great, terrible and complicated world' could place a son in such conditions as to not be able even to give hope to his own mother. Gramsci knew that he was ill; he knew that prison could kill him (as it ultimately did); he knew that appealing to Mussolini for pardon would be enough to secure his release, for him to seek care, to save his life; he knew that such a gesture on his part would also probably have been indulged and understood, precisely because not to do so meant a death sentence to which not even the Tribunale speciale dared to condemn him; but he also knew that such a gesture, however legitimate, and even though it was allowed by the laws of the time, would have been used by the enemy and its propaganda. His people, defeated, persecuted, and imprisoned, would thus have known that even he, the greatest leader of the Party in which so many – rightly or wrongly – had invested their hopes, had surrendered: even he had given in, even he had bowed his head to the Duce, the boss of their 'enemies'. It was for this very reason Gramsci did not ever make a pardon plea or allow one to be made in his name, as his loved ones repeatedly asked of him. And thus Gramsci was killed by his imprisonment, when he could have saved himself: and this, on account of his sense of duty and the ethical dimension inherent to his political choice.

The *Notebooks* do feature a reflection that can be connected to this behaviour, even if it does not concern it directly. Gramsci writes that it is no chance thing that the custom whereby the captain of a sinking ship is the last to save himself has caught on.[7] If this were not the case, there would be no guarantee that he would do everything in his power to prevent the catastrophe. Hence a type of 'ethics of responsibility' whose lack we hear so much about today.

But all this is not enough for our study, and does not answer our question as to the existence of a moral theory in Gramsci. The morality of Gramsci the individual is not in question. But what place does morality, the ethical dimension, have in the theory, the Marxism, the 'philosophy of praxis' of Antonio Gramsci?

3   Universality and Historicity

Gramsci's Marxism was characterised by a sharp rejection of all of the deterministic 'encrustations' to be found in Marx's thinking. While in Marx, there are

---

7   Q15, § 9: Gramsci 1975, p. 1762.

certainly elements of economic determinism and history-by-design, there is no such thing in Gramsci. The dimension of *necessity* takes a step back, in the face of a fresh attention toward the simple *possibility* of reaching the socialist goal, and thus toward the *freedom* of the subject.

The Gramscian subject, which is in the first place a collective one (Gramsci being first and foremost a theorist of politics) is not, however, 'free' in the absolute sense. After his youthful hyper-subjectivism – which owed so much to Bergson, Gentile, and the culture of Papini and Prezzolini's *Voce* – in his mature period Gramsci arrived at a more balanced perspective. In the *Notebooks*, the subject acts in a field of forces whose outcomes are not to be taken for granted, and thus can and must choose – within, however, a given objective situation. The subject is not absolutely free. The field of forces in which it finds itself, the historical situation in which it understands itself, prescribes the (limited) possibility of the real choices in front of it.

There is evidently a realistic first principle, in this perspective. But it is not the only one. Gramsci was a realistic author also in another sense. Also, that is, because he was attentive to the conditioning to which the single actor is always subject, and it cannot but be so. 'We are all conformists of some conformism or other, always man-in-the-mass or collective man',[8] Gramsci writes, though adding, at a later point in the *Notebooks*: 'it is nice to employ the word "conformism" precisely because it annoys imbeciles'.[9] Aldo Zanardo has commented, accurately grasping the important point: 'all the *Prison Notebooks* are a meditation on the limits of our capacity to operate, on the limits that encircle our life and our humanity and freedom'.[10]

Still, this does not mean to deny individual responsibility: Gramsci writes unambiguous pages in opposition to the tendency to 'blame everything on society' (Q16, § 12). Moreover, in accepting a framework that implies the passivity of the subject, this would be a manifest violation of Gramsci's conception of what it means to be a revolutionary. He had already written, in 1926: 'We would be wretched and irresponsible revolutionaries indeed if we were to passively leave *faits accomplis* to play out, justifying their inevitablity *a priori*'.[11]

In Gramsci's view, in a society divided into classes, in which people are conditioned in a whole series of ways – and not only economic ones – 'will' does not have, and cannot take on, a mainly normative and ethical role. Will is

---

8   Q11, § 12: Gramsci 1975, p. 1376; Gramsci 1971, p. 324.
9   Q14, § 61: Gramsci 1975, p. 1720.
10   Zanardo 1988, p. 41.
11   Gramsci 1992b, p. 471 (Letter to Ercoli [Togliatti], 26 October 1926).

collective will, a will that is before all else *political*. The space for moral freedom, properly speaking, seems limited.

This does not mean that politics is wholly extraneous to morality and can remain aloof from it. That is far from the case. As has been clearly demonstrated, there can be no party that is not upheld by ethical principles.[12] The realistic Gramsci did not compress morality into politics nor claim that ethical ends were superfluous (see Q13, §11).[13] Gramsci warned of the danger of 'moral relativism' and affirmed that historical materialism does not 'justif[y] skepticism and snobbish cynicism'.[14] It is true that the ethical principles posed for the members of a party are necessary – Gramsci specifies – first and foremost in view of its internal cohesion, and are thus necessary to reach a given end. But that does not mean that they 'lack a universal character', given that the party Gramsci has in mind aims 'to unify all of humanity'.[15]

As such, we get closer to the core of the matter that we are here examining. Like Labriola before him,[16] Gramsci considered morality a fully historical reality. He, an 'absolute historicist', held that it was unthinkable that there could be meta-historical moral principles able to act as a guide for the individual *today*, in the world in which we live. The generalisation and universalisation of a moral principle leads only to the generalisation of historically determinate beliefs (Q16, §12).[17]

Inevitably, 'Everyone acts according to his culture, that is the culture of his environment', Gramsci writes in Q11, §58,[18] in a note entitled 'Ethics'. This note subjects to critique Kant's *Critique of Pure Reason*, which Gramsci cites from memory – as is not infrequently the case in the *Notebooks*. Though Kant's text in fact reads 'Act only on that maxim whereby you can at the same time will that it should become a universal law', Gramsci's 'off by heart' version instead says 'Act in such a way that your conduct can become a norm for all men in similar conditions'.[19] It is precisely this 'in similar conditions' that is missing in Kant, and which already represents a hint toward the critique of universalism that Gramsci advances, writing in this same note: 'Kant's maxim presupposes a

---

12   See Tortorella 1998; Cacciatore 1999; and Q6, §79.

13   Gramsci 1975, pp. 1570–1.

14   Q6, §79: Gramsci 1975, p. 749; Gramsci 2011, p. 62.

15   Q6, §79: Gramsci 1975, p. 750; Gramsci 2011, p. 63.

16   See Centi 1984, p. 268.

17   Gramsci 1975, p. 1877. See Tortorella 1998, p. 65.

18   Gramsci 1975, p. 1484; Gramsci 1971, p. 374.

19   Q11, §58: Gramsci 1975, p. 1484; Gramsci 1971, p. 373.

single culture, a single religion, a "world-wide" conformism', having just himself said that 'Everyone acts according to his culture'.[20]

And yet. For a communist like Gramsci – we should add – the end of political life, the end of politics worthy of the name, the end of 'great politics' – as he calls it, in order to distinguish it from petty affairs, is to arrive at a different world, another world, in which the limits of *necessity* are removed, in which the reign of freedom is truly possible, the reign of ends, a 'moral life' worthy of the name, as Gramsci puts it.

This utopian device is also present in Marx and all Marxism: communism as the end of a 'prehistory' after which the true story of liberated man begins. The difference, though, is that in Marx the triumph of freedom through communism is presented as dialectically dependent on an inevitable movement, on account of the 'necessity' driving forward history as he sees it. In Gramsci, instead, communism (which he calls 'regulated society'), where the distinctions between leaders and led disappear and in which – as the *Notebooks* put it – bring to fruition 'a process that will culminate in a morality'[21] – his reinterpretation of Marx's utopia appears as a 'want' (rather than a 'must') on the part of the subject, a process dependent upon will and a choice that must be made, even if within the 'field of forces' given in each instance. The ultimate end of politics is its self-suppression, a moral world in which there is less politics to be done.

For Gramsci, Kant's framing of the question of morality is abstract because he postulates a meta-historical equality among humans, which, it seems to him, does not take account of their differences. Though these differences are not absolute or irreducible, there needs to be a whole historical process before they can be overcome.

In other words, it is necessary to create what could be called the preconditions of moral life, what Gramsci refers to as 'the unification of the human race'. Without this, socio-cultural differences will win out, serving the domination of some by others, and dulling any effective possibility of rational decision-making.

The 'similar conditions' that Gramsci makes explicit – and which are implicit in Kant, at least in the well-known passage cited above – are given by the fact that all humans are rational agents. Behind Gramsci's framework, instead, is a non-rationalist conception of the subject, in which ideologies play a determining role. Thus ideologies appear throughout the *Notebooks* in a wide range of

---

20   Ibid.

21   Q6, § 79: Gramsci 1975, p. 750; Gramsci 2011, p. 63.

terms – better, a 'family' of concepts that do not coincide, but are correlated amongst themselves.[22]

By way of ideologies, the individual absorbs the determinations of the socio-historical context in which he lives and is determined. There may be a rupture; the subject may not passively accept the given reality; the subject may *make a choice* – but always in a relative sense. Gramsci writes: 'Man is to be conceived as an historical bloc of purely individual and subjective elements and of mass and objective or material elements with which the individual is in an active relationship'.[23] The dialectic is an open one, certainly, but within given socially and historically connoted limits. Between 'the limits' – as we saw above – 'that encircle our freedom'.

---

22   See Chapter 5.

23   Q10, § 48: Gramsci 1975, p. 1338; Gramsci 1971, p. 360.

CHAPTER 8

Marx. From the *Manifesto* to the *Notebooks*

1 From 'War of Movement' to 'War of Position'

On first appearances, there are no works more different than Marx and Engels's *Manifesto of the Communist Party* and Antonio Gramsci's *Prison Notebooks*. The genius of the first is its impatient, assertive appeal to struggle; the second is a tormented reflection, inherently incomplete, labyrinthine and 'open'. If any work of Marx could be even superficially compared to Gramsci's *Notebooks* it would be the *Grundrisse*, also 'notebooks' published after the author's death, the preparatory material for works that were in large part destined never to be written or never to be published by their author.

Marx and Engels composed the text of the *Manifesto* during what they saw as the eve of revolutionary events, in 1847. When Gramsci was writing in prison, his hopes of revolution were now behind him and the catastrophe was already a *fait accompli*, events not playing out in the manner predicted and hoped for by so many Marxists of the Second and Third International. Gramsci was well-aware of this, and it was from this that the specificity of his reflection took its cue.

It is evident enough that no comparison between the Gramsci of the *Notebooks* and the Marx and Engels of 1848 can be considered without a historical contextualisation of the two works. No-one knew better than Gramsci how to thematise this difference: the transition from the *Manifesto* to the *Notebooks* was, to use Gramscian language, the transition from the time for 'war of movement' to that of 'war of position', from the time for 'frontal assaults' to that of the 'reciprocal siege' and 'trenches and earthworks'. Gramsci himself wrote that 'the political struggle's transition from a "war of manoeuvre" to a "war of position" ... took place in Europe after 1848',[1] strengthened also by the late Engels's self-critical reflection on these themes.

---

1 Q15, §11: Gramsci 1975, p. 1768; Gramsci 1971, p. 110.

2   Marx in the *Notebooks*

Gramsci constantly refers to Marx in the *Notebooks*, far from this playing the marginal role asserted by some. The Marx to which Gramsci refers most often, however, is not only the Marx of the *Theses on Feuerbach, Holy Family, Eighteenth Brumaire* and *Civil War in France* – references that have often been noted – but also the Marx of *Capital. Capital* is often cited in the notebooks indicated simply with the subtitle '(Critique of political economy)' and is repeatedly 'used' – so to say – in Gramsci's 'theoretical disputes' with Croce and Bukharin. And that is not to mention Gramsci's very important interpretative engagement with the 1859 'Preface' to the *Contribution to the critique of political economy*, the place in Marx where – contrary to all the economistic and determinist Marxism against which, we could say, the *Notebooks* were written – Gramsci finds a space for subjectivity, ideology and politics, with an innovative interpretation of the base-superstructure relationship that would prove central to his theoretical discourse.[2] The particular reading of the 1859 'Preface' that led Gramsci to affirm that 'it is on the level of ideologies that men become conscious of conflicts in the world of the economy',[3] was carried out, moreover, with explicit reference to the late Engels, who fought in vain against deterministic Marxism, arguing that the economy was the mainspring of history 'only in the last instance'.[4]

Sticking with the *Manifesto*, however, first we must say that Gramsci cited and used this text by Marx and Engels in a rather marginal manner. Nonetheless, it is not without significance that in prison he translated the first chapter – 'Bourgeois and proletarians' – from the German, this together with other Marx texts appearing in the seventh notebook. We can also say that there is a place in the *Notebooks* where Gramsci refers to the *Manifesto* in a most interesting context: Gramsci is struck by Marx and Engels's acclaim in the first chapter of the book (which he himself translated) for the bourgeoisie and its historically progressive – indeed, revolutionary – role, and Gramsci counterposes these famous words of praise to Bukharin's 'metaphysical conception'.[5] But how so?

---

2   See Chapter 5.

3   Q13, § 18: Gramsci 1975, p. 1592; Gramsci 1971, p. 162. We already know that in prison Gramsci translated the passages of Marx's 'Preface' on which he most concentrated his reflections: see Gramsci 2007, p. 745. This volume contains the first full critical edition of the translations that Gramsci carried out in prison: see Cospito's 'Introduzione' and the 'Nota al testo' by Francioni.

4   See the next chapter, on Engels in the *Notebooks*.

5   Q8, § 219: Gramsci 1975, p. 1080; Gramsci 2011, p. 369.

Bukharin, in his *Popular Manual of Marxist Sociology*, condemned the past – Gramsci writes – as 'irrational' and 'monstrous'. Gramsci counterposes to this the *Manifesto*'s acclaim for the bourgeoisie, considering it – and this is the most interesting point – a transposition of Hegel's famous proposition that 'all that is rational is real and the real is rational' (as Gramsci transcribes it in the second draft of this note, Q11, §18),[6] as reproposed by Engels's *Ludwig Feuerbach*.

3   The Re-evaluation of Ideologies

It would not be entirely satisfactory, however, if we are attempting to establish the relationship between the *Manifesto* and the *Notebooks*, to stop at the obvious differences in their literary and historical contexts. The eighty or ninety years between these two works did not pass in vain, and we will see in what sense that is the case; however, the *Manifesto* contains a strong proposal as to the interpretation of social reality and history – even if it is summarily expressed – and this proposal shines a light far beyond the *Manifesto*'s own time. Gramsci recognised himself in this 'conception of the world' and wrote on the basis of the theoretical field determined by Marx and Engels's analysis. Undoubtedly, he accepted the axioms from which the *Manifesto* started out: history as the history of class struggles, the proletariat as the irreducible adversary of the bourgeoise, destined to liberate the whole of humanity along with itself. But he introduced changes and corrections of no little significance, as compared to the vision set out by Marx and Engels. Here I can mention only three examples: the concept of ideology; the national/international connection; and the conception of the state. I have already mentioned Gramsci's reading of the 1859 'Preface' and the passage he opened up therein – precisely in the foundational text of economistic and deterministic Marxism – for a re-evaluation of ideologies. So, too, in the *Manifesto*, Marx and Engels put forward this vision of the connection between material relations and cultural and ideological elaborations:

> Does it require deep intuition to comprehend that man's ideas, views and conceptions, in one word, man's consciousness, changes with every change in the conditions of his material existence, in his social relations and in his social life? What else does the history of ideas prove, than that intellectual production changes its character in proportion as material

---

6   Gramsci 1975, p. 1416; Gramsci 1971, p. 449.

production is changed? The ruling ideas of each age have ever been the ideas of its ruling class.[7]

Although this does not exhaust the theme of ideology in Marx and Engels,[8] it is also true that this transparent formulation, reaffirmed in many works, connotes the work of these two authors in a decisive manner, most of all that of Marx. Ideology, a product of consciousness, is presented as *deriving* pure and simple from socio-economic relations. Thus is constructed also that fundamentally *monocausal* interpretation of socio-historical reality that has characterised such a great deal of Marxism.

In Gramsci, however, there is a determined re-evaluation of the concept of ideology, which is re-inserted into a highly variegated and articulated family of concepts, a *conceptual network* which, taken as a whole, designates an original and innovative conception of ideology. This is far from Marx's two-sided paradigm of ideology as 'false consciousness' and as a superstructure derived from and dependent on a given base. I will not insist on this point, here, because Chapters 5 and 6 are more specifically dedicated to the theme of ideology. I will just recall that ideology, in Gramsci, is a social group's representation of reality. The individual subject has a vision of the world that is not only her own, but belongs – even if not in a mechanistic manner – to the social group of which she is part. Often she shares in several conceptions of the world, even in a syncretic manner. Collective subjects are defined precisely by their ideologies. This theory thus defines social subjects in a non-economistic manner: it is a materialist, class-struggle conception of ideologies, but one profoundly different from Marx's conception, innervated by Gramsci's discourse on hegemony and the struggle for hegemony.

4　The National/International Connection

The second question to which I would briefly like to call the reader's attention is the national/international connection. The *Manifesto* offers a clear vision of the globalisation carried out by capitalism.[9] Though able to see the political centralisation, unification of local units and the birth of modern national states at work,[10] the authors pushed themselves to justify the hypothesis –

7　*MECW*, Vol. 6, p. 503.
8　See Chapter 5, Section 1.
9　*MECW*, Vol. 6, p. 485.
10　*MECW*, Vol. 6, p. 486.

even amidst this scenario – of a proletariat 'stripped of every trace of national character'.[11] As we know, this has not played out. And we know that Gramsci, also following Lenin, strongly insisted on the national character of hegemony.[12] Here, I would just like to underline that there is, of course, in Gramsci, an acute perception of the supranational dimension of questions. The national/international relationship is one of the central thematisations of his thought. Every national history is read through its relationship of oneness and difference with the supranational context in which it is situated, starting with Italy's *Risorgimento*, the birth of the Italian national state. And yet it must not be forgotten that Gramsci wrote 'To be sure, the line of development is towards internationalism, but the point of departure is "national"',[13] evidently referring to the proletariat and its historic 'movement'. For Gramsci, internationalism is a 'must' projected into the future, but today (that is, in his own time at least) the national moment cannot be disregarded, since it is in this sphere that hegemony is possible. Indeed, Gramsci continues later on:

> It is in the concept of hegemony that those exigencies which are national in character are knotted together ... A class that is international in character has – in as much as it guides social strata which are narrowly national (intellectuals), and indeed frequently even less than national: particularistic and municipalistic (the peasants) – to 'nationalise' itself in a certain sense.[14]

Ultimately, 'non-national concepts (i.e. ones that cannot be referred to each individual country)' are 'erroneous', Gramsci concludes.[15] As I have said already, within the terms of Gramsci's struggle against 'cosmopolitanism' – that is, the undervaluation of the importance of belonging to a national community – we can say, indeed, that the nation appears to him as a passage that is difficult to avoid. Is this hypothesis still valid? It is an open debate. For our purposes, here, it is only necessary to point out that even though the *Manifesto* claims, at one point: 'Though not in substance, yet in form, the struggle of the proletariat with the bourgeoisie is at first a national struggle',[16] the two registers (Gramsci's and the *Manifesto*'s) and their two 'rhythms of thought in development' are

---

11   *MECW*, Vol. 6, p. 494.
12   See Chapter 3.
13   Q14, § 68: Gramsci 1975, p. 1729; Gramsci 1971, p. 240.
14   Gramsci 1975, p. 1729; Gramsci 1971, p. 241.
15   Gramsci 1975, p. 1730; Gramsci 1971, p. 241.
16   *MECW*, Vol. 6, p. 495.

substantially different ones, despite their common inspiration, method and end goal. But one thing that was different was the historical moment. Marx and Engels peremptorily declare:

> The Communists are further reproached with desiring to abolish countries and nationality. The working men have no country. We cannot take from them what they have not got. Since the proletariat must first of all acquire political supremacy, must rise to be the leading class of the nation, must constitute itself the nation, it is so far, itself national, though not in the bourgeois sense of the word. National differences and antagonisms between peoples are daily more and more vanishing, owing to the development of the bourgeoisie, to freedom of commerce, to the world market, to uniformity in the mode of production and in the conditions of life corresponding thereto ... In proportion as the antagonism between classes within the nation vanishes, the hostility of one nation to another will come to an end.[17]

The least we can say is that a certain utopian dimension present in this vision of Marx and Engels was not wholly absent in Gramsci – but it was very much tempered.

5   Politics and the State

The third and last point: the role of politics and the state. At times, there is a tendency to turn Marx and Engels into the standard-bearers of a purely *social* revolution. This is not entirely accurate. Even in the *Manifesto*, they wrote:

> the first step in the revolution by the working class is to raise the proletariat to the position of ruling class ... The proletariat will use its political supremacy to wrest, by degrees, all capital from the bourgeoisie, to centralise all instruments of production in the hands of the state, i.e., of the proletariat organised as the ruling class.[18]

There is, undoubtedly, a *restricted* conception of the state in the *Manifesto*. And it could not but be so, for evident historical reasons: namely, the state that

---

17   *MECW*, Vol. 6, pp. 502–3.
18   *MECW*, Vol. 6, p. 504.

the authors had in front of them. Marx and Engels wrote, for example, 'The executive of the modern state is but a committee for managing the common affairs of the whole bourgeoisie'.[19] A now-famous phrase, notwithstanding the reductive and simplistic vision of politics that it seems to propose. Already in the *Eighteenth Brumaire*, in reality, it is possible to find a far more articulated and complex vision.[20] But Gramsci went much further. And it was only with Gramsci, indeed, that the concept of the state was 'extended' substantially. This was not only a matter of adding the apparatuses of consent and hegemony to the coercive apparatuses portrayed in the traditional conception. In Gramsci's theory, civil society and the state (contrary to what Bobbio claims) form a single dialectical whole in which neither term can be hypostatised as separate from the other. Civil society was no longer the 'true theatre of all history', as in Marx. As we have already seen, as early as 1843's *Critique of Hegel's Philosophy of Right*,[21] Marx stated that the subject in Hegel was the state and civil society the predicate, when in fact the opposite is true.[22] The *mature* Marx held firm to this position, right from the *German Ideology* – where the famous statement that 'civil society is the true theatre of all history'[23] appeared – up to the 1859 'Preface', where Marx reaffirms, speaking precisely of his youthful parting with Hegel in 1843–4, that 'political forms ... originate in the material conditions of life, the totality of which Hegel ... embraces within the term "civil society"'.[24] We have already said that there are also in Marx more complex readings of a relation that we have seen posed in richer, more questioning terms. Marx criticised the state/civil society dichotomy precisely when he recognised that this dichotomy is itself a facet of bourgeois society, and indicated the need to supersede it. Ultimately, Marx privileged 'civil society' in his reading of socio-historical reality, but the dialectical conception that still linked him to Hegel prevented him from falling into any radically *mechanistic* consideration of this relation – as would, conversely, so much of later Marxism. Base rather than superstructure is, without doubt, the 'mainspring' of social being: but this is just a metaphor – albeit an infelicitous one – and not the last word on Marx's interpretative model.

In the guise of returning to Hegel, Gramsci registered a novelty of history: the new relation between economics and politics in the twentieth century, the

---

19   *MECW*, Vol. 6, p. 486.

20   See Coutinho 1998.

21   See Chapter 2.

22   Cfr. K. Marx, *Critica della filosofia hegeliana del diritto pubblico* [1843], cit., p. 8.

23   *MECW*, Vol. 5, p. 50.

24   *MECW*, Vol. 29, p. 262.

extension of state intervention in the sphere of production, the organisational and rationalising effort with which politics related to and also *produced* society. While both for Marx and Gramsci classes continued to remain the subjects of the historical process, such processes did change form. And what Gramsci grasped with particular acumen was the processes that were then imposing themselves in advanced capitalist societies. This was the starting point for a profound rethinking of the role of state and political power, a central thematic focus for Gramsci as for Lenin: but with the difference that in Gramsci it was captured in all its *pervasiveness*, such as only the 'reconnaissance of a national terrain' in an advanced society could allow.

6   Against the Commodity Form

Other points of the relationship between Gramsci and Marx and Engels deserve to be studied in greater depth, though it is not possible to do so here. For example, we could look at the relatively more open character of Gramsci's conception of history, communism understood as a simple *possibility* and not as *inevitable*; and their hypotheses as to the withering-away of the state and politics once class society has disappeared.

I have tended to stress more the differences than the contiguous points and continuities between the *Manifesto* and the *Notebooks*. I will repeat again, however, that the latter are unthinkable without the former. The tendency to make Gramsci a theorist of democracy (as a political principle *different from* and, for some, *alternative to* socialism), thus an author not committed to the struggle against the rule of the commodity form, but rather to the supersession or negation of this struggle, has no basis in Gramsci's writings. It could be said – if you believed it – that Gramsci's theory is no longer adequate to today's world. But it is not right to say that Gramsci thought and wrote things that he never really did.

CHAPTER 9

Engels's Presence in the *Prison Notebooks*

1   Negative Judgements

It is well-known that Italian Marxism often sees the resurfacing of an interpretative current one of whose main distinguishing features is its stress on
the differences between Marx and Engels, with a substantially negative judgement on the theoretical activity of the latter. I do not here want to examine
this question in its entirety. I will limit myself to recalling just one moment of
this interpretative tendency, namely the singular manner in which some have
come to repudiate Engels even by basing themselves on certain passages of the
Prison Notebooks. I am referring to Lucio Colletti's book on *Il marxismo e Hegel*.
Colletti, who – as we know, certainly cannot any longer be defined a Gramscian intellectual or one of Gramscian formation[1] – cites Gramsci in order to
maintain that 'it is not necessary to identify Engels with Marx' and to recall his
judgement according to which 'the origin of many of the blunders contained in
[Bukharin's *Popular Manual*] is to be sought in *Anti-Dühring*'.[2]

This is but one of the possible examples. It serves, however, to remind us
how in at least a certain Marxism – one that has long been widespread, in Italy
and elsewhere – the idea of a sharp distinction between Marx and Engels, and
of the divergence between this latter and Gramsci, has made headway. I would
like to try to analyse whether and to what extent such an interpretation of the
relation between Engels and Gramsci is borne out by a reading of the *Prison
Notebooks*, even if limiting ourselves to studying what Gramsci wrote about
Engels specifically.

Let us begin by saying that there is no lack of negative judgements on
Engels in the *Notebooks*, tending to distinguish his elaboration from Marx's
and also to attribute it a different, lesser value. Our obligatory starting point,
in this sense, is the substantial first paragraph of the fourth notebook, which
appears under the general title 'Notes on philosophy. Materialism and idealism'.
Gramsci writes:

---

1   On Colletti's Marxist training and his relation with Gramsci, see his *Intervista politico-filoso-
     fica*: Colletti 1974, pp. 5 et sqq.
2   Colletti 1974, p. 110. We will return later on to the two Gramsci quotations.

If one wants to study a conception of the world that has never been systematically expounded by its author-thinker ... It is necessary, first of all, to trace the process of the thinker's intellectual development in order to reconstruct it in accordance with those elements that become stable and permanent – that is, those elements really adopted by the author in his own thought, distinct and superior to the 'material' that he had studied earlier and that, at a certain time, he may have found attractive ... This precaution is essential, particularly when dealing with a nonsystematic thinker, with a personality in whom theoretical and practical activity are indissolubly intertwined, and with an intellect that is therefore in continuous creation and perpetual movement ... The search for the leitmotiv, the rhythm of the thought, more important than single, isolated quotations.[3]

Passing over the suggestion that this passage also holds for its author's own work, it is clear that Gramsci is here addressing the problematic knot of studying Marx and bringing his *philosophy* into focus, almost proposing what we could – along with Althusser – call a 'symptomatic reading', that is, one able to grasp a thought that is under the surface, not always explicit, interspersed with material of little use. Gramsci's work on Marx's philosophy thus begins by assuming the non-organic, non-systematic character of the latter's philosophical thought (which is thus implicitly counterposed to Engels's attempt to systematise it, above all in the *Anti-Dühring*, to which we shall return). Gramsci adds immediately afterwards: 'among the works of the same author, one must distinguish those that he himself completed and published from those that were not published because unfinished'.[4]

He specifies that in Marx's works, there is a division between those 'published under the direct responsibility of the author' and those published 'by others after his death' for which 'it would be good to have a diplomatic text', the original not rearranged by the editor. Already on the basis of these comments on method we can speculate that there was a certain 'distrust' toward Engels on Gramsci's part. In the course of the same note, moreover, he explicates the problem:

In the study of an original and distinctive body of thought, supporting evidence contributed by other persons should only be taken up secondar-

---

3   Q4, § 1: Gramsci 1975, p. 419; Gramsci 1996b, p. 137.
4   Ibid.

ily. In the case of Marx: Engels. Naturally, Engels's contribution should not be underestimated, but neither should Engels be identified with Marx; nor must one think that everything Engels attributed to Marx is authentic in an absolute sense. There is no doubt that Engels has evinced a disinterestedness and a lack of personal vanity unique in the history of literature; there should not be the slightest doubt about his absolute personal loyalty. But the fact is that Engels is not Marx, and if one wants to know Marx, one must look for him *above all* in his authentic works, published under his own personal direction.[5]

Engels's contribution, then, should not be underestimated, but nor should what Engels wrote be attributed to Marx. Indeed, in the relevant text C in the sixteenth notebook, the second draft, Gramsci takes up this note again with the title 'Questions of method', and, without making any other substantial changes,[6] adds that

> When one or other makes an affirmation on their reciprocal agreement, this affirmation is valid only for the subject in question. Even the fact that one of them has written some chapters for a book written by the other [apparently a reference to Engels's own *Anti-Dühring*] is not an absolute reason why the book should be considered the result of a perfect agreement.[7]

Gramsci's evaluation belongs to an interpretative current that he had in mind and himself explicated, but which he kept his distance from more than may be apparent from a first reading. In the note from the fourth notebook that we are here examining, indeed, Gramsci continues by quoting both Rodolfo Mondolfo's 1912 book *Il materialismo storico in Federico Engels* and a scornful comment by Sorel (in a letter to Croce),[8] according to whom it is not worth studying Engels, given his supposedly 'scarce capacity' for original thought. Gramsci recognised the necessity of studying the differences between Marx and Engels and lamented that this had not been done, except by Mondolfo. As such, the latter's book seemed 'most useful', but, Gramsci added, that was

---

5 Q4, §1: Gramsci 1975, p. 420; Gramsci 1996b, pp. 138–9.
6 Except the terminological-conceptual clarification whereby Marx and Engels become 'the two founders of the philosophy of praxis'. On the problematisation of the *Notebooks'* transformation of Marxism into the 'philosophy of praxis', see Ciliberto 1982, pp. 272 et sqq.
7 Q16, §2: Gramsci 1975, p. 1843; Gramsci 1971, p. 385.
8 On Mondolfo's book and the letter from Sorel to Croce, see Gramsci 1975, p. 2624.

'apart from its intrinsic value, which I do not now remember'. We know that Gramsci requested Mondolfo's text in prison in 1929 and 1932, but that he did not have a copy.[9] (The text we are here focusing on can be dated to the first months of 1930, while its recomposition as a second draft, in notebook 16, is from 1933). Gramsci, then, does not seem to advance any opinion as to the merit of Mondolfo's book, also because he did not have the opportunity to check its arguments (which he did not remember well) by reading it anew. In any case, he did not agree with Sorel's aforementioned judgement, which stood in sharp counterposition to his own explicit statement that 'Engels's contribution should not be underestimated'.

The second place in the *Notebooks* where it is possible to trace out a negative estimation of Engels is a passage of the note in the eleventh notebook with the title 'The objectivity of the external world'. In this, after having critically examined Lukács's positions and interpreted their idealism as a form of reaction against 'the baroque theories of [Bukharin's] *Popular Manual*', Gramsci writes:

> Certainly in Engels's *Anti-Dühring* we can find many cues that could lead to the deviations of the *Popular Manual*. It is forgotten that Engels, notwithstanding the long time that he worked on it, left few materials for his promised work attempting to show the dialectic to be a cosmic law, and the identity of the thought of the two founders of the praxis of philosophy is exaggerated.[10]

As Valentino Gerratana has observed, for Gramsci 'there is meaning to be found in the fact that Engels never decided to give definitive form to the fragmentary materials he had collected for this work on the *Dialectics of Nature*, which ought to have developed one of the central themes of *Anti-Dühring*'.[11] That is to say, when Gramsci negatively appraised the 'metaphysical' tendencies present in Engels's elaboration, he noted that they had never produced the hypothesised results, thus raising doubts that the failure of the attempt to provide a complete demonstration of how the laws of the dialectic also embrace the natural world, was in fact due to a rethinking on Engels's own part, his work grinding to a halt because he could not demonstrate the assumptions from which he started out.

---

9   See Gramsci 1975, p. 2624; and Gramsci 1996a, pp. 248 (letter to Tania 25 March 1929) and 560 (letter to Tania of 11 April 1932).

10   Q11, § 34: Gramsci 1975, p. 1449.

11   Gerratana 1985, p. xix.

This, Gramsci says, had been 'forgotten': Bukharin continued down the same road that Engels had somehow understood to be a dead end.

In a text B in the fifteenth notebook, entitled 'Introduction to the study of philosophy', we find another passage that is critical of *Anti-Dühring*, and once again in relation to Bukharin's *Popular Manual*:

> the origin of many of the blunders contained in [Bukharin's *Popular Manual*] is to be sought in *Anti-Dühring* and in the attempt – too superficial and formal – to elaborate a system of concepts around the original core of the philosophy of praxis in order to satisfy the scholastic demand for completeness.[12]

Gramsci is clearly taking his distance from Engels, here. This again goes back to Gramsci's more general distrust toward the 'scholastic demand for completeness', for the systematic, which he certainly did not see in Marx – as we saw in the fourth notebook – and which, moreover, we could also say to be deeply alien to the *Notebooks* themselves.

It is certainly no chance thing that this last passage of Gramsci that we examined, as well as the previous one (Q11, § 34) was not included in the first thematic edition of the *Notebooks*, edited by Togliatti and Platone. The 'regard' thus shown for Engels was in reality probably dictated by the desire not to offend Soviet sensibilities, whose Diamat had two important points of reference in *Anti-Dühring* and the *Dialectics of Nature*.[13] But this does not invalidate – it is worth stressing – the meaning and the importance of the cultural initiative led by Togliatti in publishing the *Notebooks*, allowing postwar Italian Marxism to liberate itself of Soviet Marxism-Leninism, and thus decisively contributing to the affirmation of the PCI's different path.[14]

If we stop at this point, the opinion of such a great part of Western Marxism in general, and Italian Marxism in particular, may seem to have been confirmed: on the one hand stands that which so many interpreters have read as Gramsci's 'Hegelian Marxism', and on the other hand the positivistic and deterministic Marxism of Engels, on which the most illustrious theorists and leaders of the Second International nourished. While it is indeed true that in the *Notebooks* Gramsci intended radically to oppose himself to the versions of Marxism that had taken their cue from positivism and whose ultimate fruit was Bukharin's

---

12   Q15, § 31: Gramsci 1975, p. 1786.
13   See Labica 1991, pp. 151 et sqq.
14   See Chapter 12. I will also allow myself to point the reader to my own *Gramsci conteso* (Liguori 2012).

Popular Manual, it is interesting to examine how, in many passages of these same *Notebooks*, Gramsci took inspiration precisely from Engels and repeatedly used significant arguments from Engels in order to feed his own struggle and shore up own his theoretical-philosophical reconnaissance.

2   Anti-Dühring

First of all, it is worth noting how Gramsci was indebted to Engels for a formula that would leave its mark in his work, namely the 'Anti-Croce'. Gramsci wrote in the eighth notebook, again under the title 'Introduction to the study of philosophy':

> All historicist theories of a speculative character have to be reexamined and criticized. A new *Anti-Dühring* needs to be written from this point of view, and it could be an Anti-Croce, for it would recapitulate not only the polemic against speculative philosophy but also, implicitly, the polemic against positivism and mechanistic theories – degenerations of the philosophy of praxis.[15]

The idea of an 'Anti-Croce' probably came to Gramsci from Antonio Labriola, who in his *Discorrendo di socialismo e filosofia* had maintained that it was necessary to take the example of Engels's book and write 'whatever other Anti-Xs are necessary in order to fight anything else that embarrasses or invalidates socialism'.[16] In pointing to the 'Anti-Croce', Gramsci outlined a two-sided theoretical front: on the one hand, against speculative historicism, and on the other, against positivism and mechanicism, which pollute and damage the philosophy of praxis itself, indeed what Labriola called 'embarrassing and invalidating socialism'. The reference to the 'Anti-Croce' was repeated in a text B appearing in the tenth notebook, from which we can again glean indirect praise for Engels's book. Gramsci wrote that

> It would be worth the trouble of a whole group of people dedicating ten years of their life to a work of this type, an Anti-Croce that in today's cultural climate could have the same significance that *Anti-Dühring* had for the pre-war generation.[17]

---

15   Q8, § 235: Gramsci 1975, p. 1088; Gramsci 2011, p. 378.

16   Labriola 1973, p. 697.

17   Q10i, § 11: Gramsci 1975, p. 1234.

In this formulation, Engels's book appears – as it had already appeared to many Marxists of the Second and Third Internationals – as a work fundamental to the reaffirmation of Marxism against deviationism, be that neo-idealist or deterministic in the manner of Dühring or Bukharin. Our picture of the Gramsci-Engels relationship, and in particular the Gramsci-*Anti-Dühring* relationship, thus becomes more complicated. Let us attempt to understand why this is so, by concretely studying Gramsci's references to Engels's book. We can find one first positive reference to *Anti-Dühring* as early as the first notebook, in the same note 153 where Bukharin's *Historical Materialism* or *Popular Manual* also makes its first appearance. Referring to this latter text, Gramsci recalls 'Engels's very appropriate observation that even "modes" of thinking are acquired and not innate traits, the possession of which corresponds to a professional qualification'.[18] He is harking back to the 1885 'Preface' to *Anti-Dühring*. The same passage is reprised in Q4, §18, where it becomes clear that Gramsci is in reality citing a paraphrase of Engels in Croce's *Materialismo storico ed economia marxistica*, since he did not have the original at hand. The sentence from Croce picked up by Gramsci reads: 'Engels [said] ... that "the art of working with concepts is not something inborn or given with ordinary consciousness; it is, rather, a technical labor of thought that has a long history, not more and not less than the empirical research of the natural sciences" '.[19]

Engels's own formulation sounds a bit different:[20] it does not feature the expression 'technical labor of thought'. Gramsci's intention, however – repeatedly citing or recalling this quotation from Engels,[21] and connecting it to the question of which aspects of formal logic could continue to exist in historical materialism[22] – was to raise the central question of a new culture and a new and different intellectual stratum as opposed to the 'traditional intel-

---

18   Q1, §153: Gramsci 1975, p. 135; Gramsci 1992b, p. 233.

19   Croce 1968, p. 30; Q4, §18: Gramsci 1992b, p. 159.

20   'The art of working with concepts is not inborn and also is not given with ordinary everyday consciousness, but requires real thought, and that this thought similarly has a long empirical history, not more and not less than empirical natural science': MECW, Vol. 25, p. 14.

21   As well as in Q1, §153 and the relevant text C (Q16, §21) and in Q4, §18 and its text C (Q11, §44), Gramsci refers to this Engels passage in Q7, §5 and its text C (Q11, §21).

22   'The issue, for me, is not the greater or lesser originality of Engels's statement, but rather its importance and the place it occupies in historical materialism. I think one has to turn to it in order to understand what Engels meant when he wrote that, after Marx, one of the things that remains from the old philosophy is *formal logic*': Q4, §18: Gramsci 1975, p. 439; Gramsci 1996b, p. 159.

lectual bloc'.[23] Picking up again in the sixteenth notebook on the note from the
first notebook we started out from, albeit without further citing Engels, Gramsci
again recalled 'the very appropriate observation that even "modes" of thinking
are acquired and not innate traits', before adding

> The study of the 'old formal logic' has now fallen into discredit – and partly
> rightly so. But the problem of having people take an apprenticeship in
> formal logic as a sort of check on the slapdash argumentation of oratory
> reappears as soon as we pose the fundamental question of creating a new
> culture on a new social base, one that does not have traditions like the old
> class of intellectuals has.[24]

This is why Gramsci's reference to the question of the 'technical labor of
thought', inspired by Engels, repeatedly reappears in connection with his analysis of Bukharin's *Popular Manual.* This is because the audience towards which
this is addressed, the 'new class' seeking to train its own intellectuals and lack-
ing that 'apprenticeship in formal logic' which bourgeois intellectuals naturally
have, is defenceless in the face of the crude oratorical rhetoric of Bukharin's
book. This is all the more the case for the 'workers in the city', whom Gramsci compares to the ancient Greeks 'dazzled by sophisms' and 'arguments that
somehow seem brilliant and momentarily silence adversaries and leave the
listener dumbfounded'.[25]

A second theme for which Gramsci calls on *Anti-Dühring* is – even more
significantly – that concerning the objectivity of the real. The passage he cites
from Engels, taken from the fourth chapter of the first section, reads: 'The real
unity of the world consists in its materiality, and this is proved not by a few
juggled phrases, but by a long and wearisome development of philosophy and
natural science'.[26]

Among the various notes in which Gramsci quotes or mentions this passage,
it seems to me that the one which most explicitly meets the needs of our
discussion is Q11, §17, entitled 'The So-Called "Reality of the External World"',

---

23   It was thus not a rehabilitation *tout court* of formal logic. Indeed, it has been noted that
      Gramsci probably also appreciated the *Anti-Dühring's* defence of the category of objective
      contradiction (see Losurdo 1990, p. 96).

24   Q16, §21: Gramsci 1975, p. 1892.

25   Q16, §21: Gramsci 1975, p. 1889.

26   *MECW*, Vol. 25, p. 41. Gramsci cites this passage accurately enough. As we have said,
      Gramsci did not have the book in prison, so this quotation also must have been indirect,
      taken from some other, as yet unidentified, source.

where he starts out from the history of sciences conference held in London in June–July 1931, and from Bukharin's intervention at this event. Gramsci writes: 'The point that must be made against the *Popular Manual* is that it has presented the subjectivist conception just as it appears from the point of view of common-sense criticism and that it has adopted the conception of the objective reality of the external world in its most trivial and uncritical sense'.[27]

Later in this same note, Gramsci asks himself:

> Does it seem that there could exist an extra-historical and extrahuman objectivity? But who is the judge of such objectivity? Who is able to put himself in this kind of 'standpoint of the cosmos in itself' and what could such a standpoint mean?[28]

Denying, in his polemic against positivism, the dualism of man and nature, Gramsci here cites the *Anti-Dühring*, writing: 'Engels's formulation that "the unity of the world consists in its materiality demonstrated by the long and laborious development of philosophy and natural science" contains the germ of the correct conception in that it has recourse to history and to man in order to demonstrate objective reality'.[29]

Thus basing himself on Engels, and even bending his meaning somewhat, Gramsci took an original position that was, however, not isolated in the contemporary epistemological debate.[30] It is interesting to note that Gramsci, in another passage in which he recalled this same passage from Engels, also polemicises against Lukács, whom he holds guilty of falling into a form of idealism in having claimed 'that one can speak of the dialectic only for the history of men and not for nature'.[31]

As such he also evokes the other aforementioned work of Engels's that proved particularly controversial, namely his *Dialectics of Nature*. This was published for the first time in Russian and German in 1925, and Gramsci therefore probably did not know it directly; however, the work was in fact begun in 1858 and Engels himself repeatedly mentioned it in various ways, including in the 'Preface' to the second edition of *Anti-Dühring*. One of the central themes of the *Dialectics of Nature*, the dialectic of quality and quantity, also appears in the

---

27   Q11, § 17: Gramsci 1975, p. 1415; Gramsci 1971, p. 444.
28   Q11, § 17: Gramsci 1975, p. 1415; Gramsci 1971, p. 445 (translation altered).
29   Ibid.
30   On these themes, see Boothman 1995.
31   Q11, § 34: Gramsci 1975, p. 1449; Gramsci 1971, p. 448.

first section of *Anti-Dühring*: indeed, the twelfth chapter is dedicated to this. It was a question to which Gramsci returned on many occasions. For example, he writes in the fourth notebook: 'In the *Popular Manual* it is said ... that every society is something more than the mere sum of its parts. This observation should have been connected to another observation by Engels, that quantity becomes quality'.[32]

Gramsci's polemical reference point is still, above all, Bukharin, whose thought the author of the *Notebooks* saw as mechanistic, progressivist and undialectical.[33] Conversely, the reference to Engels signalled one of the moments of greatest appreciation of the Hegelian dialectic anywhere in the *Notebooks*.

One last reference by Gramsci to *Anti-Dühring* concerned the transition from the 'realm of necessity' to the 'realm of freedom'. This was, again, a reference that reappeared many times, mostly in connection to Gramsci's thesis regarding the transitory nature of Marxism itself, understood as 'absolute historicism'. Gramsci wrote:

> As a philosophy, historical materialism asserts theoretically that every 'truth' thought to be eternal and absolute has practical origins and has represented or represents a provisional value. But the difficulty lies in making people understand what it means 'in practice' to interpret historical materialism itself in this light. Such an interpretation is foreshadowed by Engels when he talks about the transition from the realm of necessity to the realm of freedom.[34]

It can be hypothesised, then, that in a future when the 'prehistory of humanity' is over, there will be a society without contradictions and thus a decline of historical materialism itself, the theory that in Gramsci's view represents the highest level of consciousness of these contradictions. This transition to the 'realm of freedom' is one of the traits of Marxism that stands furthest from our present experience and capacity to imagine. There is also the fact that on this point, too, Gramsci fully situated himself in the groove of the Marxist tradition and cited Engels to support his own reasoning.

---

32 Q4, § 32: Gramsci 1975, p. 451; Gramsci 1996b, p. 172.
33 See Bobbio 1990.
34 Q4, § 40: Gramsci 1975, p. 465; Gramsci 1996b, p. 188.

3   Engels's Anti-determinism

But the recourse to Engels, in the *Prison Notebooks*, is not limited to *Anti-Dühring*. Also particularly heavily cited are two letters by the German thinker, from 1890 and 1894. They concern the relation between base and superstructure, which Gramsci defines as 'the crucial problem of historical materialism'.[35] Gramsci writes that it is worth remembering

> Engels's statement ... that the economy is only the mainspring of history 'in the last analysis' (to be found in his two letters on the philosophy of praxis also published in Italian); this statement is to be related directly to the passage in the preface to the *Critique of Political Economy* which says that it is on the level of ideologies that men become conscious of conflicts in the world of the economy.[36]

The two Engels letters to which Gramsci repeatedly refers,[37] published in a periodical called *Der Sozialistiche Akademiker* and also quoted by Croce in his *Materialismo storico ed economia marxista*, were that of 21 September 1890, to Joseph Bloch,[38] and that of 25 January 1894, to W. Borgius.[39] In these, Engels criticised the mechanistic and economistic interpretations to which Marxism had given rise, also making a courageous self-critique:

> If some younger writers attribute more importance to the economic aspect than is its due, Marx and I are to some extent to blame. We had to stress this leading principle in the face of opponents who denied it, and we did not always have the time, space or opportunity to do justice to the other factors that interacted upon each other.[40]

Engels could thus see that, from the initial conviction that 'the determining factor in history is, *in the final analysis*, the production and reproduction of

---

35   Q4, § 38: Gramsci 1975, p. 455; Gramsci 1996b, p. 177.

36   Q13, § 18: Gramsci 1975, p. 1589; Gramsci 1971, p. 162.

37   See Q4, § 26, revisited in Q11, § 31; Q4, § 38, revisited in Q13, § 18; Q8, § 214; and Q11, § 25.

38   For more on this letter see Chapter 11.

39   In the *Notebooks* – but also in his *Prison Letters* – Gramsci also refers to a letter with a similar subject, sent from Engels to Conrad Schmidt in Berlin on 5 August 1890, in which he observes that 'too many of the younger Germans simply make use of the phrase historical materialism (and *everything* can be turned into a phrase) only in order to get their own relatively scanty historical knowledge'.

40   *MECW*, Vol. 49, p. 36.

actual life',[41] it had come to be believed that this was the '*only* determining factor':[42] which, Engels argued, had turned this 'proposition into a meaningless, abstract, ridiculous piece of jargon'.[43] In reality, for Engels, 'it is in the interaction of all these factors [economic, political, juridical, philosophical, religious] and amidst an unending multitude of fortuities (i.e. of things and events whose intrinsic interconnections are so remote or so incapable of proof that we can regard them as non-existent and ignore them) that the economic trend ultimately asserts itself as something inevitable'.[44] It is not difficult to see how close the anti-determinist Gramsci was to these arguments of Engels as he himself battled against Bukharin and so much else of Second International Marxism. This excerpt from Engels is of absolutely fundamental importance to the *Notebooks*, and it is no chance thing that Gramsci connects it to Marx's 1859 'Preface' to the *Contribution to the Critique of Political Economy*. After all, it was through interpreting this text that Gramsci constructed his *philosophical* discourse on Marxism.

There are many other passages in which Gramsci again returns to excerpts taken from Engels's works, often cited as a support for his own critical reasoning on Bukharin and even Croce's theses, and with regard to the most varied arguments: from the meaning of 'scientific' (Q6, §180, in polemic with Turati) to questions concerning art and literature, in particular Balzac;[45] from the relation between the critique of political economy and 'bourgeois' economic theories (Q10ii, §20) to the characteristics of the 'Italian revolution',[46] and so on. Gramsci also often refers to another work by Engels, *Ludwig Feuerbach and the End of Classical German Philosophy*. This text was recalled in relation to Hegel's proposition that 'all that is rational is real' (Q8, §219; Q11, §18), again for the purposes of polemic against the *Popular Manual*; as concerned the relationship between theory and praxis (Q10ii, §31), in polemic with Croce; and in relation to the contiguous problem represented by the thesis that the German workers' movement was the 'heir of classical German philosophy' (Q10ii, §10; Q11, §49).

It is not possible, here, to delve into all of these arguments. We are left with the impression that Gramsci makes recourse to Engels without the generalised preoccupation that would have been appropriate with regard to an author

41   *MECW*, Vol. 49, p. 34.

42   Ibid.

43   Ibid.

44   *MECW*, Vol. 49, p. 35.

45   See Q8, §230; Q11, §19; Q14, §41.

46   See Q9, §97; Q11, §44; Q16, §16.

deemed 'untrustworthy'. There was in Gramsci no unilateral or Manichean attitude towards Engels, as a hurried reading based on the counterposition between 'Western Marxism' and economistic and deterministic Marxism has sometimes led people to believe. Engels, for Gramsci, was one of the 'founders of the philosophy of praxis', as he repeatedly put it; and, as I have tried to demonstrate, he also made ample recourse to Engels's works, in particular in his polemic against Bukharin, against what really was a scholastic and reductive conception of Marxism.

It remains true, as we have seen, that Gramsci also cast a certain amount of doubt over Engels, this deriving from his hypothesis that *Anti-Dühring* was 'at the origin of many of the blunders contained in [Bukharin's *Popular Manual*]'. But the contradiction, here, should perhaps be sought in Engels's book rather than in Gramsci himself. While Engels criticised the encyclopaedic character of Dühring, he ended up following him onto his own territory;[47] though he took care in the 'Preface' to warn against 'presenting another system as an alternative to Herr Dühring's "system"',[48] he did produce a work that was understood precisely as having proposed a complete system. It was against this incongruence on Engels's part that Gramsci devoted his critique, and it was perhaps above all for this reason that he argued that Marx's thought should not be confused with the thought of his friend and comrade in study in struggle.

Besides, in rejecting Dühring's repudiation of Hegel, Engels 'reinhabited' the Stuttgart philosopher, with whom – as is well known – the imprisoned Gramsci also established a fruitful engagement. Indeed, faced with the rising tide of positivism, Engels and Marx fully agreed on the need to defend Hegel from whoever wanted to treat him as a 'dead dog'.[49] For Gramsci, that is, Engels very much remained one of the two 'founders of the philosophy of praxis', and the fact that this expression was not simply repeating some rhetorical formula already historically established in the workers' movement is demonstrated by the fact that Gramsci made recourse to Engels's writings when addressing some of the most crucially important questions of his own elaboration. Above all, the battle against determinism, one of the central points of the *Notebooks*.

Here, I will pass over any deeper investigation of one other theme of great interest: namely, the complex relation between Gramsci's elaborations on the transition from the 'war of movement' to the 'war of position' and Engels's indication – appearing in his 1895 'Introduction' to Marx's *Class Struggles in*

---

47   See Gerratana 1985, p. xx.
48   *MECW*, Vol. 25, p. 6.
49   See, for instance, Marx's 7 July 1866 letter to Engels: *MECW*, Vol. 42, pp. 289 et sqq.

France – according to which the proletarian army can no longer think of 'winning victory with one mighty stroke', but rather needs 'slowly to press forward from position to position in a hard, tenacious struggle', given 'how impossible it was in 1848 to win social reconstruction by a simple surprise attack'.[50] And I say 'complex' because this paragraph by Engels was read in terms of gradualism and reformism, whereas Gramsci's 'war of position' has different valences: Gramsci redefined the concept of revolution, but he did not abhor it.[51] And the same could be said of Engels.

In any case, our purpose here is not to invent any particular harmony between Engels and Gramsci. Yet it remains true that simplistic evaluations of Gramsci's consideration of Engels must be avoided, because the author of the *Notebooks* saw Engels not only – as we have seen – as having 'evinced a disinterestedness and a lack of personal vanity unique in the history of literature', whose 'absolute personal loyalty' must not be in 'the slightest doubt'; but also as an important theoretical reference whose contribution Gramsci used in order to construct his own Marxism.

---

50   *MECW*, Vol. 27, p. 512.
51   On these themes, see also Texier 1988.

CHAPTER 10

Labriola: The Role of Ideology

1   Labriola and Gramsci

The relationship between Gramsci and Labriola has been the object of various different and often counterposed readings. This has been the case ever since the first reader, commentator and publicist of Gramsci's writings, Palmiro Togliatti – whose own reading of this topic was not unvarying. Take, for example, his 1945 polemic with Ernesto Buonaiuti, who had labelled Gramsci's method 'unMarxist', which was then gradually becoming better known thanks to the reprint of *Alcuni temi della questione meridionale* and the publication of certain excerpts from the *Letters* and *Notebooks* which Togliatti himself was advance-publishing in *Rinascita*. Buonaiuti had counterposed Gramsci to Antonio Labriola, in his view far more a Marxist than the Sardinian writer. Moreover, this Catholic-modernist thinker had been a pupil of Labriola's at the University of Rome, and we may suspect that he had at least a positive *memory* – if not necessarily a positive *estimation* – of his old teacher and his doctrine.

Evidently struck and politically concerned by this counterposition – which was seemingly very unfavourable to Gramsci, who was implicitly painted as an idealist, almost as if to anticipate Croce's well-known 1947 review of the *Letters*[1] – Togliatti responded to Buonaiuti:

> scholars of Marxism recognise in Labriola a tendency towards a unilateral, limited and ultimately fatalistic interpretation of the doctrines of scientific socialism. It is this tendency that led Antonio Labriola to make profound mistakes, for example in his appraisal of Italian colonialism and, more generally, meant that his activity as a theorist of socialism in Italy bore little fruit.[2]

Perhaps this is an ungenerous reading, even if faithful enough to a view expressed by Gramsci in the *Prison Notebooks*, where he broke through the limits of Labriola's positions on colonial policy in his well-known 1902 interview[3] and

---

1   See Croce 1947, pp. 86–8.
2   Togliatti 2001, p. 96.
3   Labriola 1973, p. 957.

the equally well-known anecdote about his stance on the 'education of the Papuan', as told by Croce.[4] This was also a theoretical judgement, accusing Labriola of a 'mechanical and rather empiricist way of thinking'.[5] It was a harsh analysis, though part of a polemic – the first of the infinite postwar debates on Gramsci – trying to explain why Marxism was not the deterministic and economistic theory to which its opponents tended to reduce it. Indeed, Togliatti continued:

> Antonio Gramsci, who was an attentive scholar of Labriola, and his pupil in the true sense of that word, corrected this erroneous tendency. The Marxist does not, cannot, reduce analysis of historical and political facts to presenting a simple cause-and-effect relationship between an economic situation and the socio-political situation. But that was how Marxism was here understood by those who knew it only superficially, unaware that for a Marxist this relationship of causality is a very complicated matter, implying action and reaction, interdependence and contrast.[6]

This appraisal itself suggests the larvae of contradictions since it paints Gramsci as a *pupil* of a *fatalist* Marxist, whom the pupil himself would have to – and was able to – correct. Without mentioning the deployment of 'superficial' readers of Marxism, which Labriola ends up being objectively assimilated amongst, according to the passage here quoted: which perhaps echoes an old comment of Trotsky's, who himself passed rather contradictory judgement on Labriola, whom he both praised as a true expert on the materialist dialectic, yet also labelled as affected by a 'brilliant dilettanteism'.

An ungenerous reading, as we were saying, from Togliatti. The same man who a few years later, marking the 1954 fifty-year anniversary of the Cassino-born philosopher's death, paid homage to him with a long essay – albeit one that was interrupted and never completed[7] – in which the PCI secretary profoundly corrected himself, among other things stating that Gramsci had been 'the greatest pupil and continuation of Labriola',[8] thus reinforcing the posit-

---

4   Croce 1918, pp. 60–1.

5   Q8, §200: Gramsci 1975, p. 1061; Gramsci 2011, p. 349. In the corresponding C text (Q11, §1), Gramsci passes even harsher judgement, adding that his 'mechanical and rather empirical way of thinking' is 'very close to the most vulgar evolutionism', 'mechanical and retrograde' rather than 'dialectical and progressive': Gramsci 1975, pp. 1368–9.

6   Togliatti 2001, p. 97.

7   See Zanardo 1986.

8   Togliatti 1974, p. 324n. See also my own comments in Liguori 2012, pp. 90 et sqq.

ive element already present in his 1945 analysis. 'Continuation', an expression indicating a strong link and not later qualified in any negative sense. Above all if we consider that Togliatti's 1954 statement was delivered within the framework of a political-cultural operation that had the scope of constructing a tradition of democratic-socialist thought. As is well-known, Togliatti, extrapolating and extending some of Gramsci's own statements, posed this tradition as having begun with Francesco De Sanctis, been continued by Labriola, and ultimately culminated in Gramsci, in his youthful *L'Ordine Nuovo* writings and the *Prison Notebooks*, and finally in the 'collective intellectual' represented by the 'new party' that Togliatti himself created upon his return from the USSR.[9] This reading put great stress on *continuity*, and was thus, in fact, none too convincing, as Cesare Luporini emphasised: for him, there had been no 'linear development' of Italian Marxism across the two centuries, and still less between the two authors Labriola and Gramsci: 'There was, on the contrary', Luporini argued, 'a profound rupture', or at least 'a discontinuity and an interruption'.[10]

Moreover, it was Gramsci himself, in the *Prison Notebooks*, who examined the 'weak fortunes' of Labriola and 'his framing of the question of philosophy',[11] a judgement in which discontinuity and interruption are already implicit. A 'framing' that had to be 'redeployed',[12] Gramsci added, in explicit relation with the central question of hegemony.[13] In the *Notebooks*, then, there is undoubtedly a rediscovery of and a use for the Cassino philosopher. And Labriola's influence on the mature Gramsci has, furthermore, long been noted.[14] Labriola seems less present, however, in the cultural panorama of the younger Gramsci, during his formative Turin years where he had his first encounter with Marxism – such that Valentino Gerratana could write in 1963 that 'Labriola's teachings do not seem to have had any identifiable influence on the development of Gramsci's personality during his youth, the *Ordine Nuovo* experience

---

9   In 1961 Togliatti partially corrected this historical-theoretical judgement, though he maintained Labriola in place when he spoke of the thread linking 'Marx–Labriola–Lenin–Gramsci–PCI–our forty-year struggle' (see Togliatti 1975, p. 700).

10   Luporini 1973, Vol. 5, p. 1587.

11   Q11, § 70: Gramsci 1975, p. 1508. This is a C text: for the corresponding A text, which is partly different, see Q3, § 31.

12   Q11, § 70: Gramsci 1975, p. 1509.

13   See Finelli 2005 on the connection between hegemony and the centrality of philosophy in Gramsci's thought, which the author relates to the Sardinian communist's re-reading of Labriola in the *Notebooks*.

14   See Gerratana 1972, p. 158.

and the first period of the formation of the Communist Party'.[15] That, even if there can be no doubt – the author adds – that the young Gramsci had read and studied at least the major works of the Marxist Labriola.

While we can largely share in these considerations, there was, however, a substantial encounter between the young Gramsci and Labriola that must not be overlooked, represented by the Cassino philosopher's interpretation of Marx and Engels's theory of ideologies. Indeed, on 5 January 1918, Gramsci published the third section of his second essay, 'Del materialismo storico', giving it the title 'Le ideologie nel divenire storico'. According to Leonardo Paggi, this encounter with Labriola's Marxism even heralded 'the concept of ideology entering Gramsci's thought'.[16] A matter of no little significance. Gramsci's Marxism, indeed, was defined above all by his re-elaboration of the connection between base and superstructure, and his decisive re-evaluation of the role of superstructures: which for him largely coincided with ideologies. Gramsci's object – as against so much Second and Third International Marxism of a deterministic and economistic character, which was thus also fatalistic (to repeat the term Togliatti used, not by chance, in 1945) – was, in fact, to reappraise the freedom of the subject, and thus the possibility of revolutionary political initiative, which determinism denied, thus giving rise to a flatly reformist or else fancifully maximalist political vision.

Labriola, too, polemicised against crudely economistic interpretations of Marxism. He and Gramsci both took a stand in reaction against the persistent misunderstanding of Marxism that reduced it to an economistic interpretation of history and society. With this perspective, both reappraised the role of ideologies. This does not mean, though, that in this conceptual re-evaluation – as I will try to demonstrate – they arrived at entirely analogous results. The differences in their respective interpretations of the concept of ideology signalled the differences between their Marxisms; perhaps not to the extent claimed by Togliatti in his 1945 polemic with Buonaiuti, but certainly enough to raise doubts, even in this regard, over the hypothesis advanced by various interpreters[17] of a strong continuity between Antonio Labriola's Marxism and that of Antonio Gramsci.

---

15   Gerratana 1972, p. 157.
16   Paggi 1970, p. 18.
17   See Burgio 2005.

2   **Marx in Labriola's First Essay**

The Marxian and Marxist concept of ideology from which both Labriola and Gramsci took their cue is obviously not the one that is best-known today, namely that found in 1845's *German Ideology*.[18] This text was, indeed, only published in 1932, though its fundamental first chapter on 'Feuerbach' was published for the first time in Russian in 1924 and in German in 1926. Gramsci could, therefore, have read it, given that he was adept in both languages. Yet there is no trace of it in his writings, where he instead cites other works by the two 'founders of the philosophy of praxis', and thus we can hypothesise that he did not in fact know this text.[19] As such, neither Labriola nor Gramsci settled accounts with the concept of ideology found in Marx and Engels's 1845 work. Among other things, while shifting their study of the origin of ideas from the physiological plane of the *ideologiques'* originary sensualist-materialist framework to their own characteristic socio-historical plane, Marx and Engels did here conserve the imprint – think of their well-known metaphorical mentions of the 'retina' and the 'camera obscura' – of the originary physical and mechanical model of De Tracy and co. Both Labriola and Gramsci, however, made reference principally to another classic text in which Marx speaks of ideology and 'ideological forms', the so-called '1859 Preface' to the *Contribution to the Critique of Political Economy*. This is perhaps the best-known point in Marx's entire *oeuvre*, given that we here find an explicit, synthesised theoretical delineation of the materialist conception of history and society, with its well-known (and in my view, unfortunate) spatial metaphor of base and superstructure: and thus the suggestion of the absolute centrality of 'the economic conditions of production' and the direct and unequivocal dependence of superstructures on the subterranean movements of the 'base'. This suggestion would be picked up and made into an absolute by all the economistic-deterministic interpretations of Marxism, even though this is the only page in Marx and Engels's entire, vast intellectual production where this metaphor appears.

The importance to Labriola of the 1859 'Preface' is beyond doubt. Reading his first essay, 'In memoria del Manifesto dei Comunisti', we find ourselves faced with the somewhat paradoxical fact that Labriola never directly cites any excerpts of the text to which his own piece is dedicated (only in the third edition did a translation of the *Manifesto* appear as an appendix), while it does relate the long central passage of the 1859 'Preface'. In this, Labriola relates

---

18   However, also read Musto 2004 on the new MEGA[2] edition of the *German Ideology*.

19   See above, pp. 65–6.

Marx's argument that it is in 'ideological forms' – in Labriola's translation – 'that men acquire consciousness of conflict and in what name they are carrying it out',[20] an argument that was also particularly important to Gramsci. Here we see in Marx a conception of ideology – as Nicolao Merker has aptly demonstrated[21] – that was no longer the strictly *negative* one of the *German Ideology*. Even though it is also true that Marx here again advanced a somewhat deterministic vision of the 'revolutionary' process, almost syncretically, when he stated that in an 'era of social revolution' '[t]he changes in the economic foundation lead sooner or later to the transformation of the whole immense superstructure'.[22] Thus there remains a hiatus, it seems to me, between the role that Marx here implicitly assigns to 'ideological forms', which allow men to conceive and wage the class conflict, and his thesis seeing the transformation of the 'superstructure' as the direct and inevitable consequence of 'chances in the economic foundation'.

The Cassino philosopher was engulfed in this contradiction of Marx's, in particular in the 'first essay' that stresses the priority of the 'underlying economic movement'[23] over the 'juridical and political superstructure'.[24] Though it is true – as Gerratana notes[25] – that already in this 'first essay' there is already an outline – albeit only a metaphorical and metaphorical-spatial one – of the differentiated levels of the superstructure, when Labriola writes '*Beneath* the clamour and dazzle of passions ... *beyond* the visible movements of wills working to a design ... *above* the juridical and political apparatus ... *far behind* the meanings of art and religion ...',[26] it is still, however, true that Labriola immediately then adds that apart from this whole superstructural edifice 'stands, forms, changes and transforms the elementary structure of society, *which holds up all the rest. The anatomical* study of this underlying structure is economics'.[27] Labriola rightly appeals to another way of writing history and explaining historical changes, different to the historiography that stops at 'the most visible exterior apparatus and its ideological, religious, artistic and similar manifestations', instead seeking 'the most hidden and initially least visible changes in the

---

20   Labriola 2000, p. 60.
21   See Merker 1985, p. 21.
22   *MECW*, Vol. 29, p. 264.
23   Labriola 2000, p. 58.
24   *MECW*, Vol. 29, p. 263.
25   Gerratana 1972, pp. 167–8.
26   Labriola 2000, p. 57. My italics.
27   Ibid. My italics, except in the case of 'anatomical'.

economic processes of the underlying structure'.[28] But the image here presented by Labriola is manifestly derived from Marx's own famous depiction of it.
In this Labriola loses, at least for the moment, the anti-monistic vision that was
outlined in his 1887 text 'I problemi della filosofia della storia'. Labriola loses, *at
least for the moment*, the anti-determinism that came to him – as Beatrice Centi
has noted – from his study of Herbartism and the Herbartians, which had reinforced our author's awareness of the '*complexity of* men's ways of living'[29] and
the importance of the multiple 'factors' that *make* (that *are*) history and society.

Here, Labriola's Marxism – which is directly conditioned by its harking back
to the place where Marx most runs the risk of economistic and deterministic
interpretations – stresses the fundamental importance of the 'underlying economic movement'.[30] He knows, and says – as against the most crude and distorted readings of Marx's thought – that 'it is not a matter ... of extending the
so-called economic factor, abstractly taken in isolation, over everything else';[31]
but he adds that once 'the economy' has been conceived 'historically', it is possible 'to explain *the rest* of history's mutations through its own mutations'.[32]
Labriola's effort in the 'first essay' to defend the core of truth in Marx's theory
swamped any sense of prudence he might have had, overflowing into a strong
one-directional connection between 'the process of things' and 'the process of
ideas', as he put it.[33]

3   From One 'Essay' to Another

The 'first essay' was written in 1895. The following year came Labriola's 'second
essay', 'on the materialist conception of history'. 5 August 1895 saw the death of
Engels, with whom Labriola had been in correspondence for at least five years
and whom he had seen as a true and proper beacon, theoretically as well as
politically.

The late Engels – again, on the level of theory – had engaged in repeated
efforts to correct and rectify the most markedly deterministic interpretations
of his and Marx's thought. He did so above all through a series of private letters.

---

28   Labriola 2000, pp. 57–8.
29   Centi 1984, p. 191.
30   Labriola 2000, p. 58.
31   Labriola 2000, p. 85.
32   Ibid. My italics.
33   Labriola 2000, p. 64.

In one such exchange he had recalled the concept of 'the final analysis' (which had already appeared in the *Anti-Dühring*),[34] according to which:

> According to the materialist view of history, the determining factor in history is, *in the final analysis*, the production and reproduction of actual life. More than that was never maintained either by Marx or myself. Now if someone distorts this by declaring the economic moment to be the *only* determining factor, he changes that proposition into a meaningless, abstract, ridiculous piece of jargon. The economic situation is the basis, but the various factors of the superstructure – political forms of the class struggle and its consequences, ... forms of law and, the reflections of all these real struggles in the minds of the participants, i.e. political, philosophical and legal theories, religious views and the expansion of the same into dogmatic systems all these factors also have a bearing on the course of the historical struggles of which, in many cases, they largely determine the *form*. It is in the interaction of all these factors and amidst an unending multitude of fortuities (i.e. of things and events whose intrinsic interconnections are so remote or so incapable of proof that we can regard them as non-existent and ignore them) that the economic trend ultimately asserts itself as something inevitable.[35]

This letter is from 21 September 1890. Its addressee, Joseph Bloch, published it in the 1 October 1895 issue of *Der sozialistische Akademiker*, just after Engels's death. The expression 'in the final analysis', absent from the 'first essay', appeared repeatedly in Labriola's 'second essay' and some of the most significant parts of this essay were centred precisely on the concept of ideology.

The conception of ideology espoused by Labriola in *Del materialismo storio. Dilucidazione preliminare* can be defined as a revisiting of the framework that Marx had given for this theme in his 1859 'Preface', corrected in light of the 'supplementary elucidations' offered by Engels in his 1890 letter to Bloch.

Labriola was predisposed to harmony with Engels on this question. His own intellectual and philosophical itinerary armed him for participation in Engels's

---

34   '[T]he economic structure of society always furnishes the real basis, starting from which we can alone work out the ultimate explanation of the whole superstructure of juridical and political institutions as well as of the religious, philosophical, and other ideas of a given historical period': MECW, Vol. 25, p. 27. This was a 'retouching' of a well-known excerpt from Marx's 1859 'Preface', in which the (extremely important, though wholly embryonic) concept of 'the ultimate explanation' was, however, missing.

35   MECW, Vol. 49, pp. 34–5.

anti-deterministic battle. The inheritance of Herbartism, to which we have already referred, could be recuperated in order to arrive at a new, more dialectical proposition of the base-superstructure connection, where the former, the 'base', was determinant only 'in the final analysis'. We can, that is, share in the idea that Labriola approached a certain conception of the superstructure 'also by reflecting' – as Centi argues – 'on the Herbartian conception of the role of ideas and values',[36] or at least by carrying the inheritance of past acquisitions over to the new Marxist approach. It remains true, however, that the corrective effort carried out by the late Engels had made a significant contribution, and we see this much more clearly in the 'second essay' than the first.

Ideologies are not, therefore, 'a pure semblance, a simple artifice, a mere illusion'.[37] They are not, that is, the subject's deceit or trick, but something of which he is unaware. They are self-deceit. Meaning, they are not a conscious and immediate masking of a class's economic interests, even though these become clear *a posteriori* – as in his example of Luther and the Reformation. This is an important acquisition as against those who would reduce all reality to an immediate projection of the economic dimensions. And yet – we must note – Labriola does not emphasise a particularly important passage of Marx's 1859 text which Gramsci would fully engage with and appreciate the value of, namely the note that it is thanks to 'ideological forms' – according to Labriola's translation from the 'first essay' – 'that men acquire consciousness of conflict and in what name they are carrying it out'.[38] Here, Labriola seems to stop at rejecting the flattening of all reality to the economic dimension, without however fully appreciating the fundamental role of the ideological, as did Gramsci. Perhaps this was also because Labriola wanted above all that history be written according to a correct understanding of the canons of Marxism, while Gramsci above all wanted to *make* history, to do politics:[39] and thus to understand the avenues and resources of subjectivity not only *post factum*.

To write history, it was thus necessary to give due account of what was not the 'economic moment'. This awareness led Labriola to bring 'social psychology' back into focus, though immediately making clear that he had no intention of calling into the 'utter mysticism' of those who thought there was some sort of 'social psyche', 'collective spirit' or even 'human spirit'. 'Forms of consciousness' are themselves also determined by the 'conditions of life'. Here returns Marx's

---

36   Centi 1984, pp. 1–13.
37   Labriola 2000, p. 101.
38   Labriola 2000, p. 60.
39   Paggi 1970, pp. 18–20.

metaphor of the 'economic anatomy', which does not alone suffice to make history, since it is necessary to move from the skeleton of the 'underlying economic structure' up to everything covering this skeleton, remaining aware that 'there is no act of history that is not proceeded, accompanied and followed by determinate forms of consciousness, whether superstitious or proven in experience, ingenuous or reflected-upon, mature or incongruous, impulsive or taught, fantastical or reasoned'.[40]

'Underlying economic structure' is an expression that recurs repeatedly in the 'second essay'. 'Our doctrine', wrote the Cassino philosopher, among other things – 'is not a matter of reducing all the complicated manifestations of history to economic categories alone, but only of explaining every historical fact *in the last instance* (Engels) by *way of the underlying economic structure* (Marx)'.[41] From the Marx of 1859 to the Engels of 1890, and vice versa. From the most deterministic Marxism to Engels's (albeit partial) correction of it, and back again. The 'second essay' appears caught between the horns of this problem, without managing to find not a formulation, but an elaboration that takes the question forward from where Marx and Engels had left it.

On the one hand, it is maintained that ideologies are not semblances, but something real: 'Even though things develop and derive from others, this does not imply that they are not real things'.[42] On the other hand, Labriola returns to stressing that 'the underlying economic structure ... determines everything else', even if 'the process of derivation is rather complicated'.[43] And so on and so forth, in a continual seesawing that seems to express a fundamental torment and indecision. And yet, as compared to so much of Second International Marxism, Labriola had one of the least deterministic and economistic approaches: he was perhaps the only one to highlight – albeit with the same problem of his tormented questioning and insistence on this question – the intrinsic contradiction in Marx and Engels's concept of ideology, on the one hand a distorted consciousness of reality and on the other hand a necessary moment of class struggle.

I will make two further quick observations on the concept of ideology in Labriola. The term 'ideology' appears in the Cassino philosopher's work with a frequency and importance unusual in the Marxism of the time. Where did this highly particular attention to this term, this concept, come from? Probably from the studies that had developed among the German Social Democracy,

---

40   Labriola 2000, p. 105.
41   Labriola 2000, p. 104.
42   Labriola 2000, p. 114.
43   Labriola 2000, p. 130.

since it is unlikely that Labriola was informed of the new meaning that the term was taking on in Russian Marxist circles thanks to Bogdanov[44] and subsequently Lenin,[45] who in his *What is to Be Done?* (published in Italian in 1905) spoke of 'proletarian ideology' as against 'bourgeois ideology', thus clearly giving the term also a positive meaning as well as a negative one.

However, it is probable that Labriola's interest in the concept was substantially driven by his study and knowledge of the French Revolution and the history of eighteenth- and nineteenth-century France. The 'second essay' clearly alludes to Napoleon, the first to transport this term onto the political terrain and give it a negative connotation, when 'with a disdainful tone he defined as *ideologists*' that group of intellectuals who had dared to criticise and challenge his political moves, meaning to suggest that nothing could be expected of intellectuals other than deleterious abstractions. Labriola, though not mentioning him by name, spoke of him as 'the singular mortal on whom the qualities of military genius grafted onto indolent brigandage had, without doubt, conferred the right to mock as an "ideologue" whoever did not admire the naked fact which the simple brutality of success can be in life, as it was for him'.[46]

The second observation again concerns the theme of the various 'factors' that make history. Labriola, following in the footsteps of Marx, reproduced the 1859 Preface's map of the two levels of superstructures:

> the economic structure of society ... determines ... *in the first place and directly* all the rest of the practical activity of the members of that society, and the variation of this activity in the process that we call history, namely the formation, the friction, the struggles and the erosion of classes; the corresponding development of the relations regulating law and morality; and the motives and modes of subordination and subjection of men by men and the corresponding exercise of dominion and authority: in sum, that which the state ultimately originates from and is consisted of: and it determines, *in the second place*, the direction, and *indirectly*, in large part, the objects of fantasy and of thought in the production of art, religion and science.[47]

A little further on, the Cassino philosopher reasserts that the 'empirical view', according to which there are 'various independent factors' that combine to

---

44   See Scherrer 1989.

45   See above, pp. 55–7.

46   Labriola 2000, p. 147.

47   Labriola 2000, p. 162.

determine the process of history, is erroneous. That, because 'the true and proper positive factors – if we must use that word – of history … were and are social classes'. When the question of 'factors' returns, so, too, does the rejection of the positions expressed in *I problemi della filosofia della storia*,[48] with the – very important and interesting – affirmation that the 'factors' that make history are, in reality, social classes. This position is of course unobjectionable from a Marxist point of view, but on closer examination it seems, more than anything, to be deferring the problem. After all, the question is precisely what social classes are and how they are defined. It seems to me that Labriola at times runs the risk of giving them an implicitly *sociological* definition, since in his conception of collective subjectivities he does not seem to capture the role of ideology with due importance.

4   From Labriola to Gramsci

Is it right to say that Gramsci elaborated his conception of ideology *on the basis of Labriola*? In my view, this claim risks being misleading, insofar as it establishes a relationship of parenthood which in reality is only very partially true. In the *Notebooks*, Gramsci defined his own concept of ideology on the basis of Marx and Engels, in an intense theoretical clash mostly engaged with Croce. But many other of his youthful influences also affected its outcome: other than Labriola, above all Sorel, Barbusse and also Pareto, in a process of influence, distinction and refinement that took account of many approaches and influences.

As we have seen, Gramsci first and foremost knew and used Marx's 1859 'Preface', connecting this to the late Engels's battle against determinism and citing the latter's 1890 letter to Bloch. In another equally well-known letter to Franz Mehring dated 14 July 1893, Engels – looking at the concept of ideology – coins his well-known, later canonical definition of 'false consciousness', whose wide publicisation owes precisely to Mehring and his *History of the German Social Democracy*, in which the letter written five years previously was published for the first time as an appendix in 1898. In Engels's letter we also read that 'once an historic element has been brought into the world by other elements, ultimately by economic facts, it also reacts in its turn and may react on its environment and even on its own causes'.[49]

---

48   Franco Sbarberi rightly highlights this in Labriola 1973, p. lxiv.
49   *MECW*, Vol. 50, p. 165.

It is by combining a *dilated* reading of the 1859 'Preface' and Marx's *Theses on Feuerbach*, constantly referred to in the *Notebooks*, with the teachings of the late Engels, that Gramsci arrives at his own *positive* conception of ideology. Already for the young Gramsci, the conception of ideology in Marx (that today considered *classic*, in the sense of a distorted view of reality) was not admissible: as he argued in a 1918 article, Marx himself was an 'ideologue', 'inasmuch as he was a modern-day politician, a revolutionary'.[50] Here already, there appeared a distinction between ideologies as 'pure chatter' and ideologies as 'potential historical forces in formation', which can no longer be ignored: a distinction that would again appear in the *Notebooks*, when Gramsci settled accounts with Croce's reading of Marx. Croce was 'accused' of having absorbed various elements of Marxism, including – Gramsci says – the 'value of ideologies',[51] though the neo-idealist philosopher not only failed to recognise this debt – according to Gramsci – but also distorted Marx's theory of ideology in order to be able to criticise its systematisation.

Gramsci, then, who believed himself to be and was a Marxist, like Labriola began from the primacy of 'social reality' and the 'productive base' with respect to ideologies. But ideologies themselves are also fully part of this reality, Gramsci continues:

> How could Marx have thought that superstructures are appearance and illusion? Even his theories are a superstructure. Marx explicitly states that humans become conscious of their tasks on the ideological terrain of the superstructures, which is hardly a minor affirmation of 'reality', and the aim of his theory is also, precisely, to make a specific social group 'become conscious' of its own tasks, its own power, its own coming-into-being.[52]

Gramsci advanced an anti-deterministic reading of Marx's very most deterministic text, the 1859 'Preface'. Marxism became an ideology in the positive sense, with the scope of making a specific class, the proletariat, 'become conscious'; while the critical-destructive part of Marx's theory of ideology was, according to Gramsci, to be reserved for opposing theories alone, 'practical instruments of political domination' and 'meaningless, because they are in contradiction with actual reality'.[53] *Ideology is not negative as such*, but not all ideologies are

---

50   Gramsci, *'Astrattismo e intransigenza'*, 11 May 1918, reproduced in Gramsci 1984, p. 17.

51   Q4, §3: Gramsci 1975, p. 422; Gramsci 1996b, p. 140.

52   Q4, §15: Gramsci 1975, pp. 436–7; Gramsci 1996b, p. 157.

53   Ibid.

equal. Even Marxism – as Labriola already knew – could give rise to ideologies, when it forgot its specificity as an ideology aware of its own historicity.[54] But the 'arbitrary elucubrations of particular individuals' are one thing, the 'necessary superstructure of a particular structure' quite another.[55] This distinction was espoused in Q7, § 19, where Gramsci also stated that 'To the extent that ideologies are historically necessary they ... "organise" human masses, and create the terrain on which men move, acquire consciousness of their position, struggle, etc.'[56] Here, we are back at the 1859 'Preface', which Gramsci extensively interprets and paraphrases. But the thesis that ideologies 'organise' human masses is also taken from Marx, from *Capital* and the introduction to the *Critique of Hegel's Philosophy of Right* (Q7, § 21).[57]

Gramsci's fundamental objective was still, here, to liberate Marxism from its economistic 'encrustations' (Q7, § 24). The *negative* theory of ideology present in Marx and Marxism was read as an accusation only directed against the ideologies of 'adversarial groups'. The *positive* theory of ideology affirmed and articulated in the *Notebooks* by way of a whole family of concepts, from common sense to philosophy, a particular sense of conformism to religion, and so on, could, in a word, be defined less as 'false consciousness' as, above all, a positive 'conception of the world'. Ideology is, in this view, a site where the collective subjectivity necessary for all 'social groups' is constituted – that is, the collective subjectivity of all classes. Classes cannot be defined *sociologically*, but precisely only insofar as they have and propagate a 'vision of the world' with which they fight the 'war of position' and the struggle for hegemony that traverses every society.

---

54   Q4, § 40.
55   Q7, § 19: Gramsci 1975, p. 868; Gramsci 1971, p. 376.
56   Q7, § 19: Gramsci 1975, p. 869; Gramsci 1971, p. 377.
57   See Gramsci 1975, p. 2755.

CHAPTER 11

Togliatti. The Interpreter and 'Translator'

1   Between Fascism and Stalinism: 'For Democratic Freedoms'

Among the nearly twenty thousand entries in the worldwide bibliography of writings on Gramsci,[1] the 'book' composed by Togliatti on his old comrade in struggle, across an arc of time running from 1927 to 1964, has very few equals: both in the influence it exercised and the role it played in determining the 'fortunes' of the author of the *Prison Notebooks*. Without Togliatti's work as an editor and interpreter, Gramsci would perhaps not be the Gramsci we know today. His name would be that of an anti-fascist martyr, of an original and innovative communist, but the rich laboratory of the *Notebooks* and the high moral standing of the *Letters* would be unknown beyond a restricted circle. Gramsci would not have become the world's best-known and most-read modern Italian essayist. Gramsci is in many ways a more modern, more dynamic, *greater* writer than emerges from the 'use' Togliatti and the PCI made of him (as Togliatti himself ultimately understood and wanted to admit).[2] But the 'Togliattian' Gramsci is also full of essential insights, and when they have been forgotten or willingly ignored it has led to substantial misunderstandings of the Sardinian thinker's legacy.

For some time, now, (even when Togliatti was still alive) there has been a decline in the representation of the relation between the two communist leaders as one of total continuity. For some time, now, people have insisted – to the point of excess – more on their differences than their affinities. The time has come to go back and reread the relation between these two complex, wealthy figures and break away both from the myths of the past and the opposite attitude, which – whether perhaps through reaction or even political malice – has tended to underline only the distance between them. To read these writings today *sine ira et studio*, free of the burden of hagiography, but also free of

---

1 The *Bibliografia gramsciana*, edited by J. Cammett, M.L. Righi and F. Giasi, can be consulted online at the website of the Fondazione Istituto Gramsci: http://www.fondazionegramsci.org.

2 'Today, after having journeyed through the pages of this anthology, shot through with so many different motives, which criss-cross and at times are mixed up in each other, yet never lost – it seems to me that the figure of Antonio Gramsci must himself be seen in a more vivid light, one that transcends the historical experience of our party' (Togliatti 2001, p. 308).

any preconceived hostility, would serve to avoid many of the interpretative droughts and misunderstandings that have taken place in recent decades.

Togliatti's readings of Gramsci can be subdivided into three distinct phases: the years under Fascism, from the arrest of the Sardinian communist to his death; the period from the Liberation of Italy to the end of Stalinism; and the years between 'the unforgettable 1956' and Togliatti's death.

The first such writing – 'Antonio Gramsci un capo della classe operaia (In occasione del processo di Roma)' ['Antonio Gramsci, a leader of the working class (on the occasion of the Rome trials)'] – appeared in *Lo Stato operaio*, the theoretical-political review of the PCd'I, in October 1927. Gramsci had been arrested one year previously, and the trial against the Communist leadership group was being prepared – in June 1928 the Sardinian leader would be sentenced to twenty years' imprisonment. Togliatti's article appeared in the context of the press campaign in support of the Communists imprisoned in Fascist jails. Yet it also goes far beyond this, through the profundity of the author's reflection and the commitment with which he underlines the intellectual stature of the Sardinian communist. This was at a year's distance not only from Gramsci's arrest, but also from the deep conflict immediately previous to it, which had seen a clash between the two main leaders of the PCd'I, with their well-known exchange of letters on the struggle within the Bolshevik leadership. The most recent studies[3] and the documents that have become available only in recent years both allow for a partially new reading of this experience, taking apart the 'accusation' long levelled against Togliatti according to which he did not want to pass on the first of Gramsci's two letters[4] to the Russian Communist Party's Central Committee in the name of the PCd'I politburo. The documents today tell us that Togliatti – *alias* 'Ercoli' – (who from February 1926 was in Moscow as PCd'I representative to the International), who had been authorised by Gramsci himself to show this missive to one of the 'key' Russian comrades confidentially in advance,[5] judged it mistaken and superseded by events. Thus he asked the politburo not to send it,[6] hoping to discuss its themes shortly afterward at another (already organised) meeting, and this was agreed.[7]

---

3   Pistillo 1999; Vacca 1999c, 2012.
4   Daniele (ed.) 1999, pp. 404–12 (the letter from 14 October 1926).
5   Daniele (ed.) 1999, pp. 402–3 (attachment to the 14 October 1926 letter).
6   Daniele (ed.) 1999, p. 413 (phonogram of Togliatti's 16 October 1926 report to the PCd'I politburo) and pp. 414–19 (letter from Togliatti to the PCd'I politburo, 18 October 1926).
7   Daniele (ed.) 1999, p. 434 (phonogram of Togliatti's 26 October 1926 report to the PCd'I politburo).

Beyond Togliatti's formally correct conduct (and this point is an important one), there was also the matter of the serious October 1926 disagreement between Gramsci and Togliatti, as we learn from the second letter that Gramsci wrote, this time on his own account and addressed to Togliatti.[8] This was an eminently political conflict – one that followed a whole series of differences that had emerged during that year (on trade-union tactics, on the 'Bordiga case') between Togliatti in Moscow and the Communist leadership group in Italy, and which culminated in October's political-strategic clash, epitomised by the dramatic questioning of the possibility/necessity of building socialism 'in one country', and the possibility of revolution in the West in a period of 'capitalist stabilisation'.

On this question, Togliatti's position appears to have been not only more 'realistic', but also politically 'correct', it being a given that they were already faced with an epochal defeat. As supported by the fact that Gramsci himself, in the *Notebooks*, was unabashed about confirming the erroneous nature of Trotsky's *political line*, as against that proposed by the majority with which Togliatti sided with conviction (see Q4, §52). This notwithstanding the fact that Gramsci's letter to the Bolshevik leadership group – accused of not having proven able to manage its internal divisions in a political rather than disciplinary manner – appears, when we read it *today*, to have had an extraordinarily wealthy 'prophetic' capacity, foreseeing the risks of the degeneration of the Soviet Revolution, 'Stalinism', which was then only just beginning. The 1926 'break' between Gramsci and Togliatti comes out of this re-examination in a new light. There was, certainly, a bitter clash, a deep divergence, which the 8 November 1926 arrest of Gramsci prevented from being overcome: the division was left crystallised, particularly in the eyes of later observers: after all, in reality the dialogue had continued during Gramsci's prison years.

The real rupture (neither definitive nor of an organisational-disciplinary character) between Gramsci and the PCd'I was consummated later, in the face of the 1929 turn and the politics of 'social-fascism'. The imprisoned Gramsci and Togliatti (living between Moscow and Paris) continued their discussion at a long distance as well as by personal intermediaries – Tania, Sraffa and the 'virtuous circle' of letters that remarkably managed to hold these figures together throughout a whole decade – in difficult conditions, also on account of the serious errors being made by the Italian and other Communists as regards how to help Gramsci in prison and work towards his liberation.[9] Moreover, the

---

8   Daniele (ed.) 1999, pp. 435–9 (26 October 1926 letter).

9   See Spriano 1977, pp. 155 et sqq.; and more generally on the campaigns for Gramsci's release, Natoli 1995 and 1999.

readings that have insisted on the supposed 'break' between the imprisoned Gramsci and the Communist movement[10] – sometimes in good faith, but often with malice and pretexts, for example the speculation on Grieco's 'strange' letter of 1928[11] – run aground on a document that, according to what we now know, invalidates the very roots of this theorem. Namely, the request to the Italian authorities, prepared by Gramsci together with Sraffa on 18 April 1937, only nine days before his death, to be allowed to leave Italy for the Soviet Union.[12] This would have been an inexplicable step for any man who felt betrayed, isolated and abandoned by his comrades.

This was, in synthesis, the context within which Togliatti's first writings dedicated to Gramsci fell. In the first of these, from 1927, Togliatti did not mention the previous year's disagreements, but *on the contrary* forcefully reaffirmed all of Gramsci's merits as concerned the struggle against 'Bordighism' and overcoming the sectarian and extremist 'first period' of the PCd'I. In this article, the issues of dispute that had opposed Gramsci to Bordiga in the 1920s returned, point-by-point. Togliatti rebuffed charges of 'intellectualism'; defended the legitimacy of arriving at Marxism having started out from Hegel, with the related sense of historicity and of the dialectic that this guaranteed; he recalled Gramsci's study of glottology; he exalted his intuitive understanding of the role of the Factory Councils; he denied the idea that in this period Gramsci did not have in mind the question of the party, as 'part' of the class deeply connected to the masses; he did not hesitate to recall that he himself and many other leaders of the PCd'I had abandoned Bordighist positions only thanks to Gramsci. This historical reconstruction was carried out in the heat of the struggle, and could not always be explicit, but provided a substantially accurate framing of what Gramsci was and had been and the essential connotations of his thought. Togliatti was taking a clear, political position, one that resounded with its defence of Gramsci and reaffirmation of his *leadership* in full view of the Russian party and the International.

With the 'turn' of 1929, meaning the launch of the politics of 'social fascism' and its imposition on all the parties of the International, the distance grew between the imprisoned Gramsci and Togliatti. The latter, now at the head of the PCd'I, had fully accepted – after one last effort at the July 1929 Tenth Plenum of the Communist International[13] – Stalin's new course, which effect-

---

10   See, for example, Natoli 1998.
11   See Spriano 1977 and 1988; Fiori 1991; and Vacca 1999a, pp. 78–106.
12   See the document in Spriano 1977, pp. 155–6; and also Vacca 1999a, p. 120.
13   At the tenth plenum of the Comintern in July 1929, Togliatti, Grieco and Di Vittorio sought

ively overturned the political perspectives of 1926 and returned to gambling on an incipient catastrophic crisis of capitalism. A new revolutionary wave was at the gates, it was said. The dissent that Gramsci showed from his Turi prison cell on this point is well-known. He upheld, instead, the thesis of the need for a 'democratic' phase as a way out of fascism, advancing the watchword of a republican constituent assembly. Still, Gramsci's deep dissent with respect to the party line never led to any 'disciplinary' procedure, including the supposed expulsion about which so many tales have been told. His contact with Togliatti was never interrupted, thanks to the Tania-Sraffa 'virtuous circle' on which he long relied.[14]

What is real and meaningful, though, is the fact that Gramsci appeared little in *Lo Stato operaio* between 1931 and 1933.[15] His dissent with regard to the 'turn', perhaps even more than his 1926 letter, advised maximum caution. But Gramsci was not 'condemned' as a heretic, nor expelled like Leonetti, Tresso and Ravazzoli,[16] who were opposed to the course taken by the international Communist movement. Perhaps it would not have been difficult to mix him up in the rising clamour against 'Trotskyism'. But Togliatti chose silence. And

---

to uphold Gramsci's lesson – the non-sectarian, 'popular', and not narrowly 'proletarian' character of the 'Italian revolution' – that is, a vision linked to Italy's national specificities. They did so in the face of pressure from the International, ultimately capitulating with a declaration of principles that almost seems to have been designed for posterity. Togliatti said 'It is right to pose these questions in discussions with the comrades at the centre of the Party? If the Comintern says it is not right, then we will not pose them any more; each of us will continue to think these things and not speak about them any more; we will just say that the anti-fascist revolution will be a proletarian revolution. But each of us will continue to think that it is not at all certain that we will lead this revolution right from the outset, and that we will conquer leadership of it only in the course of the struggle'. And, moreover, 'We have always said that it was our Party's task to study Italy's particular situation ... If the Comintern asks us to do so no longer, we will not do it any more ... but since it is impossible for us to prevent ourselves from thinking about such things, we will keep them to ourselves and limit ourselves to making general statements. But I do say that this study must take place' (cited in Ragionieri 1976, p. 717). On this episode, see also Agosti 1996, pp. 126–9.

14   Even a scholar like Aldo Natoli, who is often excessively 'suspicious' of Togliatti and the PCd'I, has admitted that in the early 1930s 'Gramsci, for his part, displayed his confidence in Sraffa, and was certainly well aware that this latter had a direct relation with Togliatti' (Natoli, 1997, p. xxxiv).

15   See Liguori 2012, pp. 34 et sqq.

16   [Alfonso Leonetti, Pietro Tresso and Paolo Ravazzoli, 'the three', were the founders of Italian Trotskyism. Leonetti would later rejoin the Communist Party – DB.]

when the political decisions of the USSR and the International allowed it – with the Comintern's Seventh Congress and the 'popular front' policy, which did not coincide but did at least converge with the aforementioned 'constituent assembly' proposal, 'a joint action of all anti-fascist groups to bring down the monarchy and the Mussolini régime'[17] – Gramsci's presence on the pages of the PCd'I and Comintern press again became conspicuous, as well as in demonstrations and anti-fascist agitation by Communists in Italy and beyond. Togliatti's choices were dictated by the maximum caution: after all, he was the leader of a party reduced to very little, caught between prison, clandestinity, and exile, for which the support of the Soviet Union was the inescapable condition for continuing the struggle and continuing to exist. Moreover, after the Tenth Plenum Togliatti interpreted the International's new policy with conviction. The salient fact did not, however, lie in the motivations of Togliatti the individual, but rather in his understanding of the fact that the whole historical situation had radically changed in just a few years. On the one hand there was the gradual strengthening of Nazism in Germany; and on the other, the closing down of any space for real, open debate in the Communist movement. It was in this situation that Togliatti succeeded not only in saving himself and his party, but also Gramsci. 'Ercoli' put forward 'Gramsci's politics' (obviously as interpreted and *translated* by Togliatti himself, adapting them to the actual conditions of operation) as soon as there was political space for this.

In Togliatti's 1937–8 written contributions upon Gramsci's death, there was no little of the dross which marked the climate now reigning in the International, the state of affairs usually known as 'Stalinism'. Gramsci became a 'faithful Leninist and Stalinist' who from his prison cell advanced 'that rather important watchword: Trotsky is Fascism's whore'; Bordiga was 'Trotskyist scum', allegedly having reached a partial compromise with the régime. This was also an attempt to save Gramsci's name and to bind it to the International now dominated by Stalin, and also to defend the specificity of a political tradition which just a few months later Togliatti would have to save in the teeth of the PCd'I leadership group itself.

Indeed, in 1938, with a new wave of Stalinist repression in full flow, the Comintern dissolved the Italian party's central committee, which had been heavily criticised by the International in Togliatti's absence. In a secretariat meeting on 12 August 1938, some of the PCd'I's main leaders expressed the opinion that it was necessary to review critically the 'oscillations' of the Party between 1926 and 1928–9 – that is, first Gramsci and then Togliatti – in relation

---

17   Tosin 1976, p. 98; Lisa 1973.

to the Bolshevik leadership group, and publicly to take a position against Gramsci's 1926 letter, which Angelo Tasca in France had just recently made known
for the first time. Togliatti opposed this decision, crushing in the egg a revised
apparaisal of Gramsci's positions which could have entailed the 'condemna-
tion' of the Sardinian leader by the international Communist movement.[18] This
was a fundamentally important episode, indicating that 'Togliatti's manage-
ment' of Gramsci's legacy – even in 1938 – was no easy choice.

If we go beyond certain expressions that we find in these texts, linked to
the tragic conditions of the time, we cannot but note that Togliatti outlined
a substantially accurate picture of Gramsci's thought and works from the First
World War onwards. He was not only a martyr killed by Fascism, not just a 'great
Italian' who fought for freedom, but also a Marxist and a revolutionary of some
consequence: not just an intellectual, but a political fighter. Nor did these texts
straightforwardly eulogise him: Gramsci had also committed errors (and this
was, moreover, a self-critique by Togliatti), for example when the *Ordine Nuovo*
group did not organise on a national basis during the *biennio rosso* of 1919–20,
leaving the leadership of the communist wing of the Italian Socialist Party to
Bordiga; or in 1922, when it had not immediately initiated a political struggle
against the Bordighist leadership. While the argument is forced, in places, the
reconstruction of historical events captures the substance of the processes that
the two Communist leaders had lived through together. He remained silent on
the conflicts of 1926 and 1929–33: a price paid on the altar of safeguarding the
memory and legacy of Gramsci through the tempests of Stalinism. Not a price
that could be paid light-mindedly; but nor should it be exaggerated, except on
condition of drawing an undue equivalence between the consciousness and
freedom of today's readers with those of the actors of the time. What must be
stressed above all, in Togliatti's 1937–8 writings, is that he captured the essence
of Gramsci's teachings, in pointing to the 'working class as the first, the only, the
truly *national* class, which looks to resolve all the problems that the bourgeoisie
and the bourgeois revolution have not resolved'.[19] The ability to understand
that the Communist movement, while remaining internationalist, necessarily
had to delve deep into national realities if it was to play an effective role and not
limit itself to purely describing events or minoritarian agitation, was the axis of
Gramsci's teachings which Togliatti placed at the centre of his own political
activity, marking a whole period of struggles and conquests: above all starting
with the end of Fascism. It was a conviction, then, that was not only clearly

---

18   Spriano 1977, pp. 118–21; Agosti 1996, p. 214.
19   Togliatti 2001, p. 78. My italics.

apparent from the 1930s onwards, but simultaneously directly connected to Gramsci's thought, to which Togliatti could pay full tribute in the new stage of the international Communist movement beginning in 1934–5:

> His fundamental idea was that after fifteen years of Fascist dictatorship, which has disorganised the working class, it is not possible for the class struggle against the reactionary bourgeoisie to resume its development on the same positions that the proletariat had reached immediately after the First World War. A period of struggle for democratic freedoms is indispensible, and the working class must be at the head of this struggle.[20]

The Togliattian Gramsci and Togliatti's postwar politics – a *democratic and national* politics – were already clearly present from 1937–8 onwards.

2   'Gramsci's Politics' in Liberated Italy

Returning to Italy in March 1944, Togliatti made the 'Salerno Turn', which meant not only a rejection of the Communists' previous policy towards the monarchy and the institutional question, within the terms of the struggle against Nazi-Fascism, but also for the Italian Communist Party (PCI) itself to operate in a new and different way. The novelty of Togliatti's policy can be summarised, above all, in his conception of the 'new party' and his emphasis on the democratic and national character of the PCI's activity. While this outlook was perhaps above all rooted in certain moments of Togliatti's own 1930s experience (the popular front era, the Spanish Civil War experience, reflection on the new characteristics of Fascism and mass society), the references to Gramsci in support of this new policy were very frequent in this period.[21] It would be a mistake to underestimate the undoubtable distinctions between Gramsci's prison-era elaborations and Togliatti's theoretical-political elaboration. For example, Gramsci's 'war of position' was a strategy of much wider relevance than the PCI's postwar 'policy of anti-Fascist unity', indicating new modes of anti-capitalist struggle and of the transition to socialism which Togliatti and his party were only in part able to master or attempt to put into action. It should not be forgotten that the political elements that Togliatti was able to deploy from Salerno onwards, in a situation that was new in so many aspects, distanced him from

---

20   Togliatti 2001, p. 89.
21   Liguori 2012, pp. 55 et sqq.

Gramsci *in a positive sense*, also in merit of his acceptance of pluralism and democratic politics.

We can say that Togliatti realised a politics of Gramscian inspiration within the limits allowed by his realism in the post-Yalta Conference world. In 1944, Gramsci was an unknown for most people, even among PCI militants themselves. It was Togliatti who made him the reference point of the politics and culture of the Italian Communists. It was a precise choice, one explained first and foremost by their common political and cultural formation, along with their 1930s reflections, which though separate were not divergent. It was a complex relationship, with light and shadows, but also depth. It is also explained by the need to assert the peculiarity of Italian Communism, to reaffirm (though without breaking with the USSR, even at the price of often being syncretic) a political line that Togliatti had advanced whenever the relations of force internal and external to the international Communist movement had allowed it. If it is true that in presenting his politics as 'Gramsci's politics', Togliatti was forcing the issue somewhat, it is also true that this also provided the 'new party' with a strong anchor, overcoming the resistance of those more attached to the USSR or illusions of insurrection.

When, in liberated Italy, he again became able to speak of Gramsci, Togliatti recalled the Sardinian Communist's indication of a 'national' politics, a policy of alliances between workers, peasants and intellectuals,[22] pivoting on the 'national function of the working class'. The 'Salerno policy' was thus totally at one with his reading of Gramsci. The policy of anti-Fascist unity had a fundamental point of reference in Gramsci. In his speech at the Naples San Carlo theatre of 29 April 1945, referring to the 1924–6 period, Togliatti said that

> The central idea of Gramsci's political activity was the idea of unity: the unity of the workers' parties in the struggle to defend democratic institutions and overthrow Fascism; the unity of the workers' parties with democratic forces ...; the unity of the socialist working masses with the Catholic working masses in the towns and countryside, the unity of workers, the unity of workers and peasants, the unity of those who work with their hands and those who work with their minds, for the creation of a great bloc of national forces, on the basis of which it would be possible to block the way to Fascism's final advance and to save – as still would have been possible – our country.[23]

---

22   Togliatti 2001, p. 42.
23   Togliatti 2001, p. 33.

This political line, unity – clearly being projected onto the postwar situation – was in reality above all grounded in Gramsci's prison reflections indicating the objective of a Constituent Assembly. Togliatti here remained within the groove of Gramsci's indications, even if in the mid-1930s these could have said little or nothing on the new situation that would be created with the defeat of Nazi-Fascism. Togliatti continued to cohere to this political outlook, albeit in a national and international setting that was rapidly changing. Again in 1947 he warned:

> We Communists would be in trouble if we believed that Antonio Gramsci's legacy was ours alone. No, this is a legacy for all, for all Sardinians, for all Italians, for all workers who fight for their emancipation, whatever their religious faith or political belief.[24]

This 'Gramsci for all' – long polemicised against 'from the Left' – was an important moment of a struggle for hegemony that Togliatti believed to be more open than it really was. With the end of the unity of anti-Fascist forces, a historical period was brought to a close and Togliatti's reading of Gramsci partly changed. It continued to be a political-cultural operation of wide relevance, whose importance appeared even more clearly in the Cold War years. For Togliatti and the PCI, Gramsci also served the establishment of a relationship with intellectuals. The PCI attempted to speak to all of these latter – above all those of a neo-idealist culture – by way of Gramsci, offering a terrain of unity/distinction with their prior Crocean and Gentilian formation. 'The intellectual vanguard' were called upon to be 'the inheritors of all that is positive and progressive in the development of our country's culture'.[25] Its attitude towards Croce himself was far from unvarying, and alternated between more conciliatory and bitterer tones. Among the former could be counted the view that Gramsci had understood

> that the new Italian idealist culture represented a step forward in the development of our national culture ... that it was not possible to take a strictly negative attitude towards this new intellectual current, and stated, rather, that we would have to carry out an operation with regard to this philosophical current analogous to what Marx and Engels did in their own

---

24   Togliatti 2001, p. 128.
25   Togliatti 2001, p. 112.

time, when, faced with Hegelian formulas, they turned Hegel's dialectic on its head, as they themselves put it.[26]

Among the latter – and still as regards writings on Gramsci – we could count the reaction to Croce's review of the *Lettere dal carcere*,[27] which sought to counterpose Gramsci to the PCI. 'As a thinking man, he was one of our own', the liberal philosopher had written, listing the points of similarity between Gramsci and neo-idealism ('His renovated concept of philosophy in its speculative and dialectical tradition, and not in a positivist, classifying one; his wide perspective on history; uniting erudition with philosophising; his very vivid sense of poetry and art in their original character; and, with this, opening of the road to recognising the originality and autonomy of ideal categories'), counterposing this to 'today's Communist intellectuals'. Perhaps on account of this last, instrumental statement, but more probably on account of another (hardly contestable) statement of Croce's counterposing Gramsci to the 'philosophical catechism written by Stalin', Togliatti reacted to what 'Don Benedetto' had said with unusually harsh sharpness.[28] In any case, the seed of Gramsci's Marxism had already been sown: an anti-dogmatic, anti-deterministic, anti-fatalist Marxism, much more dynamic and enduring than so many 'philosophical catechisms'. Indeed, Togliatti had himself stressed this as early as 1945, in polemic with the Catholic-modernist historian Ernesto Buonaiuti.[29]

With 1948 and the beginning of the 'Cold War', the PCI's politics changed partly: the 'Salerno policy' was denatured in the harshness of the clash, and the Party's cultural policy, ideological battle and attitude toward intellectuals became more inflexible. The originality of the Italian Communists had not gone away, but the contradiction between 'the Italian road' and adherence to international Communist ranks decreed – even in the PCI and in Togliatti – that the Party was again weighed down by a heavy Stalinist and Zhdanovite encumbrance. Togliatti's strategy was founded on the hypothesis of a long period of collaboration between the democratic parties, dictated not only by the Yalta accords but also an analysis of Fascism as an epochal threat, thus making Togliatti afraid of a possible return to reactionary forms of bourgeois hegemony. At least up until 1953, the stress on the risk of involution (for example at the 1952 Bari Conference)[30] was so strong as to leave the Communists barely sensitive

---

26   Togliatti 2001, p. 111.

27   Croce 1947.

28   Togliatti 2001, pp. 129 et sqq.

29   See chapter 10, p. 142.

30   'Does this not mean Gramsci's analysis, Gramsci's conclusions, namely that in the current

to the processes of modernisation now underway in Italy. This error of judgement, constituting the principal limit of 'Togliatti's Marxism', appears all the more serious because a very different reading of capitalism's capacity to expand was available precisely in Gramsci, in *Americanism and Fordism*. Not by accident, this text long remained a dead letter, and Felice Platone's preface to a 1950 edition of the twenty-second notebook was concerned to warn the reader against considering Gramsci's analyses to be still-current, including as regarded the United States, 'a country with a Fordism rather different to what Gramsci knew ... America today lives under the nightmare of a new economic crisis, and looks with apprehension at its growing crowd of unemployed'.[31] It was necessary to wait as long as the early 1970s before the importance of *Americanism and Fordism* began to be recognised.[32]

In this period, between 1948 and 1953, the Party was ever more convinced of the need to attach itself to a national-democratic tradition, indeed one to which Italian Marxism was heir by way of its connection to Gramsci. And while in 1945 Togliatti, polemicising against Buonaiuti, had significantly questioned the relationship between Labriola and Gramsci, from 1948 he insisted on the continuity between them. The publication of the *Quaderni del carcere* with the publisher Einaudi between 1948 and 1951[33] contributed decisively to giving the PCI its own particular identity. And for precisely this reason it did not fail to arouse surprise and even disorientation.[34] The *Notebooks*, indeed, appeared as a radical alternative to the Marxist-Leninist orthodoxy of a Stalinist stamp. Togliatti was well aware of the problematic consequences that their publication might entail.[35] The thematic ordering, 'cutting' and positioning of the texts also provided the means by which he sought to avoid a collision between Soviet orthodoxy and Gramsci's bequest, suggesting that the latter be read through the prism of 'national specificity' and not the great disputes of the 1920s and 1930s international workers' movement.

The subdivision of the *Notebooks* on a thematic basis, which could be criticised from a philological point of view and was not free of censorship, did

---

period of our national life, Fascism is ever-present, a danger and threat still incumbent upon us?' Togliatti 2001, p. 178.

31   Gramsci 1950, p. 15.

32   An oversight corrected thanks to De Felice 1972.

33   On the reverberations of the publication of Gramsci's *Letters* and *Notebooks* and the problems that this entailed, see Liguori 2012. See also Chiarotto 2011.

34   See the accounts of Natta 1977, p. 274 and Luporini 1974, p. xxviii.

35   As early as 25 April 1941, in his letter to Comintern leader Dimitrov: cited in Vacca 1999a, pp. 130–1.

have the merit of favouring their assimilation and cultural impact,[36] though also opening the way to forms of syncretism. As regards culture, a classic subdivision of knowledge was here deployed, largely concealing the connection between his prison reflections and the history of the Communist movement. The rupturing effect of the *Prison Notebooks* was enormous, leading to profound renovations of various fields, from history to literature, from studies of folklore to political thought, pedagogy, and so on. The 'reconnaissance of the national terrain' was, however, almost solely historiographical: from the *Risorgimento* to the Southern question to the history of intellectuals. It was Togliatti himself who pushed in this direction: again in 1952, in search of the right terrain for an encounter with culture, he stressed the need to value the progressive national tradition.[37] This was also a way of shifting away from the Stalinist-Zhdanovite model without forcing a politically unsustainable open break.

For many, Gramsci thus became above all a 'great intellectual'. We have seen how Togliatti had already in 1927 and 1937–8 – in a very different historical situation – rebuffed the separation between an 'intellectual' and a 'political' Gramsci. Even in 1923, he had polemicised with Giuseppe Prezzolini, who had written, with regard to the *Ordine Nuovo* experience:

> To me it seems being thrown into militant political activity dampened the creative qualities of these youths, who matched an original intellect and faith in a way that does not often happen. This was good for their Party, but I, as a reader, greatly regretted it.[38]

We note, in these words, the ill humour of the *liberal* intellectual (even if considered a *sui generis* one, as Italian liberals have often been) with regard to an almost incomprehensible choice: that the young revolutionary intellectuals of *L'Ordine Nuovo* should have chosen marriage with the working-class cause and to commit themselves wholly to this cause. That this represented a moment of strong *discontinuity* in this history of Italian intellectuals was clear to Togliatti, who polemically wrote – reviewing Prezzolini's book – that

> There has always been a sharp separation between our culture and our life, almost an abyss. 'Intelligence' has been separated from other fac-

---

36 Gerratana always recognised the merits of the thematic edition of the *Notebooks* and never indulged its 'demonisation': see his preface in Gramsci 1975, p. xxxiii.

37 Togliatti 1974, p. 201 et sqq.

38 Prezzolini 1923, p. 122.

ulties, either held apart from them, or because of an incapacity to understand the necessity of an organic link between it and all the other forms of life, or because of an inability to translate into practice the coherence reached and demonstrated in the mind.[39]

The PCI's postwar attempt at an encounter with the Crocean 'great intellectuals' was important to the consolidation of Italian democracy: it was an effort to win to democratic positions a layer who had in the past often been displaced onto conservative or even reactionary positions. This meant also making Gramsci a 'great intellectual', even describing him (and this is not in itself mistaken) as 'one of the great minds of today's Italy'.[40] It was necessary, in other words, to give the other intellectuals the example of a democratic 'great intellectual', an example to follow, linking them to the popular masses and their party. The negative side of this operation lay in the fact that the status of a 'great intellectual' was never even partially questioned. While for Gramsci the question of the intellectuals concerned the forms of cultural organisation, the apparatuses of hegemony, for Togliatti it concerned the ideological plane. There was a risk, here, of privileging intellectual elites. The 'traditional intellectual' who stood with the Left ultimately occupied the same position as in liberal culture and society, even if the branding was different. It denatured the *break* represented by *L'Ordine Nuovo* and the Resistance, running the risk of a new continuity, even a new *transformismo* among the intellectuals. Of course, they were no longer entirely separate from society and politics, but their relationship with the working class was not that foreseen by Gramsci, namely, the fusion and reclassification of their roles and tasks. It was a more limited, albeit still important relation: *alliance*.

Moreover, there were tensions concerning Gramsci's cultural legacy even within his and Togliatti's party. And the latter's struggle always appeared 'on two fronts': against liberal deviations and against rigid Zhdanovism. One telling episode which demonstrates how Gramsci and his historiographical teachings constituted an object of contention among those who remained faithful to the various Marxist-Leninist 'catechisms' was the conflict between a group of Communist historians and Arturo Colombi, who in a meeting of specialists at the Istituto Gramsci accused the historians of excessive disregard for the model provided by Stalin's *Short Course of the History of the CPSU(B)*, instead preferring to use the categories and terminology of the *Notebooks*. In the letter

---

39   Togliatti 1967, p. 490.
40   Togliatti 2001, p. 149.

that Togliatti subsequently wrote to Donini, director of the Istituto Gramsci, in support of the historians, we read:

> if today, in Italy, we have managed to establish ample contacts with the world of culture and penetrate into it, this is dependent on the fact that we have avoided taking the position of judges standing on the outside, and have instead sought to develop our competence, favouring and carrying out objective research, not rejecting or, worse still, ignoring what comes from other sources; we have entered into debate and remained there, without showing any pretense of infallibility ... Perhaps it was better to start out from Gramsci and delve deep into the novelty of his historiographical thought ... Gramsci expressed himself as the scholars of his time and his country expressed themselves, without ever conceding anything in the substance of his views ... In every country, Marxism must be able to fight on the terrain of its national culture, of its traditions, of its mode of being and development, if it wants to become an active and determining element of this development.[41]

On the one hand, Togliatti here again affirms the specificity of Gramsci's cultural contribution; on the other hand, in the years 1948–54 he explained that Gramsci's research was driven by politics, by the demands of the struggle. Speaking at Turin University in 1949, the PCI secretary focused on Gramsci's cultural formation, evoking the climate in which this had taken place, whose limits could only be overcome 'by making men rediscover the unity of being and thought, and for this unity to be rediscovered in concrete history, in concrete struggles to transform and renovate the country, thus creating new economic and social relations for Italy'.[42] The meaning of the political-cultural operation initiated by the Communist leader was to advance from the early-twentieth-century separateness between intellectuals and the people, to the new connection attempted by *L'Ordine Nuovo*, and toward the hypothesis of a new reconciliation in the difficult 'Cold War years'. And it was harking back to Gramsci that Togliatti made this call. Though doubtless marked by limits, this effort was also rich in meaningful results.

Togliatti also began to clarify that Gramsci's prison reflections was not at all *für ewig*, but rather had started out from a *political* demand: the necessity of explaining the epochal defeat of the workers' movement, and the resumption

---

41   See Vittoria 1992, pp. 275–6.

42   Togliatti 2001, p. 143.

the struggle. Everything – the history of Italy, the study of intellectuals – had its centre and propulsive force within this demand. Here began 'a new science of our history and of our politics'.[43] And already before 1956, Togliatti pointed to the *fully political* terrain of Gramsci's research. In 1954, reviewing the first volume of Gramsci's pre-prison writings, concerning the years 1919–20, he forcefully stressed that 'his prison writings did not, then, stand outside the political struggle that preceded them; they were an integral part, almost the crowning part, of this struggle'.[44]

3   After '56: The 'Theorist of Politics'

With 1956 there began a new phase not only in the history of Togliatti's readings of Gramsci, but in the Communist leader's whole elaboration: a period that would culminate in the *Memoriale di Jalta*. Both the need to rethink the politics of the PCI – looking for the way to a new strategy, after the failure of the course attempted in the 'East' – and the deep crisis in its relations with intellectuals, led to a reinterrogation of Gramsci. The Sardinian Communist again became an original point of reference, even if one deployed in defence of the tradition of October 1917. According to Togliatti, he had 'opened the way to the study of the various forms that the dictatorship of the working class can take in its various phases and in different countries. What is in discussion, here, is a new chapter of Leninism, one whose complete elaboration is now being worked on by the international workers' movement'.[45]

Gramsci had indicated new hypotheses for the struggle for socialism. If we add to this the publication of his pre-prison writings, the interest that they aroused in anti-dogmatic Marxism, and the end of the long period in which the history of the Communist movement had been the de facto property of party leaders, we can well understand how these factors collectively led to the image of the 'great intellectual', interested in what existed *für ewig*, being put away in favour of Gramsci, theorist of politics, who theorised *for the purpose of praxis*. It was no accident that many of Togliatti's directly political interventions in 1956 took recourse to invoking the author of the *Prison Notebooks*. This was a reread Gramsci, interrogated in close relation to the strategic problems of the Communist movement, whose necessarily 'national' existence was

---

43   Togliatti 2001, p. 178.
44   Togliatti 2001, p. 189.
45   Togliatti 2001, p. 233.

relocated in a precise international and internationalist panorama; a Gramsci looked to as the origin of the 'Italian road to socialism'; a Gramsci who also ultimately became an object of political contention, among those tendencies within and without the PCI critical of Togliatti's handling of deStalinisation.[46] The interpretation of Gramsci advanced by Togliatti in 1956–8[47] was built on the connection between Gramsci and Leninism. To be 'Leninists' meant to reaffirm the link with the Bolshevik tradition, reducing Stalin's role and harking back to the original *raisons d'être* of the Communist movement. But it also meant to relaunch the 'Italian road to socialism', that is, to be 'national' in a new way, reprising the creative reading of Leninism that Gramsci had taken forward on the basis of his distinction between 'East' and 'West' (war of position, hegemony, historic bloc) and with a 'reconnaissance of the national terrain', similar to that which Lenin had carried out in Russia. Indeed, Togliatti drew from Lenin the conviction that 'the working class's revolutionary movement can and must develop through different paths in different historical situations'.[48]

It was necessary, then, to be Leninists in the sense of a capacity to *translate* Leninism into Italian – as Gramsci had attempted – advancing 'towards socialism along a national road, determined by the historical conditions of our country. It is this national road that he wanted to open to us'.[49] From here came the perspective, with a basis in Gramsci, that the Italian Communists should elaborate an ever more autonomous outlook, this being a practice that had been partially abandoned and was now necessary to resume. This meant a bind of continuity and innovation with respect to the Communist tradition – yet it discounted two limiting factors. Firstly, it did not shed light on the peculiarities that made it impossible to box Gramsci within the terms of a purely Leninist horizon, his thought not being just 'a variant' of Leninism, but rather a theory and strategy with its own autonomous significance. Secondly, to insist on Gramsci as the point of origin of the *'Italian* road to socialism' implied giving up on identifying him as a possible new reference point for the whole Communist movement, or at least one for the West.

---

46   Among the Gramsci studies taking Togliattianism as a polemical target, we ought to mention at least Caracciolo and Scalia (eds.) 1959, with essays by Caracciolo, Guiducci, Tamburrano, Tronti and others.

47   The three Togliatti essays to which I am here referring – 'Attualità del pensiero e dell'azione di Gramsci [1957]', 'Il leninismo nel pensiero e nell'azione di A. Gramsci (Appunti) [1958]' and 'Gramsci e il leninismo [1958]' – could be considered a unitary whole.

48   Togliatti 2001, p. 261.

49   Togliatti 2001, p. 209.

There was in Togliatti, then, a prudent historicism that allowed for greatly important theoretical-political innovations in Italy, but was careful to avoid a break with the Soviet model. This choice led Togliatti as far as stiffening the base-superstructure connection, to the end of upholding the supposed superiority of Soviet 'democracy'; if change had taken place at the base level, then full liberation on the superstructural, political level must necessarily sooner or later follow.[50] And yet Togliatti had repeatedly insisted and here again insisted on the dialectical character of the base-superstructure relationship and on the non-mechanical, non-one-directional nexus between them (as clearly indicated by Gramsci). Indeed, he argued that already in *L'Ordine Nuovo* 'there were the seeds of the *Notebooks*' most profound reflections on the reciprocal relationship between base and superstructure, and on the unity of economics and politics throughout the whole complex of social reality'.[51] The distinction between the different parts of the real – Togliatti recalled, following in Gramsci's footsteps – 'is only methodological, not organic'.[52]

The interpretation that Togliatti proposed in 1956–8 was, in any case, a notable step forward in terms of reading 'Gramsci according to Gramsci', rich in indications and cues that still today remain valid. From here, he began a discovery of a different Gramsci, 'a theorist of politics, but above all ... a practical politician, that is, a fighter ... It is in politics', Togliatti maintained, 'that the unity of A[ntonio] G[ramsci]'s life must be sought'.[53] This was a red thread that ran 'from his youthful days', 'up to his arrest and even after'. The reading of the *Notebooks* is lit up by this last insight: and Togliatti here prompted a whole new phase of studies, situating them at a new level constructed around the texture of Gramsci's political militancy. He moreover delineated the figure of a great thinker of the Communist movement being lowered down into the international debate, one who had reached theoretical maturity within the terms of a precise horizon and a certain historically determinate situation.

4   The Final Chapter: Gramsci, a Man

The final chapter of Togliatti's readings of Gramsci was dedicated to an important work of historiographical and theoretical fine-tuning, which accompanied and stimulated the publication or re-edition of Gramsci's works. A fundamental

---

50   Togliatti 2001, pp. 206–7.
51   Togliatti 2001, p. 202.
52   Togliatti 2001, p. 233.
53   Togliatti 2001, p. 213.

moment of the new historiographical stage, made possible by deStalinisation, was Togliatti's essay 'La formazione del gruppo dirigente del Partito comunista italiano nel 1923–24' ['The formation of the PCI leadership group, 1923–24']. Freeing historical reconstruction from the direct influence and demands of politics, Togliatti encouraged and theorised a true 'historiographical revolution', writing:

> I hold it to be a great error, in expounding the history of the workers' movement and in particular the history of the party of which one is a member and has been and is a leader, to maintain and force oneself to demonstrate that this party and its leadership always made the right move in the best possible way. With this, we end up representing it as an uninterrupted triumphal procession. And this is a false representation, far from reality and contradicted by it.[54]

In the introductory essay to the correspondence between Gramsci (in Moscow and Vienna) and Togliatti, Scoccimarro, Terracini and Leonetti, a volume also including documents and articles from the time – largely unedited material from the Angelo Tasca and PCI archives – Togliatti filled in voids of unawareness; lit up shadowy areas; made explicit elements and evaluations that had previously only been mentioned or implied; and reaffirmed critical judgements in new ways, in forms that did not demonise, and with more balance in his analyses and assessments. This was a masterclass in style, very innovative with respect to the praxis hitherto followed by the Communist Parties' leaderships, and helping the renovation of Communist historiography.

Beyond the substance of the matter, this historiographical method was never again to be contradicted. In this regard, it is a fact of no little significance that the columns of Togliatti's review *Rinascita* played host to documents, letters, and analyses concerning the historical experience of the PCI. One of the most telling cases, on this point, was the publication – while Togliatti was still alive – of the 1926 exchange of letters on the CPSU's internal struggle.[55]

Togliatti's last text dedicated to Gramsci was a short article appearing in *Paese sera* upon the publication of *2000 pagine di Gramsci*,[56] two months before the Communist leader's death in Yalta. As we have said, this was an opportunity for an – also partly self-critical – balance-sheet of the relationship between the

---

54   Togliatti 2001, pp. 280–1.

55   See *Rinascita*, 1964, no. 22, and Togliatti's brief clarification of this same topic in issue 24.

56   Gramsci 1964.

Sardinian thinker and the leaders and intellectuals of his party – first among them Togliatti – who had interpreted his *oeuvre* in relation to the concerns and demands of praxis, of politics. Gramsci was more than the founder of the 'Italian road to socialism' – Togliatti argued – and was of such depth as to foster a more general reflection, one now made urgent by the crisis of the international Communist movement. Touchingly, Gramsci also re-emerged here as 'a man', a dramatic example of the tension between theory and praxis, between a person's limits and the struggle to overcome them. It was an example that Togliatti had never ceased to look up to with admiration and reverence.

Many interpretative elements of the years from 1927 to 1964 obviously strike us as belonging to their own time more than ours. Others, however, remain fundamental to an understanding of Gramsci and his legacy. Politics as the motor of all his research; his dialectical vision of the base-superstructure and society-state nexus, the centre of his Marxism; the conviction that 'the national' remained a barely avoidable moment of the struggle for hegemony. How could we fail to see the aptness and usefulness of such interpretative keys – the fulcrum of Togliatti's reading of Gramsci – today, now that we are faced with so many culturalist, neo-idealist and even 'liberal' interpretations of the Sardinian Communist?

CHAPTER 12

Hegemony and Its Interpreters

1   After '56: Between Dictatorship and Democracy.

Probably everybody today recognises that the concept of hegemony is the most important theoretical-political category of the *Notebooks*. For some thirty years now, all of the works that have concerned themselves with Gramsci's thought, taken as a whole, have also addressed the concept of hegemony. It will obviously not be possible, here, to devote our attention to each and every one of them. I will limit myself to noting works specifically dedicated to hegemony and those works that have made some specific contribution to illuminating this category.

This theme has not always been in the forefront in the reception and study of Gramsci's thought. Indeed, full awareness of its relevance, its novelty, and its specificity only emerged and began its rise as late as the 1970s. It should be noted, nonetheless, that already in 1958, beginning his contribution to the Rome 'Gramsci studies' conference, Giuseppe Tamburrano lamented the fact that the 'conception of hegemony' was 'an aspect of Gramsci's political thought that has not been sufficiently studied and delved into'.[1] This was, without doubt, a truthful statement. The category of hegemony had been somewhat left in the background of the reconstruction of 'the great national intellectual' Gramsci's thought that was long dominant in the postwar period, especially following the first publication of the *Letters* and the *Notebooks*. This had been a great *hegemonic* operation, which had evidently been unable to insist on this theme explicitly, or not needed to do so in order to be driven forward.

The debate on hegemony can be said to have begun – after 1956 – with the onset of the theoretical-strategic reflection on the new question of *what is to be done?*; it was thus that the debate on Gramsci returned, his work being seen as a *terrain* of reflection and examination of the political questions facing the workers' movement (both Socialist and Communist) internationally. Indeed, in two talks on 'Gramsci and Leninism' at the 1958 Rome conference, Togliatti replied to the polemic, also concerning Gramsci, advanced by certain parts of the Socialist and Communist intelligentsia. His response both underlined how much Gramsci's mature reflection owed to the encounter with Lenin, and

---

1   Tamburrano 1973 p. 277.

indicated the extent to which in the *Notebooks* Gramsci had, in reality, begun to write a 'new chapter' of Leninism. As concerned hegemony, Togliatti stated that 'there is a difference, but not one of substance'[2] between the terms 'hegemony' and 'dictatorship' – since even if it was true that 'hegemony' referred to civil society, and was thus a 'broader concept', it should not be forgotten that for Gramsci the difference between civil and political society 'is purely methodological, and not organic. Every state is a dictatorship, and every dictatorship presupposes not only the power of one class, but a system of alliances and mediations'.[3]

This was a philologically accurate, but politically weak response. Tamburanno himself had grasped this, insisting with some justification – at Rome and after – upon the specificity of the concept; even if he was pressuring the PCI secretary on the basis of rather instrumental positions, given his tendency to uphold the democratic character of Gramsci's thought also to the end of denying the legitimacy of the Communist tradition. In his intervention appearing in the volume *La città futura*, the most important moment of the polemic against the PCI on the terrain of post-'56 readings of Gramsci, Tamburrano stressed that Gramsci had insisted on the fact 'that it is not enough to conquer the instruments of political dominion; it is necessary [to obtain] the *consent* of the masses with an interest in socialism *before* the conquest of state power. This means ... *democratically* conquering and *democratically* maintaining proletarian power'.[4] Resuming this polemic in his 1963 monograph on Gramsci, Tamburrano reminded Togliatti – not wrongly – that 'if it is true that every state is a dictatorship in the Marxist sense, it is also true that this fundamental dictatorship can be exercised democratically or in an authoritarian manner'.[5] Therefore, for Tamburrano the theory of hegemony meant 'the examination and overcoming of the Leninist theory of the state',[6] and as such 'the theory of hegemony is a democratic theory and a *new* line of thought in Gramsci and the communist doctrine'.[7]

---

2   Togliatti 2001, p. 232.
3   Togliatti 2001, p. 233.
4   Tamburrano 1959 p. 61.
5   Tamburrano 1977, p. 290.
6   Tamburrano 1977, p. 285.
7   Tamburrano 1977, pp. 288–9.

2   1967: Political and Cultural Leadership

The second chapter of this brief history of the fortunes of the concept of hegemony was written by Norberto Bobbio on the occasion of the 1967 Gramsci
conference in Cagliari. In his well-known talk on 'Gramsci and civil society',
Bobbio argued that in Gramsci 'the moment of force [was] instrumental and
thus subordinate to the moment of hegemony, while in Lenin ... dictatorship
and hegemony went hand in hand, and thus the moment of force was primary
and decisive'.[8] But this was not the essential difference Bobbio recognised,
since it could also have been due to different contingencies of history. For Bobbio, instead, the essential difference, the peculiarity of hegemony in Gramsci,
lay – coherent with his vision of civil society – in his shifting the accent onto *cultural* leadership. Though up until 1926 the term had appeared in Gramsci with
the same meaning that it had in the Leninist tradition (that is, 'in the sense
of the *political leadership*' of the working class with respect to allied classes), in
the *Notebooks* there was an *extension of the concept of hegemony*, which came to
mean 'also *cultural leadership*'.[9] Also and above all cultural leadership, since he
was emphasing precisely the role of the 'so-called private organisations, such
as the church, trade unions, schools, and so on' – as Gramsci put it in his famous 7 September 1931 letter to Tania – through which 'the hegemony of a social
group over the entire national society' is exercised. In sum, Bobbio glossed, this
meant not only the party but 'all the other institutions of civil society (understood in the Gramscian sense) that have some connection with the elaboration
and spread of culture'.[10]

1967 also saw an essay by Luciano Gruppi in *Critica marxista*, which – if I
am not mistaken – represented the first text dedicated entirely to the concept
of hegemony. In 1972 Gruppi was also the author of the first book whose title
referred to hegemony, which was, indeed, the central – if not only – topic of
this small volume.[11] At the forefront of Gruppi's 1967 essay was his argument
that 'with the term *hegemony*, Gramsci wanted above all to emphasise the
leadership moment in the *dictatorship of the proletariat*, the capacity to guide
a system of alliances ... For Gramsci, the concept of *hegemony* customarily
included both *leadership* and *dominion* simultaneously'.[12] In substance, we are

---

8   Bobbio 1969, p. 61.
9   Bobbio 1969, pp. 59–60.
10   Bobbio 1969, p. 61.
11   Gruppi 1967, 1972.
12   Gruppi 1967, p. 78n.

thus not very far here from Lenin's teachings, the term being interpreted above all as the working class's capacity to guide a system of alliances. Gruppi also maintained that the concept of hegemony, if not the term itself, was present as early as the *Ordine Nuovo* years – albeit not yet having fully matured – but was obfuscated when Gramsci was subject to the influence of Bordiga.

In the 1972 book, the reference to Lenin was, certainly, no lesser, but there was greater emphasis on the originality of Gramsci's conception. If, on the one hand, 'hegemony' – Gruppi wrote – 'is the capacity to lead, to conquer alliances, the capacity to provide a social base to the proletarian state', still within the terms of the Leninist theory of the dictatorship of the proletariat,[13] on the other hand the author emphasised the development of this term throughout Gramsci's reflection and the oscillations present in the *Notebooks*, while also recognising the aspect of hegemony already mentioned by Bobbio, as something that concerned 'culture, morality, and conceptions of the world'.[14] Gruppi sought, however, to overcome the unilateral character of Bobbio's vision with an opportune reference to the concept of the 'historic bloc', that is, stressing that 'hegemony tends to construct a historic bloc, that is, to realise the unification of different social and political forces held together through the conception of the world that hegemony has outlined and propagated'.[15]

3   The 1970s: Hegemony and Hegemonic Apparatus

It was in the 1970s that reflection on hegemony, as on all of Gramsci's reflection, made a decisive qualitative leap. The concept began to impose itself as central to the theoretical toolbox of the *Notebooks*, as well as being studied even beyond the traditional ambit of political theory. It is telling, for example, that pedagogical reflection – now increasingly looking to our author – underlined, with Angelo Broccoli, that 'every relation of hegemony [is] necessarily a pedagogical relation'.[16]

Returning to the study of political science and philosophy, Nicola Auciello's 1974 contribution on *Socialismo ed egemonia in Gramsci e Togliatti* brought clearly into focus the 'two principal meanings' of 'hegemony' in the *Notebooks*, namely political leadership and intellectual and moral leadership. As distinct

---

13   Gruppi 1972, p. 15.
14   Gruppi 1967, p. 92.
15   Gruppi 1967, p. 99.
16   Broccoli 1971, p. 139.

from Gruppi, the author denied that hegemony meant leadership and dominion both at once. The 'exercise of dominion', as he saw it, was functional 'to the growth of hegemony', and thus the expansion of hegemony turned into the 'gradual reduction of the state-force element' up until the very extinction of the state.[17] This was the specificity of Gramsci's understanding of the concept, which was thus inflected on the terrain of democracy, though Auciello set himself apart from Tamburanno's reading, defined as 'having a democracy-centred pretext'. In polemic with Bobbio, moreover, Auciello also recalled the 'economic-structural foundation of hegemony', since 'the degree to which a social group is able to expand its hegemony is, above all, of an *objective* character – related, that is, to its economic position'.[18]

In 1975, Christine Buci-Glucksmann's book on *Gramsci and the State* appeared in France, and it was translated into Italian the following year. This was the first book to be able to make partial use of the new critical edition of the *Notebooks*. The author captured well the qualitative leap between *On the Southern Question* and the *Notebooks*: in 1926, hegemony was still only a strategy of the proletariat, whereas the first notebook 'reverses the terms: hegemony, specified by the new concept of hegemonic apparatus, involves first and foremost the practices of the dominant class',[19] even if in the first notebook these concepts (hegemony, hegemonic apparatus) were not yet attached to the question of the state (as they would be in the seventh and eighth notebooks). Later, however, the *extension of the concept of the state* took place, in Buci-Glucksmann's view, precisely by way of 'incorporating the hegemonic apparatus into it'.[20]

The concept of hegemony derived from Lenin, whereas 'hegemonic apparatus' was an innovation of Gramsci's, referring to the dominant class and that class only. Buci-Glucksmann, who was Althusserian in training, here distanced herself theoretically from Althusser, that is, from any structural-functionalist perspective, as she argued that 'the concept of hegemony' cannot simply reduced to the Marxist notion of 'dominant ideology',[21] since 'the hegemonic apparatus is intersected by the primacy of class struggle'.[22] Indeed, she maintained that in Gramsci there is 'no theory of hegemony ... without a theory of

---

17   Auciello 1974, pp. 107 and 119.

18   Auciello 1974, p. 120n.

19   Buci-Glucksmann 1980, p. 47.

20   Buci-Glucksmann 1980, p. 49.

21   Buci-Glucksmann 1980, pp. 58–9.

22   Buci-Glucksmann 1980, p. 48.

the crisis of hegemony'.[23] So in the first place she rejected Poulantzas's argument in *Political Power and Social Classes* that reduced the concept of hegemony 'only to the political practices of the dominant classes';[24] secondly, she clarified a class in power is hegemonic insofar as it 'really does carry the whole of society forward: it has a universalist aim, and not an arbitrary one'.[25] On the contrary, for Gramsci, 'the arbitrary moment, recourse to the more direct or more concealed forms of authoritarianism and coercion, mark a "developing crisis of hegemony"'.[26]

A further contribution of Buci-Glucksmann's concerns the genealogy of the concept of 'hegemony': she writes that it was a widely-used or even 'commonplace' term in the Third International, and not only in Lenin and Stalin. Gramsci's concept of hegemony – even if not always using this term – was present from the *Ordine Nuovo* years onward, according to Buci-Glucksmann. It was from 1924 onward, in the years when he was most in touch with the debates in the International and in the Bolshevik leadership, that Gramsci elaborated this concept, on the basis of Lenin's theory of class leadership within an alliance policy. Even if it was only in 1929 that he established this as a concept in its own right, as we have seen already.

4   1975–6: Hegemony and Democracy

The mid-1970s saw the well-known debate in *Mondoperaio* on 'hegemony and democracy', the political-instrumental motivations of which are today rather too apparent.[27] It was, indeed, with an eye to the political situation and the rise of Bettino Craxi's 'new socialist course' that the Italian Socialist Party's official review hammered the Communist Party on the cultural terrain, attacking the supposed continued existence of undemocratic elements in its cultural tradition. The reflections of Massimo Salvadori came in reaction to some of the Communists' 'in-house' elaborations, according to which – as Salvadori put it – 'Gramsci carried out a sort of theoretical "rotation", at the beginning of which he was internal to Leninism and Lenin's perspective and at the end of which he opened the way to the current strategy of the PCI, precisely through his elabor-

---

23   Buci-Glucksmann 1980, p. 58.

24   Poulantzas 2008, p. 88, cited in Buci-Glucksmann 1980, p. 59; see also the interesting considerations in Coutinho 2012.

25   Buci-Glucksmann 1980, pp. 57–8.

26   Buci-Glucksmann 1980, p. 58.

27   See Liguri 2012, pp. 251 et sqq.

ation of the "theory of hegemony".[28] Salvadori arrived at the conclusion that hegemony in Gramsci was, in substance, nothing other than the dictatorship of the proletariat, and that Gramsci was no different to Lenin: 'Gramsci's theory of hegemony is the highest, most complex expression of Leninism'.[29]

The other interventions by exponents of the Socialist milieu were also on this same wavelength. Surprisingly, Bobbio asked himself whether it was legitimate for a reformist party to 'make use' of a revolutionary thinker in order to justify its own reformist politics.[30] The novelty represented by Gramsci with respect to the Leninist tradition – proclaimed by Bobbio himself in 1967 – was abruptly (and instrumentally) set to one side. Lucio Colletti thus concluded, lightly enough, that Gramsci was substantially extraneous to the democratic tradition.[31] It is easy to see – even from these very brief mentions – that the Socialist intellectuals at the forefront of the cultural offensive on hegemony and democracy refused to see the novelty of the *Notebooks'* elaboration. Not in the sense that it was reformist rather than revolutionary, but in that – as concerned the concept of hegemony – it addressed itself to understanding the socio-historical reality before elaborating as strategy for the workers' movement. Hegemony was a category read in relation to the extension of the state, and the morphological novelty that this entailed, *consequently* also transforming the concept of revolution also.[32]

5   1977: The Forms of Hegemony

The best – even if often indirect – responses to the polemical stances of the Socialist intelligentsia came from one of two main 'Gramsci appointments' organised for the fortieth anniversary of his death. The first was in Frattocchie in January 1977, organised by the PCI, with the title 'Egemonia Stato partito in Gramsci'. The second was the conference held in Florence in December of that year,[33] a conference that – dedicated to the theoretical-political categories of the *Notebooks* – gave much more space to the theme of 'passive revolution' than to 'hegemony'. This seems symptomatic of the profound influence that the

---

28   Salvadori 1977, pp. 33–4.
29   Salvadori 1977, p. 49.
30   Bobbio 1977, pp. 55 et sqq.
31   Colletti 1977, p. 63.
32   Mancina 1976.
33   The interventions are collected in Ferri (ed.) 1977–9.

political situation necessarily had on the activity of the Communist 'collective intellectual' in the dramatic year of 1977.

The talk given by Valentino Gerratana at Frattocchie was at the outset of the author's long research on a theme which he described as follows: 'the instruments and institutions of hegemony' are not independent 'of the historical subjects of hegemony ... The historical forms of hegemony ... vary according to the nature of the social forces that are exercising hegemony'.[34] What Gerratana made out in the *Notebooks* was, first and foremost, a general theory of hegemony, understood as a category for historical interpretation, and thus possible to refer to different classes and even 'social and political groups acting within one same class'. (Think of the moderates *versus* the 'Party of Action' in the *Risorgimento*: think of the hegemony exercised by way of *trasformismo*.) Gramsci had not, however, proposed the bourgeois model as 'the model of political strategy also valid for the working class'; where 'the class referent of hegemony changes', Gerratana argued, 'its instruments and institutions – in a word, the apparatus of hegemony itself – must also change'.[35]

If an exploiter class needs 'forms of hegemony that arouse a consent translatable into a mandate, the consent of its subaltern allies', then a class that fights to put an end to all exploitation wants 'a hegemony without subaltern allies, a hegemony that is a permanent education in self-government'. This would require, Gerratana argued, institutes and instruments 'of a profoundly innovative character'.[36]

In Frattocchie, Biagio de Giovanni also put forward some specifications on the concept of hegemony, which were also addressed to the current political situation. Ever since Gramsci's time there had been a situation of spreading hegemony, coinciding with the expansion of the state. Now, however, unlike in the past, it is 'through pluralism that the struggle between hegemonies can move forward':[37] that is, there is nothing preventing the clash for hegemony taking place on the terrain of political democracy, and, indeed, this terrain should be sought after, remembering, *inter alia*, that the subject of hegemony is above all a class and not a party.

---

34   Gerratana 1977, p. 40.

35   Gerratana 1977, pp. 43–5.

36   Gerratana 1977, pp. 50–1. Gerratana 1997 does link Gramsci with Lenin, but adds that while for the latter this concept lost its relevance 'in the new perspectives of socialism' after the Russian Revolution, the opposite view matured in Gramsci's thinking. This was also central to his famous 1926 letter.

37   De Giovanni 1977, pp. 57, 72.

6   Hegemony and 'Prestige'

In 1977 the *New Left Review* published a far-reaching essay by Perry Anderson, translated into Italian the following year for Laterza. Anderson negatively stressed what he saw as the gradual semantic slippages in the term, as he worked through the supposed 'antinomies' in the *Notebooks*. Hegemony was a term that 'originated in Russia to define the relationship between the proletariat and peasantry in a bourgeois revolution' and 'was transferred by Gramsci to describe the relationship between the bourgeoisie and proletariat in a consolidated capitalist order in Western Europe'.[38] The two meanings both gave an important place to the search for consensus. But – Anderson's critique argued – coercion is fundamental to the relation between antagonistic classes: and Gramsci seemed to undervalue it, or better, his theory led to this fact being underestimated. In reality, it is impossible – Anderson maintained – to conquer hegemony before conquering power and the state.

A few years later, Gianni Francioni responded to Anderson's essay, showing that it was now impossible to take forward readings of the *Notebooks* that did not take due account of their 'internal history'. Studying the dating of the various notes and bringing attention to the distinction between A and C texts, Francioni showed that Anderson's thesis as to the 'supposed *three-stage metamorphosis* in Gramsci's conception of hegemony' was in fact mistaken. For Francioni, this was simply demonstrated: 'if we look up the first appearance of each of the formulations on which Anderson bases his thesis of "three moments" of hegemony in Gramsci, thus not stopping short at the second drafts of these texts (which is all that Anderson cites) but rather retracing their path and dating their first outlines in the *Notebooks*', then the logical-chronological hypothesis of the English historian collapses: 'what Anderson sees as the destination of Gramsci's "extension of the concept" instead marks one of its starting points'.[39] Not having taken account of the diachronic structure of the *Notebooks* had prevented the English historian from grasping the manner in which Gramsci's reasoning played out and in which his elaboration advanced, thus bringing him to the mistaken conviction that there was a fundamental theoretical contradiction at the very heart of Gramsci's prison elaborations.

Returning to the late 1970s, we still have to mention a contribution from the Catholic camp, which also believed that it had grasped a basic contradiction

---

38   Anderson 1976.
39   Francioni 1984, p. 161.

in Gramsci. Carmelo Vigna[40] asserted the supremacy of cultural hegemony over political hegemony in the *Notebooks*, the supremacy of 'truth' over force, even though Gramsci had remained caught up in the contradiction deriving from the fact that his political baggage had impeded him from going beyond politics and fully overcoming Lenin and Machiavelli, and thus recognising that a discourse of 'truth' must necessarily be meta-political. This, according to the author, decisively led to Gramsci keeping silent on Christianity and its values.

1979 also saw Franco Lo Piparo's book *Lingua intellettuali egemonia in Gramsci*, which was destined to have a wide echo on account of the novelty of its interpretative thesis, which located the origin of Gramsci's concept of hegemony in his youthful interest in glottology and the fundamental category of 'prestige', which he had begun to use in the political field (with the meaning of 'ethical-cultural leadership')[41] from 1918 onwards. In order to operate such a genealogical hypothesis, Lo Piparo firstly interpreted the category of hegemony only in terms of 'consent' (as opposed to 'force' and 'coercion'), and secondly relativised the influence of the Soviet tradition (as principally reconstructed by Buci-Glucksmann and Anderson). He did not deny that the Comintern debate had influenced Gramsci's eventual choice of this term in the *Notebooks*.[42] But he held that 'hegemony' was used up until 1924 simply to mean 'supremacy' and 'dominance', whereas the concept and problematic that the mature Gramsci indicated with this term had instead appeared in the term 'prestige'. As such, according to Lo Piparo the concept of hegemony should be seen as 'an elaboration and enrichment of the linguistic concept of prestige'.[43]

Indeed – it should be remembered – even in the *Notebooks* we can read that 'consent is born of prestige "historically" … deriving from the ruling group's position and function in the world of production'.[44] The two terms seem to indicate two concepts that although not identical, are closely related. Moreover, Lo Piparo stretches himself to assert that both 'hegemony' and 'prestige' come from and belong to[45] a *liberal* view of the world, which not only appears in the young *Gramsci* but is also clearly present in the mature Gramsci, a view exemplified in the liberal Ascoli's opposition to the protectionist Manzoni and

40   Vigna 1979, pp. 11 et sqq.
41   Lo Piparo 1979, p. 137.
42   Lo Piparo 1979, p. 105.
43   Lo Piparo 1979, p. 145.
44   Q12, §1: Gramsci 1974, p. 1519.
45   Lo Piparo 1979, p. 147n.

his demand for 'state language support and protection'. But, we must ask, is this enough to believe that the same went for the mature Gramsci, also on the socio-historical plane? And would there have been the 'mature Gramsci' that we know, if it had not been for the decisive 1923–4 period, the discovery of a Leninist self-critique and the founding of the West-East distinction, which was first geopolitical and then categorial and morphological?

7   The 1980s: A Non-modern Gramsci?

The 1980s saw a decline in the number and quality of contributions to this debate, both in regard to interpreting Gramsci and as concerned the concept of hegemony.[46] But here I do want to mention Nicola Badaloni, who in 1987 again insisted on the relation between hegemony and the concept of the historic bloc:

> What should be recognised as the central theme of A. Gramsci's Marxist thought, it seems to me, is the fact that he was not ready to attribute the hegemonic function in advance and for every determinate situation to either the movements embedded in the base or those promoted in the superstructure by what he called the 'historic bloc'. After all, in different conditions and contexts either the one or the other could represent its principal productive objectification.[47]

The 'theoretical-practical principle of hegemony' was understood, therefore, 'as a synthesis of economic development and critical awareness', within a perspective in which 'the economy is no longer a "reified" object, but depending on human choices, it becomes, in various ways and despite many impediments, a conscious activity'.[48] He grasped the theory of hegemony thus outlined as something extremely polyvalent; it was not pre-defined, but rather open to the most varied inflections, even on the terrain of individual subjectivity. Badaloni wrote:

> hegemony means, ... for Gramsci, a historical opening, also at the individual level, to a multiplicity of practices of life, willed or undergone by

---

46   *Hegemony and Socialist Strategy* (Laclau and Mouffe 1985) had almost no echo in Italy, and was translated only in 2011, after the success of Laclau's works on populism.

47   Badaloni 1987, p. 29.

48   Badaloni 1987, p. 31.

various social groups. These can be conscious or unconscious, but are never determined *a priori* in such a manner as to definitively establish one of them as dominant. Gramsci wrote this splendid passage on the terrain of individual life choices: 'The critical comprehension of the self operates … by way of a struggle between political "hegemonies" with conflicting bearings, first in the field of ethics, then the field of politics, thus arriving at a superior elaboration of one's own conception of the real'.[49]

Another interesting contribution is that of Gian Enrico Rusconi, written in 1987 and published in 1990. This work was symptomatic of the particular climate of the 1980s, often critical towards the *Notebooks*' legacy following the assertion of other paradigms, what we could call *other hegemonies*. Rusconi maintains that there are two theories of hegemony in Gramsci. One – neither current nor modern – was above all the will to assert a 'vision of the world'.[50] The other, conversely, was identified in 'a communicative process founded on the search for consent by way of persuasion … hegemony understood as communication', the author wrote, 'harked back to a consensual theory of truth, with political action founded on a communicative theory of action'.[51] Here, we arrive at Habermas, and thus the affirmation – to use Rusconi's words – of an 'adult pluralist society' in which Gramsci and what Rusconi called his 'mature concept of hegemony' could only survive if it was heavily amputated.

8   The 1990s: Hegemony and Interdependence

After the events of 1989 the panorama of Gramsci studies changed partly: with a reawakening of interest, above all, in the concept of hegemony. This was the result of the combination of various factors, though each was itself fully independent (the need to rethink the theory and strategy of the Left; the author's advance into new geographical and disciplinary areas; reflection on globalisation and the destiny of the nation-state). A first rereading marked by its originality and extensive relevance was that carried out by Giuseppe Vacca, according to whom 'the concept of hegemony contains … at least *in nuce*, a new conception of politics'.[52] For this author, the horizon of Gramsci's thought

---

49   Badaloni 1987, p. 45. On this application of the theory of hegemony to understanding the invidiual, see Ragazzini 2002.

50   Rusconi 1990, p. 224.

51   Ibid.

52   Vacca 1991, p. 5.

was the crisis of the nation-state and the international scenario. It was thus that politics-hegemony could be developed by a class and a doctrine that conceived the state as tendentially liable to decline. Meaning, an 'economically and politically international' class: 'a subject that develops its faculties entirely within a horizon that transcends the traditionally-established functions of national states',[53] Vacca wrote. As such, 'the decisive terrain for the consolidation of politics-hegemony' was, for Vacca, linked to a 'supranational and global horizon';[54] moreover, 'the foundation of the theory of hegemony must necessarily be a principle of integrating political action within a vision of the human race based on unity and solidarity: *the principle of interdependence*'.[55]

This was undoubtedly an innovative reading, one that raised no few questions. To me, it seems that the economically unified world to which Gramsci alludes is, in fact, a post-revolutionary one; and to transport this vision into a *non-revolutionary* epoch can itself be misleading – in terms of understanding Gramsci – because it risks expunging class struggle from the theoretical-political panorama. As such, to suggest this idea again in the epoch of globalisation seems liable to lead to even greater misunderstandings. Vacca writes: 'the "philosophy of praxis" posed itself the task of uniting the human race in solidarity'.[56] But it must be asked: did there exist, for Gramsci, a nebulous, undifferentiated human race, one that was not organised, for example, into exploiters and exploited? And what does 'unite in solidarity' mean? If the author's thesis is meant to be understood as an assertion of the need to struggle against the obstacles to such a unification, then his reading is a legitimate one. But to me it still seems rather incongruous to use the term 'interdependence', which evokes a more 'pacified' world than exists in reality. Also because in another essay from this same period, Vacca wrote

> The idea that 'the doctrine of hegemony' must constitute a 'complement to the theory of the state-force' ... postulates *a permanent subordination of politics-power to politics-hegemony*. Its project cannot be pursued without superseding the nation-state and integrating it into supranational regroupments co-ordinated amongst themselves.[57]

---

53   Vacca 1991, p. 21.
54   Vacca 1991, p. 36.
55   Vacca 1991, p. 86.
56   Vacca 1991, p. 108.
57   Vacca 1999a, p. 240.

However, in my understanding Gramsci maintained that the pole of hegemony *completes* the state-force, rather than substituting for it. Even so, it can also be said that there are phases in which force is 'subordinated to hegemony', predictably enough. But that this might become 'permanent' is *only* a prediction (albeit one that we could share in). Meanwhile, the overcoming of the nation-state in 'supranational regroupments co-ordinated amongst themselves' seems further still from the extinction of the state and the affirmation of a regulated society as foreseen by Gramsci – if it is not something else entirely. Vacca does add, however, that 'the nation-state will probably still be the decisive site of political struggle for a very long time. The principal terrain for shifts in the relations of forces is, therefore, a national one'.[58]

9   Hegemony and Globalisation

Again in 1997, upon the sixtieth anniversary of Gramsci's death, there were no few references to the theme of hegemony. At the Cagliari conference,[59] for example, this theme was debated from a standpoint that was rather uncommon in Italy – but widespread in the Anglo-Saxon world – using the concept of hegemony for the study of international relations. This was also thanks to the presence of the two scholars Stephen Gill and Robert Cox at Cagliari (the latter also spoke of 'global hegemony', that is, hegemony in the epoch of globalisation). However, it was Mario Telò who best and most richly framed the question, insisting on the centrality of the nation-state in Gramsci also as concerned the international scenario. Gramsci remained 'anchored to the idea that the principal international actor is the hegemon-state, and not an internationalised or transnationalised economic-political system'. And, he added, 'hegemony is not only an attribute of the hegemon-state, but arises from the complex of social, ideological and political relations internal to the hegemon nation-state'.[60] It is interesting to note, in Telò's argumentation, the critique that he turns against the aforementioned Anglo-American writers on account of their assigning little importance to the *institutional* dimension of the struggle for hegemony, which is undoubtedly present in Gramsci. As such, he grasps a particular limit of many English-language interpreters engaging with Gramsci, and not only those occupied with international relations.

---

58   Vacca 1999a, pp. 245–6.

59   On the 1997 Cagliari debate, see above, pp. 36 ff.

60   Telò 1999, pp. 62–3.

In 1997, other authors directed their attention to hegemonic relations as concerned the processes of the crisis of the nation-state, arriving at somewhat different conclusions. Pasquale Voza, for example, wrote:

> 'There is no state without hegemony', Gramsci said ... And yet now, we must say, there is a capitalist hegemony *without a state*, that is, without the active social and cultural mediation of the nation-state. The *fortresses* of this capitalist hegemony cannot be reduced within the traditional limits of the 'ideological state apparatuses', but rather are articulated and intersect in a weft of powers and knowledges at the supranational level, which combine to develop the public spirit and the new processes of social regulation.[61]

10   The Word 'Hegemony'

I want to mention briefly two further studies. In his book *Gramsci storico* – which proposes to interpret the *Notebooks* in their entirety – Alberto Burgio emphasises two considerations that concern the concept of hegemony. Firstly, hegemony is always also economic: 'Gramsci repeatedly maintained that the ideological hegemony of the dominant subject' – Burgio writes – 'is rooted in its economic hegemony, of which "intellectual and moral" leadership is a function'. It is 'the materialist – structural – foundation of the hegemonic relation'.[62] The 'hegemonic function' thus has 'two sides', the 'economic' and the 'ethical-political'. And the hegemonic or organic crisis, likewise, can be either structural or superstructural.[63] These were not new concepts, but were worth reaffirming at a moment when new 'culturalist' readings of Gramsci and his categories were becoming widespread. However, I believe that the second of Burgio's insights is truly original: the 'hegemonic relation', even if 'dictated by partial interests', constitutes an increase in the critical capacities of the subalterns, 'through the very fact that it transmits consciousness':

> Education implies an increase, however instrumentally, in the cultural level ... the 'expansion' of the dominant subject – while it sanctions an

---

61   Voza 1999, pp. 105–6.
62   Burgio 2002, p. 100.
63   Burgio 2002, pp. 156 et sqq.

increase in its power and capacities for control – lays the bases of a more intense conflictual element in society.[64]

The hegemonic relation is thus *ambivalent* – Burgio explains – because 'the increased leadership capacity of the dominant subject entails (or rather, coincides with) the constitution of now autonomous subjectivities, which are potentially conflictual'. The author adds that with the twentieth century, 'with the dynamic function performed in the background of bourgeois "expansion" now set aside, the hegemonic relation now consists in the exchange between favourable (or less discriminatory) conditions and readiness to acquiesce to the conservative resistance (or despotic offensive) of the dominant subject'. Fordism and Fascism were, in this sense, two sides of the same coin: it was not necessary in all cases – even in the 'contemporary dictatorships' of which Gramsci spoke from within a Fascist jail – to take recourse to pure force and coercion.[65]

Finally, a note on Giuseppe Cospito's essay in the collective work *Le parole di Gramsci*. All that I will mention from this work here is a peculiar methodological trait, namely its attempt to give 'voice' back to Gramsci, after so many decades of interpretative contributions, which have at times seemed to have sat on the text to the point of encrusting its surface and making it unrecognisable. This hermeneutic exercise was both necessary and arduous, on account of the particular difficulty of Gramsci's text – Cospito recalling that

> even as regards the word 'hegemony', Gramsci ... adopted a term from commonplace language and attributed it – sometimes even in the course of one same note – not only sometimes very varied meanings, but also ones that stood rather far both from its everyday usage and the meanings crystallised in various traditions of philosophical and political thought.[66]

It was also this lexical originality that made Gramsci one of the most difficult – as well as among the most fascinating – authors of the twentieth century. It is also for this reason that it has been possible and necessary that people would exercise themselves so much in their efforts to interpret Gramsci's text. And we can be certain that this history is not yet over.

---

64   Burgio 2002, p. 103.
65   Burgio 2002, p. 189.
66   Cospito 2004, p. 74.

CHAPTER 13

Dewey, Gramsci and Cornel West

1   Marxism and Pragmatism

Cornel West is one of the most visible intellectuals in the United States. He has taught philosophy and theology at Princeton and Harvard. Engaged in public life and an interlocutor of politicians such as Jesse Jackson and celebrated intellectuals like Richard Rorty, as well as being close to the Black Church, he has pointed to his Christian inspiration – as well as pragmatism and his own reading of Gramsci – as the source of his theoretical elaboration. Indeed, he has defined his conception as 'prophetic pragmatism'. And it is not by accident that in his 'genealogy of pragmatism', a long opening chapter is devoted to Ralph Waldo Emerson, the greatest religious thinker in the United States: while West does not share in his transcendentalism, he, too, considers religion an ethical resource and spur to action. West also defines himself as a 'neo-Gramscian pragmatist'. I would like to try to explain the meaning and the significance of this definition.

The history of relations between Marxism and pragmatism is rather variegated. For a long time, there prevailed an attitude of mutual repulsion, at times intersected with more directly political experiences, above all during the Cold War years when 'American philosophy', in particular Dewey, were bitterly fought – to use Lukács's words – as part of the 'dominant imperialist philosophy' of the postwar period. For the Hungarian philosopher, pragmatism had been 'an ideology of capitalist agents consciously anchored in capitalist immediacy', of the supporters of the 'American form of life'; on the philosophical plane, it was accused of rejecting 'the objective study of reality independent of consciousness', instead studying only the practical use of single actions in an environment taken to be essentially immutable.[1] This picked up on a judgement of Lenin's in *Materialism and Empirio-Criticism* – a work marked by the thesis of the 'objectivity of the world' and cognitive activity as purely 'reflecting' this – in which Lenin said (speaking of James) that '[f]rom the standpoint of materialism the difference between Machism and pragmatism is ... insignificant and unimportant'.[2]

---

1   Lukács 1981, p. 779.
2   Lenin 1972, p. 416.

While Lenin and Lukács identified the rejection of subject-object dualism as one of the distinctive themes of the pragmatist tradition, in Italy this very element favoured a certain positive reception of pragmatism, within the ambit of neo-idealist culture. Croce again attempted the same operation of assimilation-neutralisation with regard to the pragmatists, Dewey in particular, that he had attempted with regard to Gramsci upon the first appearance of the *Lettere dal carcere*:

> It is to these philosophers' credit that they have stated that consciousness is not a 'copy' of reality but its 'invention', if I also recall that when I was very young I heard my Neapolitan teachers instilling the idea that consciousness is not 'Ab-bild', that is, a copy of reality, but its creation: and I persuaded myself of this when I reached such an age as to be able to understand it properly.[3]

Giulio Preti expressed another take, already in 1946 maintaining that Marxism and pragmatism were 'meeting on this terrain: that the basis and the essence of man and all spiritual life is practical-sensory activity, in virtue of which man ... is influenced by his external environment, but in turn influences it through his *labour*'.[4] For Preti, Dewey was the thinker who 'though not a Marxist ... most resembles Marx, sharing – *in his concrete cultural analyses if not wholly in terms of theory* – his historical materialism'.[5] Ten years later, in *Praxis ed empirismo*, Preti resumed his comparison of Dewey and Marx; pragmatism and Marxism are both philosophies of praxis. Preti here used 'Marxism' to mean the philosophy of the 'young Marx'. And 'pragmatism', explicitly, to mean 'the pragmatism of J. Dewey'.[6] Preti maintains that both of them are philosophies of praxis, if by this we mean 'an active, effective and voluntaristic orientation toward the world, intending not to *interpret* the world, but rather to *change* it'.[7] Interpretation is here understood already to mean change, and change to be the only valid interpretation. In which knowledge of 'truth' requires an active disposition toward the real, the result of operations carried out 'in and on the real'.

---

3 Croce 1951, p. 21.
4 Preti 1946, p. 59.
5 Preti 1946, p. 60.
6 Preti 1975, p. 12.
7 Ibid.

2   The American Pragmatism of the Prison Notebooks

Gramsci occupies a strategically-important role in the possible encounter between Marxism and pragmatism, as proposed by Cornel West. However, in the
Notebooks the name John Dewey is mentioned only once, indirectly, in a cita-
tion of a passage by Vittorio Macchierò in Q4, §76. Gramsci does, however, show
some knowledge of William James, who appears right from the first notebook,
§34 of which is entitled 'American pragmatism'.

> Could one say about American pragmatism (James) what Engels said
> about English agnosticism? (I think in the preface to the English edition
> of *Socialism: Utopian and Scientific*).[8]

Gramsci began this first notebook on 8 February 1929. In a letter to Tania
Schucht of 25 March of that same year, (indirectly) responding to an acquaint-
ance's request for book recommendations, Gramsci wrote that 'the best Psychology manual is that by William James'.[9] Here, he was referring to the *Principles of
Psychology*, first published in Italian in 1905 by Milan's Società Editrice Libraria.
In this first notebook, we find two other brief mentions of pragmatism. Firstly in
§78, entitled 'Bergson, positivist materialism, pragmatism', which reproduces
extracts from an article by Balbino Giuliano on Bergson, who was criticised for
asserting the 'practical origin of every conceptual system';[10] and secondly in
§105, entitled 'American philosophy' where Gramsci asks himself, in regard to a
book by Josiah Royce, 'Can modern thought [Marxism] go beyond empiricism-
pragmatism and become widespread in America without a Hegelian phase?'.[11]
In later notebooks, Gramsci repeatedly cites the Italian pragmatists (Calderoni and even more so Vailati), above all in reference to the theme of language,
common sense and metaphors.[12] Moreover, the books Gramsci had in prison
included Mario Calderoni and Giovanni Vailati's volume *Il pragmatismo*, edited

8   Gramsci 1975, p. 26; 1992, p. 120. Gramsci seems to be referring – the Gerratana edition's
        critical apparatus suggests – to Engels's definition of agnosticism as a 'shamefaced' mater-
        ialism.

9   Gramsci 1996a, p. 249. For a broader picture of the *Notebooks*' author's relations with (US
        and Italian) pragmatism, see Meta 2010.

10   Gramsci 1975, p. 86; 1992, p. 183.

11   Gramsci 1975, p. 97; 1992, p. 194.

12   See Q4, §18 (an A text, redrafted in Q11, §44); Q4, §42 (an A text, redrafted in Q11, §48), Q7,
        §36 (an A text, redrafted in Q11, §24); and the B text Q10, §44.

by Giovanni Papini.[13] It was only in the seventeenth notebook (1933–5) that Gramsci returned to American pragmatism, in a B text entitled 'Introduction to the study of philosophy. Pragmatism and politics'. If every philosopher is a politician, Gramsci argues, then this is all the more true of the pragmatist 'who constructs philosophy in a way which is in an immediate sense "utilitarian"'. Pragmatism 'tends to create a "secular morality"', a 'popular philosophy' and an '[immediate] "ideological party" rather than a system of philosophy'.[14] Gramsci referred to James's *Varieties of Religious Experience*, which appeared in Italy in 1904,[15] with regard to the method of judging theories according to the different practical consequences they would have if they were realised. The traditional philosopher, Gramsci continued, was only a politician in a mediated sense: for he 'has a higher aim, sets his sights higher and tends (if he tends in any direction) to raise the existing cultural level', while the pragmatist 'judges from immediate reality, often at the most vulgar level'.[16] Thus, Gramsci insisted, 'Hegel can be considered as the theoretical precursor of the liberal revolutions of the nineteenth century. The pragmatists, at the most, have contributed to the creation of the Rotary Club movement'.[17]

Thus pragmatism did appear in some measure in the *Notebooks*, including American pragmatism. Gramsci's evaluation of pragmatism was not a positive one, though, in my view, it was not entirely negative. After all, themes like 'secular morality', 'popular philosophy' and philosophy-as-politics, which Gramsci aptly attributed to pragmatism, were not in reality so distant from some of the fundamental points elaborated by Gramsci in the *Notebooks*.

3   Gramsci and Dewey

It remains true that Gramsci seems almost entirely ignorant of Dewey. But if a link can be found for an encounter between pragmatism and Marxism, this is possible precisely through a connection between Gramsci and Dewey or, at least, among some of the moments of their respective intellectual paths. I do not wish to go so far as to assert – as has been done – that 'the convergences between Dewey's thought and Gramsci's are far from accidental' or even that

---

13   See Gramsci 1975, p. 3123, on works that he had in prison but did not cite.

14   Q17, § 22: Gramsci 1975, p. 1925.

15   Gramsci refers to James's work but does not cite this text directly, suggesting an indirect source.

16   Q17, § 22: Gramsci 1975, p. 1925.

17   Ibid.

there is a clear 'parallel ... and a substantial, non-episodic crossover among the most significant "categories" of each of their "philosophies"':[18] Eugenio Garin has warned of the risks of 'forcing' certain cultural 'encounters', himself referring to Croce's reception of pragmatism.[19] We must not forget that on many levels these two authors were very far apart: Gramsci did not ascribe scientific method a preponderant role in the process of democratising society, as did Dewey, and nor could he have accepted Dewey's thesis according to which the idea of classes is only 'a survival of a rigid logic that once prevailed in the sciences of nature, but that no longer has any place there'.[20] This notwithstanding, Gramsci and Dewey were united by both being educated as young men in philosophical environments which, although different, were similarly influenced by the revival of Hegelianism, and thus a conception of the subject-object relationship which rejected the theory that the one 'mirrored' the other, as well as the cognisability of 'external objectivity understood in ... a mechanical way'.[21] Much of Gramsci's polemic against the positions expressed by Bukharin at the Second International Congress of the History of Science and Technology, which took place in London in 1931,[22] was of this bent. But above all it is here worth remembering the passage from the *Notebooks* in which Gramsci polemicises with Bertrand Russell, who had maintained that it was possible to imagine

> even without man ... two points on the surface of the earth, one of which is farther north and the other farther south. But in the absence of man, what would be the meaning of north and south, and 'point' and 'surface' and 'earth'? ... In the absence of human activity, which creates all values, including scientific values, what would 'objectivity' be? ... For historical materialism thought cannot be separated from being, man from nature, activity (history) from matter, subject from object.[23]

It does not seem any chance thing that Russell was a severe critic of Dewey's, denouncing 'Dr. Dewey's world' in which 'it seems to me ... human beings occupy the imagination'.[24] To have common theoretical adversaries does not, of course, mean to share theoretical positions that coincide. Nonetheless, even if

---

18   De Cumis 1978, pp. 306–7.
19   See Garin 1975, p. 517n.
20   Dewey 1988, p. 56.
21   Gramsci 1975, p. 1415; 1971, p. 446.
22   See the volume *Science at the Crossroads*, with the papers of the London congress.
23   Q4, § 41: Gramsci 1975, p. 467; Gramsci 1996b, p. 190.
24   Russell 1967, p. 827. See his whole chapter on Dewey.

the 'coincidences' of Dewey and Gramsci's positions were perhaps 'accidental', they undoubtedly seem to exist, on this terrain.

4   Dewey and Marxism

Turning to West and his attempt to conjugate Gramsci's legacy with pragmatism, or, more exactly, with the legacy of Dewey, who in his view represented the peak of the American pragmatist tradition, it is worth noting how West, perhaps bearing in mind the Marxist judgements of Dewey modelled on Lukács's characterisation of him as the 'philosopher of imperialism', forcefully affirms Dewey's position among the ranks of the democratic left. As he writes in *The American Evasion of Philosophy*, 'the implausible notion that Dewey slid into institutional conservatism holds only if one wrongly views his brand of anti-Stalinism in the forties as conservatism, for his critique of American society remained relentless to the end'.[25] Moreover, for West 'it is misleading to characterize Dewey as a liberal in the tradition of Jeremy Bentham and John Stuart Mill':[26] he was, certainly, influenced by this tradition, but all things considered he rather decisively established his distance from it. According to West's reconstruction, Dewey upheld a vision of the world that 'includes socialist and Jeffersonian dimensions yet is ultimately guided by Emersonian cultural sensibilities'.[27] Dewey's project of a 'creative democracy', West underlines, differed from that which he calls Roosevelt's 'liberal program'. Dewey, indeed, opposed Roosevelt's reformist efforts, which left too much power in the hands of narrow financial-capitalist elites. He sought to create a third party, and moreover supported the Socialist Party candidate Norman Thomas in the presidential elections of 1932, 1936 and 1940.[28]

As regards the theoretical plane, West emphasised Dewey's lack of knowledge of Marx, basing this assertion both on Max Eastman's account and the statements of Dewey himself.[29] Dewey remained 'a stranger'.[30] Despite not seriously studying Marx, he stuck by his deep prejudices, indeed being an 'extreme

---

25   West 1989, p. 221.

26   West 1989, p. 102.

27   West 1989, p. 103.

28   West 1989, p. 107.

29   West 1989, p. 102. In fact, it seems to me that we can deduce that Dewey did have some real knowledge of Marx, given that, as we shall see later on, he was able to distinguish between Marx's dialectic and the Marxist (determinist-economistic) dialectic.

30   West 1989, p. 107.

critic' of Marxism.[31] West advances a series of hypotheses to explain this missed encounter, retracing a number of elements of Dewey's biography. Here, I want to limit myself to the more strictly theoretical plane alone. In his 1939 text *Freedom and Culture*, Dewey asked: 'Is there any one factor or phase of culture which is dominant, or which tends to produce and regulate others, or are economics, morals, art, science and so on only so many aspects of the interaction of a number of factors, each of which acts upon and is acted upon by the others?'[32]

For the pragmatist Dewey, the answer was obvious. He rejected any monocausal explanation of reality, asserting that 'probability and pluralism are the characteristics of the present state of Science',[33] as against the *'necessity* and search for a *single* all-comprehensive law', which he attributed not only to Marxism but also the whole 'intellectual atmosphere of the forties of the [nineteenth] century'.[34] What West draws most from this position of Dewey's is the theme of pluralism, contiguous to that of *difference*, which has profoundly interested the African-American author in his search for a theoretical framework allowing him to tackle the racial conflict without *reducing it* to *something else*. From this point of view, Dewey's concept of pluralism also allows West to avoid the dreaded spectre of 'cognitive nihilism' hanging over discussion of difference, all the better to thematise and scrutinise it. Dewey conceived of Marxism as a rigidly monocausal theory. To use the language typical of pragmatism, Marxism was thus a case of a *monist* theory: 'the isolation of any one factor, no matter how strong its workings at a given time, is fatal to understanding and to intelligent action'.[35] According to West, Dewey does not think that all factors (the economic, social, political, cultural, and so on) can have the same weight or that there are not *dominant* factors. He thinks, rather, that this *dominant* weight and role cannot be determined *a priori*, but only after 'empirical study'. Obviously, West makes clear, this search is itself necessarily based on a theory, but it must be kept open to review. It is interesting to note a factor that West himself underemphasises: according to Dewey, in Marx's 'original formulation' there was 'an important qualification' which later Marxists 'tended to ignore'.[36] That is, Marx admitted that once 'political relations, science etc.', or superstructure, are 'produced, they operate as causes of subsequent events,

---

31   Ibid.
32   Dewey 1988, p. 74.
33   Dewey 1988, p. 123.
34   Ibid.
35   Dewey 1988, p. 79.
36   Dewey 1988, p. 118.

and in this capacity are capable of modifying in some degree the operation of the forces which originally produced them'.[37] Marx's dialectic is not, therefore, as rigidly *monocausal* as that of Marx*ism*. If we held onto this original framework, according to Dewey, the methodological consequence would be of great significance, since 'observation of existing conditions [could tell us] just what consequences at a given time are produced by secondary effects which have now themselves acquired the standing of causes'. This being so, '[t]he only way to decide [which factors are of greatest significance] would be to investigate ... to abandon the all-comprehensive character of economic determination. It would put us in the relativistic and pluralistic position of considering a number of interacting factors – of which a very important one is undoubtedly the economic'.[38] Unlike Marxism (the crudely determinist version that Dewey knew), Marx, at least, did not seem to be so far away from Dewey's own method. And certainly Gramsci's Marxism does not seem to be at a great distance from this latter.

5   West's Gramsci

West's 'reply' to Dewey's considerations on Marxism is explicit enough: Dewey did not know Gramsci, because if he had done then he could not have had such a negative vision of Marxism. Gramsci's conception – West writes – 'focuses on a notion of historical specificity and a conception of hegemony which preclude any deterministic, economistic, or reductionist readings of social phenomena'.[39] Gramsci does not adopt a one-dimensional theory of power. This is the reason why the pragmatist Cornel West proclaims himself a neo-Gramscian: the Sardinian thinker, unlike *monocausal* Marxism that aprioristically hinges on the centrality of class conflict, helps him to read the specific conflicts of the society in which he lives, in the first place the racial struggle. This is evinced with particular clarity also in another essay of West's in which the author's 'neo-Gramscianism' is placed in tension not with pragmatism but with the post-structuralism drawing on Derrida and Foucault. West openly declares that he is inspired by the theory of difference propounded by the school of thought that took its cue from these authors, but inserts it within a 'neo-Gramscian framework' with the aim of seeking to avoid the 'reductionist elements' present

---

37   Ibid.

38   Ibid.

39   West 1989, p. 218.

in Foucault and the *'idealist* tendencies' present in Derrida. West's interest in these authors, however, comes from their effort to 'dismantle the logocentric and a priori aspects of the Marxist tradition'.[40] West clarifies:

> The neo-Gramscian rejection of the base/superstructure metaphors of economism (or logocentric Marxism) entails that it is no longer suffi-cient or desirable to privilege the mode of production and class subjects in an *a priori* manner and make causal claims (whether crude or refined) about racist ideology owing to simply material factors. Instead, follow-ing Antonio Gramsci, the metaphor of a 'historic bloc' replaces those of base/superstructure.[41]

West does not spare even Gramsci certain accusations of 'logocentrism'. That is, he does not accept the centrality of class conflict, which does remain present in Gramsci. However, he does understand that Gramsci's approach allows for the recognition of different subjectivities and conflicts. West forces the concept of the historic bloc to the point of totally unravelling the base/superstructure metaphor and renouncing the centrality of class conflict. He uses Gramsci to provide a corrective to post-structuralism, preventing it from slipping into a true and proper 'cognitive nihilism', which would mean to give up on 'explain-ing and transforming history and society'.[42] It is this reasoning that leads West to affirm that

> Culture is as much a structure as the economy or politics; it is rooted in institutions such as families, schools, churches, synagogues, mosques, and communication industries (television, radio, video, music). Similarly, the economy and politics are not only influenced by values but also promote particular cultural ideals of the good life and good society.[43]

Here returns Dewey's thinking on the interconnection between economics, morality, culture, and so on. But the Gramscian aroma of this passage takes its cue from the *Notebooks'* analysis of hegemonic apparatuses and the 'trenches and earthworks' in which the struggle for hegemony is articulated. West does not only study Gramsci; he uses him in his political-cultural analysis, seeking to empower an emancipatory praxis. To use a well-known Gramscian term, we

---

40   West 1992, p. 17.
41   West 1992, p. 24.
42   Ibid.
43   West 2000, p. 12.

could say that West *translates* the categories and the sense of the *Notebooks'* studies into American, the reality of the modern-day United States. In so doing, he also arrives at statements that are not entirely justifiable, from a philological standpoint. But a discourse can never be *faithfully* translated from one language to another: something is always lost in translation, all the more so if we want to conserve its original theoretical and practical force. And when we are talking about pragmatism and Gramsci, this is a concern of no little significance.

CHAPTER 14

The Modern Prince

It is difficult to exaggerate the importance of Machiavelli's place in Gramsci's *Prison Notebooks* reflection. The Florentine *Segretario* ['secretary'] appeared on many different 'pathways' of Gramsci's reflection: a moment in the history of Italy and Europe, an important figure in the history of intellectuals, an emblem of the renewed evaluation of politics in Marxism, an example of a 'precocious' Jacobinism, a philosopher of immanence and of praxis. It seems that Gramsci projected himself onto Machiavelli, or used him as a mirror;[1] indeed, there were many points of convergence between them (though there was no lack of differences, which we will proceed to discuss). Both wrote after their respective defeats; both contemplated the situation in which they were immersed in light of the international context and with reference to foreign 'models' (in Gramsci's case, Soviet Russia, for Machiavelli, the great nation states of Europe); both sought to *translate* these historical experiences *into Italian*, obviously with all the adaptations and alterations that a good *translation* must entail.

1   Against Stenterello

Gramsci's engagement with Machiavelli had a long past. In a letter from Turi prison to his sister-in-law Tatiana on 23 February 1931, Gramsci himself recalled that his interest in Machiavelli went back to his university education in Turin. It was probably a lecturer in Italian literature, Umberto Cosmo, that gave the young Sardinian his interest in the author of *The Prince*, or at least reinforced it. Cosmo had a significant influence on the Sardinian student, among other things encouraging him to study Dante and De Sanctis and introducing him to 'lifetime friend' Piero Sraffa. Gramsci wrote:

> When I saw Cosmo for the last time in May 1922 (he was at that time a
> secretary or adviser at the Italian Embassy in Berlin) he still insisted that
> I should write a study of Machiavelli and Machiavellianism; it was fixed

---

1 'It is not hard to see the extent to which Gramsci's Machiavelli borrowed from Gramsci himself': Garin 1997, p. 59.

in his mind, from 1917 onward, that I ought to write a study of Machiavelli, and he reminded me of this on each meeting.[2]

Despite this account – which suggests that he had a specific, deep interest in studying Machiavelli (and Machiavellianism) going back to at least 1917 – we do not find Gramsci making many references to the Florentine secretary in the years preceding his arrest and imprisonment. As a militant journalist in the 1910s – also drawing on Croce – he did not, of course, repudiate politics as force,[3] and nor did he have any love for reformism and the parliamentary system, especially in the form that it had assumed in Italy, going under the name of 'Giolittism'. However, the young revolutionary took a clear distance from those inspired by a *'raison d'état'* that allegedly harked back to Machiavelli. Gramsci was hostile to the 'varied scheming formulas of our flabby Machiavellianism',[4] and he compared this latter to Jacobinism, which up until 1921 he interpreted as a negative phenomenon wholly internal to bourgeois politics. In the 18 May 1919 *Avanti!* Gramsci wrote that 'Messrs. Statesmen in France and Italy ... are realists, naturally descended from Machiavelli, and they have explicitly put *raison d'état* back on the altar as the sovereign criterion of our international co-existence ... These Machiavellis of capitalist realism are, essentially, Jacobins: they make a fetish of laws and treaties'.[5]

That said, Machiavelli is one thing, 'Machiavellianism' quite another. Already on 21 December 1915, Gramsci had written – in the guise of a 'history lover' polemicising against the rhetoric of the radical Antonio Fradeletto: 'Up until the French Revolution there was no effective, widespread national sentiment in Italy: the expressions of Italianness among literati and historians were just literature and rhetoric of more or less good coin, according to the writer: Machiavelli does not stand for his whole century'.[6] Subsequent years also saw repeated positive references to the Florentine secretary. 'Italy', Gramsci wrote on 2 November 1918, 'is the cradle of the experimental method that Machiavelli applied to the social sciences and Galileo applied to the physical sciences'.[7] And on 7 November of the following year: 'Just as Machiavelli

---

2 Gramsci 1996a, p. 399.

3 Paggi 1984, p. 393. Paggi emphasises how this reading, which concerned also his reading of Machiavelli, entered into crisis with Fascism's coming to power.

4 As he put it in a 22 March 1916 article, in Gramsci 1980, p. 210.

5 Gramsci 1987, p. 28.

6 Gramsci 1980, p. 41.

7 Gramsci 1984, p. 389.

took religion to be nothing but a means for consolidating princely power, so, too, does that Machiavelli to the power of sixty-four called Giolitti take social-ism to be a means for the "ordinary administration" of the state. And the Giolittian state certainly has none of the ideal beauty, none of the attributes proper to Machiavelli's "principality".[8] The opinion that the young Gramsci developed of Machiavelli and his work can also be deduced from his cita-tion, in a 10 March 1917 *Avanti!* article, of a piece of verse by Giuseppe Giusti 'Behind the tomb/Of Machiavello/Lies the skeleton/of Stenterello'. Gramsci adds the comment 'There is a whole horde of Stenterelli surrounding each single Machiavello'.[9] The coupling/counterposition of Machiavelli and Stenter-ello – which he again picks up on in the *Notebooks* – repeatedly appears in Gramsci's writings in these years,[10] in order to signify the poverty of forces and protagonists of political life (*in primis* Giovanni Giolitti) as compared to the per-haps cynical, but nonetheless great and serious, means of doing politics that the Florentine secretary represented. Again in October 1926, just before his arrest, Gramsci repeated Giusti's motto, writing that 'Our "Machiavellis" are the works of Marx and Lenin, and not the editors of *Voce repubblicana* and the honour-able Arturo Labriola, who, moreover, follow Mr. Niccolò Machiavelli only in the sense of the lines "Behind the tomb/Of Machiavello/Lies the skeleton/of Sten-terello"'.[11]

We can say that in the years of Gramsci's journalistic activity and political activism,[12] he had read Machiavelli's works – probably under the influence of his two principal sources of inspiration as a young man, De Sanctis and Croce – and that they did influence his thought, but not with such central importance as would be the case in his *Notebooks*.

---

8   Gramsci 1987, p. 288.

9   Gramsci 1982, p. 84.

10   See for instance Gramsci 1966, p. 325; Gramsci 1984, p. 614.

11   Gramsci 1971b, p. 351.

12   It is also worth noting that in a 1922 letter to Leon Trotsky – who had asked him for information on Italian futurism – Gramsci recalled that 'In Milan recently a political weekly called *Il principe* has been founded, looking back to or seeking to invoke the same theories that Machiavelli preached in sixteenth-century Italy: that is, the struggle between local parties that lead the nation toward chaos must be overcome by an absolute monarch, a new Cesare Borgia, who places himself at the head of all the leaders of the parties in struggle. The review is led by two futurists ...' (Gramsci 1966, p. 527).

2   The Machiavelli Question

It was in his prison years that Gramsci deepened his study of Machiavelli's thought. This was not only because the dramatic circumstances in which the Sardinian communist found himself forced him to continue his political struggle by means of theoretical reflection. The historic defeat that the communist movement had suffered also led him to deepen the rethinking of Marxism that he had begun in the years 1923–4. This rethinking posed fundamental questions of strategy and tactics, as well as their philosophical presuppositions, and this also concerned some of the political categories he considered fundamental: the revolutionary party and the foundation of a new state. In this context, the great 1920s resumption of studies on Machiavelli, including those surrounding the 1927 fourth centenary of the Florentine secretary's death,[13] was doubtless also of some significance. In another letter to Tatiana, from 14 November 1927, we read:

> Find out if the 'Tutto Machiavelli' ['Machiavelli *Collected Works*'] has come out in the Florence publisher Barbera's 'Tutte le Opere' [*Collected Works*] collection and how much it costs; I fear, though, that it might cost a bit much, at least a hundred *lire* or so. *The finest pages* of the Treves edition will be sufficient, if that is the case. On the occasion of the Machiavelli centenary I read all the articles published by the five daily papers I read at that time; later I got the special issue of *Marzocco* devoted to Machiavelli.[14]

Already the previous year, soon after his arrest, Gramsci had sent one of his first letters to his sister-in-law (who together with Piero Sraffa was the principal link between the prisoner, his Party and more generally the outside world); this 27 December 1926 missive, sent from his temporary confinement in Ustica, had requested works including 'Francesco Ercole's book on Machiavelli'.[15] Now he not only asked for Machiavelli's works, but added a comment that already shone light on certain future developments in his interpretation:

> I was struck that none of the people writing on the centenary related Machiavelli's books to the development of states across Europe in the

---

13   On the 1920s debate (Chabod, Croce, Ercole, Gentile, Gobetti, Mussolini, Russo and so on), see Donzelli 1981, pp. xxxv et sqq.

14   Gramsci 1996a, pp. 132–3.

15   Gramsci 1996a, p. 24.

same historical period. Diverted by the purely moralistic question of so-called 'Machiavellianism', they did not see that Machiavelli was the theorist of nation states ruled by absolute monarchies: that is, in Italy he theorised what Elizabeth energetically accomplished in England, what Ferdinand the Catholic did in Spain, what Louis XI did in France and Ivan the Terrible did in Russia, even if he did not know and could not have known of any of these national experiences, which in reality represented the historic problem of the age, and which Machiavelli was enough of a genius to intuit and systematically to expose.[16]

In December 1927, Gramsci argued that Machiavelli was not the theorist of realpolitik, as anti-democratic interpreters and anarchists had asserted in the 1920s; and also that he was not only or mainly the theorist of politics *tout court* as Croce had claimed,[17] since in order fully to understand his thought it was necessary to historicise it, setting it in relation with the question of the birth of nation states. When Gramsci began drafting his *Notebooks* in 1929, he began precisely from these considerations in one of his very first notes of theoretical reflection:

> *On Machiavelli.* All too often Machiavelli is considered as the 'politician in general', good for all seasons: this is certainly an error in politics. Machiavelli linked to his times: 1) internal struggles within the republic of Florence; 2) struggles among the Italian states for a reciprocal balance of power; 3) struggles of the Italian states for a European balance of power. Machiavelli is influenced by the examples of France and Spain which have attained strong national unity ... Machiavelli is wholly a man of his times and his art of politics represents the philosophy of the time that leans toward absolute monarchy, the structure which permits bourgeois development and organization.[18]

So already in the first pages of this first notebook (written in the second half of 1929) we find a note entirely dedicated to Machiavelli, indeed taking his name. In the 'work plan' at the start of the *Notebooks*, however, the topic 'Machiavelli' does not appear. Gramsci had not initially intended to deepen his study of the

---

16   Gramsci 1996a, p. 133.

17   In the first notebooks, he still makes approving references to Croce's thesis, demonstrating the many aspects of the 'Machiavelli question' and also that the *Notebooks* were themselves a 'laboratory', particularly the first ones.

18   Q1, § 10: Gramsci 1975, pp. 8–9; Gramsci 1992a, p. 103.

Florentine secretary,[19] except in terms of his history of intellectuals: point 3 of this list is the 'Formation of Italian intellectual groups', which would have been where Machiavelli made his appearance, above all from the third notebook onward.[20] Indeed, Gramsci wrote to his sister-in-law Tatiana on 17 November 1930 that:

> I am fixed on three or four principal subjects, one of which is the cos-mopolitan function that Italian intellectuals played up until the eight-eenth century; a theme which I will then split up into various sections: the Renaissance and Machiavelli, and so on. If I were able to consult the necessary material, I believe that it would be possible to put together a really interesting book that still does not exist; I say 'book', by this I just mean the introduction to a certain number of monographic works, because the question is posed differently in different epochs, and, indeed, I think I would have to go all the way back to the times of the Roman Empire.[21]

In the very first notebooks there is no lack of references to Machiavelli, including ones of considerable interest. In Q1, § 10 (which he goes back to in Q13, § 13), for instance, the prisoner continues down the route of historical contextualisation, stating that Machiavelli was fiercely opposed to 'the residues of feudalism, not the progressive classes' or the 'productive classes, peasants and merchants'. Having read *The Art of War* – a work that was well-known from the early 1920s onward[22] – and its affirmation of the need to substitute mercenary militias by arming the peasants, Gramsci was convinced that Machiavelli wanted to show the 'urban bourgeoisie' the need to 'have the support of peasants as a mass, and create a secure and loyal armed force'.[23] Again in the extremely significant Q1, § 44, Gramsci wrote on the relations between moderates and democrats in the Risorgimento:

> The history of the Communes is rich with experiences in this respect: the emerging bourgeoisie seeks allies among the peasants against the Empire and against its own local feudalism ... even Machiavelli ... had posed the problem (within the terms and preoccupations of his time, of course):

---

19   In this regard, see also the hypotheses advanced by Gallo 2012, pp. 92–4.
20   See Frosini 2012.
21   Gramsci 1996a, p. 364.
22   Paggi 1984, p. 401.
23   Q1, § 10: Gramsci 1975, pp. 9; Gramsci 1992a, p. 103.

the need to forge links with the peasants in order to have a national
militia that could eliminate mercenary companies is seen quite clearly
in Machiavelli's military writings.[24]

The alliance between the progressive urban classes and the peasant masses was
part of the basis for the parallel between Jacobinism and Leninism that Gramsci
had borrowed from the great French historian Albert Mathiez.[25] By 1921 this had
also led him to a new, positive evaluation of Jacobinism. It was on this basis
that Gramsci could define Machiavelli as a 'Jacobin'; as he wrote in a letter to
Tania on 7 September 1931 ('through the organisation of the army ... Machiavelli
wanted to organise town's hegemony over country, and so he can be called
the first Italian Jacobin')[26] and in a note that he would later develop in the
thirteenth notebook: 'No formation of a national popular will is possible unless
the masses of peasant farmers enter *simultaneously* into political life. This is
what Machiavelli wanted to happen through the reform of the militia; it is
what the Jacobins achieved in the French Revolution. This is what Machiavelli's
[precocious][27] Jacobinism consists of'.[28]

In the second notebook – which from 1929 to 1933 Gramsci dedicated 'almost
entirely to a systematic working-through of old magazines that he had accu-
mulated over the years'[29] – we find two notes entitled 'Niccolò Machiavelli'
(which became a 'section heading'), based on supplements and articles from
Nuova Antologia in 1927. Q2, § 31 takes its cue from an issue of that magazine
entirely dedicated to the Florentine secretary, in which Gramsci's attention and
his critique are above all concentrated on what he sees as Guido Mazzoni's mistaken interpretation of *The Mandrake*; for its part, Q2, § 41 takes its cue from an
article by Luigi Cavina entitled 'Il sogno nazionale di Niccolò Machiavelli in
Romagna e il governo di Francesco Guicciardini', again on the topic of national
militias. In Q2, § 116, Gramsci asks 'was the nationalism of Machiavelli so strong,
after all, as to overcome "the love of art for art's sake"? Research along these
lines would be very interesting: did the problem of the Italian state concern
him more as a "national principle" or as a political problem interesting in itself,

---

24   Q1, § 44: Gramsci 1975, pp. 43–4; Gramsci 1992a, pp. 139–40.

25   See the entry in the *Dizionario gramsciano 1926–37* (Medici 2009). See also Lelio La Porta's
        pieces in the same volume: 'Machiavelli, Niccolò' and 'Moderno Principe'.

26   Gramsci 1996a, pp. 458–9.

27   Gramsci added this word between the lines.

28   Q8, § 21: Gramsci 1975, pp. 952–3, Gramsci 2011, p. 248.

29   Francioni 2009a, p. 4.

especially given its difficulty and Italy's great historical past?'[30] In other words, should Machiavelli be read in the light of the history of his times, or as a theorist of politics 'in and by itself'? Despite the clear statements in Q1, § 10, in these first notebooks we find diverse interpretative orientations and approaches to Machiavelli.

3   The Fourth Notebook: Marx and Machiavelli

Gramsci's reflection on Machiavelli and on *The Prince* makes a qualitative leap in the considerable section of the fourth notebook entitled 'Notes on Philosophy', where it takes on the problematic weight that would then feed into the thirteenth notebook's 'Brief notes on Machiavelli's politics'. This new complexity in Gramsci's reflection on the Florentine secretary came from the fact that here converged both the question of reading Machiavelli from a Marxist point of view, and the rethinking of Marxism from the point of view of the specificity of politics, which Machiavelli represented (that is, the question of reflecting on the fundamental categories of political science, in the first place the revolutionary party that wants to found a new type of state). Indeed, it is in the fourth notebook that Gramsci writes:

> *Marx and Machiavelli.* This topic could give rise to a twofold task: a study of the real connections between the two as theoreticians of militant politics, of action; and a book that extracts from Marxist thought an orderly system of politics along the lines of the *Prince*. The topic would be the political party in its relations with the classes and with the state ... the protagonist of this 'new prince' should not be the party in the abstract ... but rather a determinate historical party operating in a precise historical environment, with a particular tradition, in a distinctive and quite specific combination of social forces.[31]

The idea was not only to reflect theoretically on the redefinition of the modalities and role of the revolutionary party after its 1920s collapse: to write of the 'new prince' meant – Gramsci adds – 'to write a book that is, in a certain sense, "dramatic", an unfolding historical drama in which political maxims are

---

30   Gramsci 1975, p. 25; Gramsci 1992a, p. 342.
31   Q4, § 10: Gramsci 1975, p. 432; Gramsci 1996b, p. 152.

presented as a specific necessity and not as scientific principles'.[32] Therefore, Gramsci meant to take Machiavelli's most famous work as a model – as would become clearer and made explicit in the eighth notebook – in order to write a book 'for the masses', so to say, a political book like Marx and Engels's *Manifesto*, in which elements of theory, historical examples and a reasoned appeal for mobilisation would come together as one. In Gramsci's interpretation, this was what Machiavelli's *Prince* had succeeded in doing: 'Machiavelli wrote books of "immediate political action"'.[33] These had been studied and even become an immediate source of inspiration, but only among the 'powerful'. Which showed that 'Machiavelli was really of use to the absolute states in their formative stage because he was the expression of the European, more than Italian, "philosophy of the age"'.[34]

Again in the fourth notebook, we find two further notes dedicated to Machiavelli and Marx. The first, Q4, § 4, which is entitled 'Machiavellianism and Marxism', is crossed out (in such a way as to leave it still legible, as Gramsci does for all his first drafts), yet there is no second draft, except partially so in Q4, § 8, another A text, entitled 'Machiavelli and Marx'. Gramsci first recalls 'Foscolo's lines "even as he tempers the sceptre of the rulers, strips them of their laurels and lets the people see, etc." Croce writes that this proves the *objective validity* of Machiavelli's views, and this is absolutely true'.[35] Here he recognises Machiavelli's elaborations as a 'science', useful to everyone. Then, in Q4, § 8, he establishes the differences between Marx's anthropology and that of the Florentine secretary:

> The basic innovation introduced by Marx into the science of politics and of history, in comparison with that of Machiavelli, is the demonstration that 'human nature', fixed and immutable, does not exist and that therefore, the concrete content (as well as the logical formulation?) of political science must be conceived as a historically developing organism. In Machiavelli, two basic elements have to be considered: (1) the affirmation that politics is an independent and autonomous activity that has its own principles and laws, different from those of morality and religion in general (this position of Machiavelli's is of great philosophical significance, because it implicitly alters the conception of morality and religion,

---

32   Ibid.

33   Q5, § 127: Gramsci 1975, p. 657; Gramsci 1996b, p. 657.

34   Q6, § 50: Gramsci 1975, p. 723; Gramsci 2011, p. 39.

35   Q4, § 4: Gramsci 1975, p. 425; Gramsci 1996b, p. 144.

it alters the whole conception of the world); (2) the practical and immediate content of the art of politics, which is studied with realistic objectivity, in accordance with the first affirmation.[36]

As he wrote his fourth notebook, Gramsci identified the historicisation of human nature as the 'innovation' that Marx had contributed. He also agreed with Croce that Machiavelli's determining insight was the autonomy of the political, recalling Croce's old definition of Marx as the 'Machiavelli of the proletariat'.[37] However, he went much further, bringing into relief the essentially *philosophical* dimension of Machiavelli's thought, seeing him as the author of an 'original conception of the world' that could be defined with the same expression that Gramsci used to define Marxism: the *philosophy of praxis*.[38] He writes:

> In his treatment, in his critique of the present, [Machiavelli] articulated some general concepts that are presented in an aphoristic and nonsystematic form. He also articulated a conception of the world that could also be called 'philosophy of praxis' or 'neohumanism', in that it does not recognise transcendental or immanent (in the metaphysical sense) elements but is based entirely on the concrete action of man, who out of historical necessity works and transforms reality.[39]

As he dealt with the problems of his own time, Machiavelli expressed a more general conception of politics (and a philosophy) that went beyond them. He was the theorist of nation states (and so can only be explained in relation to his 'European' time) but he expressed – even if a 'nonsystematic' form – 'general concepts', that is, the fundamental terms of a science of politics and a philosophical conception that is valid also outside of his own period.

Turning to Q4, §8, we see that Gramsci again referred to Foscolo's thesis that '"Machiavelli revealed" something real', and stated that in reality the Florentine secretary was thinking about 'those who are not in the know', 'the revolutionary class of the time, the Italian people and nation, the democracy that gave birth to Pier Soderini rather than Valentino. Machiavelli wanted to educate this class, which needed to produce a "chief" who knew what to do and a people

---

36   Q4, §8: Gramsci 1975, pp. 430–1; Gramsci 1996b, pp. 150–1.

37   Q4, §56: Gramsci 1975, p. 503; Gramsci 1996b, p. 231.

38   On Machiavelli and the philosophy of praxis, see Frosini 2003, pp. 162 et sqq.

39   Q5, §127: Gramsci 1975, p. 657; Gramsci 1996b, p. 378.

who knew that the chief's actions were also in their interest'.[40] That is, Gramsci advanced a 'national' and 'democratic' interpretation of Machiavelli, a great theorist of politics but also one who was situated within his own time and 'served' determinate class interests (as we can infer also from the hypothesis that he was an antecedent of mercantilism and the physiocrats).[41] The democratic character of such a perspective is not nullified by his acceptance of the Prince's 'dictatorship': this prepares the achievement of greater freedom, just like the 'dictatorship of the proletariat' in the Leninist vision. He simply wants – Gramsci adds in Q14, § 32 – to 'educate the people' as to the fact that 'there can only exist one politics, a realistic politics, in order to achieve the desired end', since 'only he wants the end wants the means suitable to achieving it'.[42] On this basis, we can say that 'Machiavelli's position ... ought to be compared to those of the theorists and politicians of the philosophy of praxis' because 'they, too, have sought to construct and spread a popular, mass "realism"'. The barrier that Machiavelli faced was, however, a quite different one, which related to the social subject that would be responsible for getting Italy up to speed with Europe. That is, Gramsci argues in the fifth notebook, the 'medieval Italian bourgeoisie' had proven unable fully to overcome the Middle Ages by freeing itself from the burdensome presence of the Papacy and of the Church in order to 'create an autonomous state state'; instead, it had 'remained within the feudal and cosmopolitan medieval framework'.[43]

In this same note Q5, § 127 – a B text, much like many others in the fifth and sixth notebooks that Gramsci never had the time to revisit and re-elaborate, but that did establish convictions that would remain at the basis of his later elaborations – the author 'translated' the 'prince' of Machiavelli's thought into modern language:

---

40   Q4, § 8: Gramsci 1975, p. 431; Gramsci 1996b, p. 151.

41   Gramsci says as much not only in Q8, § 78 but also in a letter to Tatiana of 14 March 1932, with the declared aim of seeking the opinion of his friend, the great economist Piero Sraffa: 'Could we say that Machiavelli was a "mercantilist", if not in the sense that he consciously considered himself a mercantilist, at least in the sense that his political thought corresponded to mercantilism; that is, that he said in political language what the mercantilists said in terms of economic policy? Or could we even go so far as to say that in Machiavelli's political language (especially in *The Art of War*) the first germ of a physiocratic conception of the state is breaking through?' Gramsci 1996a, pp. 548–9.

42   Gramsci 1975, pp. 1690–1.

43   Q5, § 127; Gramsci 1975, p. 658; Gramsci 1996b, p. 379.

If one had to translate the notion 'Prince' as it is used in Machiavelli's book into modern political language, one would have to make a series of distinctions: 'Prince' could be a head of state or head of government, but 'Prince' could also be a political leader who wants to conquer a state or establish a new type of state; in this sense, 'Prince' could also be translated in modern terms as 'political party'.[44]

He thus translated Machiavelli's 'prince' as 'political party'. Gramsci was thinking in particular of the Communist Party – not only, or not still, the party that he wanted to re-construct and re-establish, but the party and revolutionary experience that, beyond the necessary work of 'translation', represented a model for Gramsci and the communists of his time: the Communist Party of the Soviet Union. Continuing the note, indeed, Gramsci writes:

> In reality, in certain states, the 'head of state' – that is, the element that balances the various interests struggling against the predominant but not absolutely exclusivistic interest – is precisely the 'political party'. With the difference, however, that in terms of traditional constitutional law the political party juridically neither rules nor governs. It has 'de facto power', it exercises the hegemonic function, and hence the function of balancing various interests, in 'civil society'; however, 'civil society' is in fact so thoroughly intertwined with political society that all the citizens feel instead that the party rules and governs.[45]

4   The Eighth Notebook: The Modern Prince

At the beginning of the eighth notebook, in which the author initially planned[46] to collect and order his reflections on the history of Italian intellectuals (a project that he never realised), Gramsci drew up a new research programme, which is at the same time a summary of the work that he had thus far completed in Turi,[47] with the title 'Principal essays'. Machiavelli appears twice in this list,

---

44   Q5, § 127; Gramsci 1975, pp. 661–2; Gramsci 1996b, p. 382.
45   Ibid.
46   As is evident from the title at the beginning of the first page: 'Loose notes and jottings for a history of Italian intellectuals'.
47   Francioni 2009b, pp. 3–4. According to Francioni, the list of 'Principal essays' dates from late 1930, even if there may have been later additions (p. 5). Apart from this list, however, it

firstly in the seventh entry 'Machiavelli' and then in the last one, 'Machiavelli as a technician of politics and as a complete politician or politician in deed'.[48] This latter may have been added subsequently.[49]

This first list is followed by another, which Gramsci entitled 'groupings of subjects', and here in the second line we find '2. Machiavelli'. This list – although spatially contiguous with the previous one[50] – was in reality written at a different time and seems to have been a new work plan, which can probably be dated to April 1932[51] and which at least in part prefigured the subdivision of the notes in the 'special notebooks'.

The importance that Machiavelli assumed in Gramsci's reflection can also be deduced from these two 'work plans', that is, from the significant presence of the Florentine secretary's name. Machiavelli's appearance here is also connected to the fact that the great economic crisis that had struck the capitalist West without giving rise to any revolutionary wave had confirmed and reinvigorated Gramsci's anti-deterministic and anti-economistic vision of the base-superstructure relationship, thus encouraging a further extension of Gramsci's reflection on the political sphere.[52]

It is in the first part of the eighth notebook ('miscellany') that we find the first appearance of the famous expression 'the Modern Prince' in the *Prison Notebooks*. Indeed, this is the title of Q8, § 21, which begins: 'The Modern Prince. This can serve as the general title for the collection of ideas on political science that may be assembled into a work of political science that would be conceived and organised along the lines of Machiavelli's *Prince*'.[53] This was the development of what we already saw in the fourth notebook, namely Gramsci's intention to bring together under the title 'Modern Prince' not only

---

seems that Gramsci began this notebook starting with what appears as its second half in November 1931, with the 'third series' of his 'notes on philosophy'; only in January 1932 did Gramsci definitively abandon his plan to gather together his notes on intellectuals in this notebook (p. 8), instead devoting the first half of the notebook to miscellaneous notes.

48   Q8: Gramsci 1975, pp. 935–6; Gramsci 2011, pp. 233–4.

49   Francioni 2009b, p. 5.

50   The Gerratana edition (Gramsci 1975, pp. 935–6) strongly suggests that the two lists were contiguous: they appear together, with no explanation of how one is meant to follow from the other. In the anastatic edition (Gramsci 2009, Vol. 13, pp. 29–31) we see that the first list occupies the first page of Gramsci's notebook and only the first line of the other side, which is thus almost entirely blank, while the second list appears on the first half of the third page. Thus we see their lack of spatial contiguity.

51   Francioni 2009b, pp. 9–10.

52   See Donzelli 1981, p. xviii.

53   Q8, § 21: Gramsci 1975, p. 951; Gramsci 2011, p. 246.

his observations and notes on Machiavelli and his most famous work, but moreover all those that would be useful for a treatise of 'political science' built on the model of *The Prince*. In order to clarify this very point, Gramsci revisited his interpretation of Machiavelli's book, already outlined in the fourth notebook, in a famous passage that would appear in its second version at the beginning of the thirteenth notebook.[54] Gramsci writes:

> The fundamental characteristic of the *Prince* is precisely that it is not a systematic treatment; it is, rather, a 'living' book in which ideology becomes 'myth', a fantastic and artistic 'image' between utopia and scholarly treatise in which the doctrinal and rational element is personified by the 'condottiere', the 'anthropomorphic' and plastic symbol of the 'collective will'. In describing the process of formation of a 'collective will', Machiavelli does not resort to pedantic disquisitions on the principles and criteria for a method of action; instead, he presents it in terms of the 'qualities and duties' of a concrete personage and thus stimulates the artistic imagination and arouses passion.[55]

So it was necessary to take *The Prince* as an example in order to awaken a 'collective will', Gramsci considering this work to be 'a historical example of the Sorelian "myth"', that is, of a political ideology that is not presented as a cold utopia or as a rationalised doctrine but as a concrete "fantasy" that works on a dispersed and shattered people to arouse and organise its collective will'.[56] His would be a book for the *mobilisation* of the masses, and not just a theoretical study. Its subject would be the Communist Party ('a determinate historical party', as we read in the fourth notebook),[57] but it would also be addressed, in the first place, to its militants. He knew that in twentieth-century society 'the modern Prince, the myth-Prince cannot be a real person, a concrete individual. It can only be an organism ... the political party'.[58]Also because a modern 'condottiere' – as a 'concrete individual', a 'Duce' – would give rise to an action that '[i]n almost every case ... typifies a restoration or reorganisation'; 'it is not typical of the founding of new states or new national and social structures (as was the case in Machiavelli's *Prince* ...)'.[59]

---

54   Q13, § 1: Gramsci 1975, p. 1555.

55   Q8, § 21: Gramsci 1975, p. 951; Gramsci 2011, p. 246.

56   Ibid.

57   Q4, § 10: Gramsci 1975, p. 432; Gramsci 1996b, p. 152.

58   Q8, § 21: Gramsci 1975, p. 951; Gramsci 2011, p. 247.

59   Ibid.

From this moment onward there would be a very strong inter-relation in the *Notebooks* between reflection on the *Prince* and reflection on the *modern Prince*, between reflection on Machiavelli and his time and Gramsci's reflection on his own time. Indeed, we find one such example of this interconnection in this same note, where Gramsci asks 'Why was there no absolute monarchy in Italy in Machiavelli's own time?' and answers by turning 'back to the Roman Empire (the question of the intellectuals and of the language question) in order to understand the medieval communes and the role of the church'. Similarly, he repeats his thesis that '[t]here never was an effective "Jacobin" force – precisely the force that creates the national-popular collective will', before immediately asking whether 'the conditions for this will' existed, and beginning to speak of the formation of the unitary Italian state, a process whose consequences reverberated through history, ultimately arriving at Fascism.[60] Gramsci continues by saying that when it comes to conceptions of the world, we again 'find an absence of "Jacobinism" and a fear of "Jacobinism" ... The modern Prince must be the promoter of moral and intellectual reform, which constitutes the terrain for a subsequent development of the national popular collective rooted in a complete and accomplished form of modern civilisation'.[61] Indeed, Gramsci adds, 'the modern Prince should focus entirely' on 'two basic points': 'the formation of a national popular collective will, of which the modern Prince is the active and operative expression, and intellectual and moral reform'.[62] He continues:

> As it grows, the modern Prince upsets the entire system of intellectual and moral relations, for its development means precisely that every act is deemed useful or harmful, virtuous or wicked, depending on whether its point of reference is the modern Prince and whether it increases the Prince's power or opposes it. The Prince takes the place, in people's consciousness, of the divinity and of the categorical imperative; it becomes the basis of a modern secularism and of a complete secularisation of life and of all customary relations.[63]

Gramsci made this restatement in peremptory, totalising terms, because it reflected the dramatic situation in which he and the Italian Communists found themselves, dedicated to the hard and unequal struggle against Fascism – but

---

60   Q8, § 21: Gramsci 1975, p. 952; Gramsci 2011, p. 248.
61   Ibid.
62   Q8, § 21: Gramsci 1975, p. 953; Gramsci 2011, p. 249.
63   Ibid.

also because the Party was seen as the founder of a 'new type of state', an initial cell with a strong tendency toward expanding and asserting itself in order to give rise to a 'complete and total form of modern civilisation'. These considerations all help us better to understand what Gramsci was writing, but they also perhaps constitute the antipode of what his Party would become in the – in many ways novel – situation that came about after the end of Fascism. Not only accepting the great compromise that the republican Constitution represented, but actively promoting it, the Communists accepted democratic methods and thus would make the 'modern Prince' something partly different from what Gramsci had prefigured and theorised. However, Togliatti's 'new party' was also in several regards inspired by the *Notebooks*, as it sought to become a 'collective intellectual' and promoter of 'intellectual and moral reform', at least within the limits that subjective capacities and objective conditions set to the realisation of Gramsci's teachings in the *Notebooks*.

Returning to the eighth notebook, we can also find many examples of the interconnection between the *Prince* and the 'modern Prince' in Gramsci's notes in the 'miscellaneous' section – all of which would be revisited in the thirteenth notebook – with titles like 'Machiavelli' or 'modern Prince', as the focus of the argument turns back and forth between the Florentine secretary, the problems of 'political science', or the (Communist) Party and its tasks. Notes 42, 52 and 56, for example – each of them entitled 'Machiavelli. The modern Prince' – deal with 'big politics' and 'minor politics', Gaetano Mosca's 'political class', and 'Croce's conception of politics-passion'. Notes 58, 61, 62, 69, 86 and 114 come under the heading 'Machiavelli', and these, too, show the interconnection between his comments on political science and those concerning Machiavelli: for example, with regard to the question 'what is politics?', a theme that Gramsci links to the 'advance' that Croce had made 'in the study of Machiavelli and of political science';[64] or with regard to the 'conception of criminal law'.[65] Gramsci also addressed topics that more directly concerned Machiavelli. Particularly worth mentioning is Q8, § 84, entitled 'Machiavelli. What is and what ought to be'. Here, Gramsci deals with the question of 'political realism', which is here understood in a conservative sense, the negation of any transformative dynamic:

'Too much' political realism has often led to the assertion that the politician should only work within 'effectual reality', that he should not be inter-

---

64   Q8, § 61: Gramsci 1975, p. 977; Gramsci 2011, p. 271.
65   Q8, § 62: Gramsci 1975, p. 978; Gramsci 2011, p. 272.

ested in what 'ought to be', but only in what 'is'. This erroneous approach
has led Paolo Treves to find the exemplar of the 'true politician' in Guicciardini and not in Machiavelli. One must distinguish between the political scientist and the politician in action. The scientist must operate only
within effectual reality, insofar as he is just a scientist. But Machiavelli is
not just a scientist; he is a passionate man, an active politician, and therefore he must concern himself with what 'ought to be'.[66]

Machiavelli was a 'politician in action, who wanted to create new relations
of force' and – by writing *The Prince* – to point the way to effective political
action, just as Gramsci wanted to do by writing the *Notebooks*. Their theory
is *for praxis*, for politics, and for a politics of transformation. For Gramsci,
Machiavelli was a revolutionary, because if 'what ought to be' is not an 'arbitrary
act' or 'passing fancy', but a 'concrete will' with a bearing 'on effectual reality'
(as in Machiavelli's case), then this reality must be understood in a dynamic
sense, as 'a relation of forces in continuous shifts of equilibrium'.[67]

It is thus possible to 'apply ... one's will to the creation of a new equilibrium
among really existing and active forces – basing oneself on the force with a
progressive thrust in order to make it prevail'.[68] So what 'ought to be', also, is
understood in a realistic sense ('as a realistic interpretation and as the only
historicist interpretation of reality'). 'The Savonarola-Machiavelli opposition' –
Gramsci writes in the eighth notebook, as he would repeat in the thirteenth,
criticising Russo's theses[69] – 'is not the opposition been what is and what
ought to be, but between two different notions of "ought to be"'.[70] However,
while Savonarola's is 'abstract and nebulous', Machiavelli's is 'realistic', even
though it did not 'become direct reality, for one cannot expect an individual or
a book to change reality but only to interpret it and to indicate a line of action.
Machiavelli had no thought or intention of changing reality; he only wanted
to show concretely how the concrete historical forces ought to have acted to
change existing reality in a concrete and historically significant manner'.[71]

This was also what Gramsci proposed to do, though he was far more of a
'politician in action' than Machiavelli was. Yet now he was prevented from

---

66   Q8, § 84: Gramsci 1974, p. 990; Gramsci 2011, p. 283.
67   Ibid.
68   Ibid.
69   Russo 1931.
70   Q8, § 84: Gramsci 1974, p. 990; Gramsci 2011, p. 283.
71   Ibid.

acting, as a prisoner in enemy hands with ever more faint hopes of release. Whether he, too, was writing only 'to show how historical forces ought to have acted', or he still believed he could play an active role in the revolutionary process, remains an open question.

Other fundamentally important passages of Gramsci's reading of Machiavelli appear in the eighth notebook, and they are revisited in the thirteenth notebook. In Q6, § 52 Gramsci had spoken of the 'tragic split' in Machiavelli, who was 'unable to detach himself from the republic, but ... understood that only an absolute monarchy could resolve the problems of the time'.[72] Now he remarked that *The Prince* did not fail to mention 'the moment of hegemony and consensus, along with the moment of authority and force'.[73] Gramsci invoked Machiavelli's 'Centaur' and his 'dual nature' as the symbol of a theory that fit together the moments 'of force and consent, domination and hegemony'.[74] So it is quite mistaken to counterpose to the Florentine secretary an 'anti-Machiavellian' Bodin: this latter 'laid the foundations of political science in France on a terrain that was much more advanced than that which Italy had to offer to Machiavelli', with quite different 'historic tasks': 'The question that concerned Bodin was not the founding of a territorial and unified (national) state but the balancing of conflicting social forces within a state that was already strong and firmly in place'. Thus it was 'not the moment of force that interested Bodin but the moment of consent'.[75]

We already touched on the double meaning of Gramsci's reference to Machiavelli, and indeed in the ninth notebook – one of the first notebooks Gramsci had, but used for 'translation exercises' up until April 1932[76] – there are several notes entitled 'Machiavelli' (revisited in the thirteenth notebook) dealing from anything from the relation between politics and the military art (Q9, § 19), to bureaucracy (Q9, § 21), 'relations of force' (Q9, § 40), 'organic and democratic centralism' (Q9, § 68), representative systems (Q9, § 69), the origin of wars (Q9, § 70), and Caesarism (Q9, § 133, 136). So the heading 'Machiavelli', did not only cover interpretations of the Florentine secretary and his works, but also concerned the 'modern Prince', the volume modelled on *The Prince* (and Marx and Engels's *Manifesto*) that Gramsci wanted to write.

---

72   Gramsci 1975, p. 725; Gramsci 2011, p. 39.

73   Q8, § 48: Gramsci 1975, p. 970; Gramsci 2011, p. 265.

74   Q8, § 86: Gramsci 1975, p. 991; Gramsci 2011, p. 284.

75   Q8, § 114: Gramsci 1975, p. 1008; Gramsci 2011, p. 299.

76   Francioni 2009c, p. 5.

5   A Jacobin Force

The thirteenth notebook – one of the four large-format ones (a 21.8 by 31.2 centimetre book), along with notebooks 10, 12 and 18 – was the notebook in which the Sardinian communist began to collect all his notes under headings such as Machiavelli and 'modern Prince'. According to Francioni it was composed between April 1932 and November 1933,[77] and between 1932 and 1934 according to Gerratana.[78] He did not work starting from the first notebooks. In the thirteenth notebook, Gramsci began copying out notes beginning from the eighth notebook (the first sixteen), then continuing with seven[79] notes from the fourth notebook, and finally notebooks 1, 7, and 9 – demonstrating that it was in the eighth notebook that his project for the 'modern Prince' fully took shape. This notebook did not prove large enough to contain all the notes that were meant to be in it, and Gramsci sought to continue this effort gathering notes on this question in his eighteenth notebook, which was entitled *Niccolò Machiavelli II*. However, here he would ultimately copy out only three notes (from the third notebook). As his illness continued to worsen, Gramsci interrupted this work, preferring to dedicate his remaining energies to other single-subject notebooks, but also to writing new texts encapsulating new reading and reflection. So in notebooks 14, 15 and 17 there are new notes on Machiavelli and his thought as well as (in greater number) new reflections on 'political science' with the title 'Machiavelli'.

Completely full of the prisoner's writings, except for its very last few lines, notebook 13 contained 39 C texts (all revisions, without the original title) and a single B text (Q8, §25). Of these forty notes, thirteen deal with Machiavelli, his thought, his works, and interpretations of him; while twenty-seven of them concern 'political science', with considerations that were evidently functional to his writing an 'orderly system of actual politics along the lines of *The Prince*', which was hypothesised as early as Q4, §10[80] and brought into focus in the eighth notebook. In particular, the last fifteen notes here copied out did not regard Machiavelli, eleven of them from the ninth notebook and the other four from the first, with an ever greater privileging of the 'modern Prince' over *The Prince*.

---

77   Francioni and Cospito 2009, p. 153.

78   Gramsci 1975, p. 2410.

79   Eight, if we also include Q13, §23, written on the basis of A texts from notebooks 4, 7 and 9.

80   Gramsci 1975, p. 432; Gramsci 1996b, p. 152.

The first main section of the thirteenth notebook is devoted to questions regarding the interpretation of Machiavelli's thought. It takes Q8, §21 as its starting point, though without the original *incipit* ('The Modern Prince. This can serve as the general title for the collection of ideas ...'). In this section – other than various changes of no great importance – there are two telling additions,[81] concerning the same theme: the famous *Exhortatio* in Chapter 26 of *The Prince*, the 'conclusion' that for Gramsci 'is linked to the book's "mythical" character', to the fact that it is not a 'work of "science", in the academic sense, but of "immediate political passion", a party "manifesto" '.[82] Gramsci writes:

> The 'mythical' character of the book to which I have referred is due also to its conclusion; having described the ideal condottiere, Machiavelli here, in a passage of great artistic effect, invokes the real condottiere who is to incarnate him historically. This passionate invocation reflects back on the entire book, and is precisely what gives it its dramatic character.[83]

And soon after he adds:

> in a dramatic movement of great effect, the elements of passion and of myth which occur throughout the book are drawn together and brought to life in the conclusion, in the invocation of a prince who 'really exists'. Throughout the book, Machiavelli discusses what the Prince must be like if he is to lead a people to found a new State; the argument is developed with rigorous logic, and with scientific detachment. In the conclusion, Machiavelli merges with the people, becomes the people; not, however, some 'generic' people, but the people whom he, Machiavelli, has convinced by the preceding argument – the people whose consciousness and whose expression he becomes and feels himself to be, with whom he feels identified. The entire 'logical' argument now appears as nothing other than auto-reflection on the part of the people – an inner reasoning worked out in the popular consciousness, whose conclusion is a cry of passionate urgency. The passion, from discussion of itself, becomes once again 'emotion', fever, fanatical desire for action. This is why the epilogue of *The Prince* is not something extrinsic, tacked on, rhetorical, but has to be understood as a necessary element of the work – indeed as the ele-

---

81   On the origin of the changes introduced in this C text, see Frosini 2013.

82   Q17, §26: Gramsci 1975, p. 1928.

83   Q13, §1: Gramsci 1975, p. 1555; Gramsci 1971, p. 125.

ment which gives the entire work its true colour, and makes it a kind of 'political manifesto'.[84]

The Prince's conclusion reveals the work's true *raison d'être*: for it is here that Machiavelli becomes 'popular consciousness', a true and proper 'organic intellectual' who understands the need to operate in 'sentimental connection' with the 'people-nation'[85] and has thus chosen the mediation of 'passional, mythical elements'[86] in order to educate, convince and encourage mobilisation and action, in order to awaken a 'national-popular collective will', an 'effective Jacobin force'.[87] Such an attempt failed in Machiavelli's own time, also because he was an exceptional case among the Italian intellectuals, on account of 'the international position of Italy (seat of the universal church)', which determined a situation of backwardness and posed obstacles to the process of constituting a unitary state. Gramsci asked if the conditions to overcome such a barrier now existed, repeating that Machiavelli had understood the fundamental point, in this sense: namely, the still-present need for the engagement of the peasant masses and for their *simultaneous* irruption into political life.[88] This was the same discourse on the 'driving forces of the Italian revolution' that had been present in Gramsci since the *Lyons Theses*. That is, a politics of alliance, principally the worker-peasant alliance, which came to Gramsci from Lenin and which in the Italy of the 1930s he still saw as central to the political development of the 'modern Prince'.

---

84   Ibid.
85   Q11, § 67: Gramsci 1975, p. 1505.
86   Obviously Sorel's conception of 'myth' exerted a fundamental influence here. See the interesting considerations on this point in Frosini 2013.
87   Q13, § 1: Gramsci 1975, p. 1560; Gramsci 1971, p. 132.
88   Q8, § 21: Gramsci 1975, p. 953; Gramsci 1996b, p. 248.

References

Agosti, Aldo 1996, *Palmiro Togliatti*, Turin: Utet.

Anderson, Perry 1976, 'The Antinomies of Antonio Gramsci', *New Left Review*, 1/100, available at: http://newleftreview.org/I/100/perry-anderson-the-antinomies-of-antonio-gramsci.

Asor Rosa, Alberto 1973, 'Un "Ordine Nuovo"', in *Intellettuali e classe operaia*, Florence: La Nuova Italia.

Auciello, Nicola 1974, *Socialismo ed egemonia in Gramsci e Togliatti*, Bari: De Donato.

Badaloni, Nicola 1987, 'Teoria gramsciana delle dislocazioni egemoniche', *Critica marxista*, 2–3.

Baratta, Giorgio 2004, '*Americanismo e fordismo*' in Frosini and Liguori (eds.) 2004.

Bobbio, Norberto 1968, 'Sulla nozione di società civile', *De Homine*, 24–5.

———— 1969, 'Gramsci e la concezione della società civile', in *Gramsci e la cultura contemporanea*, Vol. I, edited by Pietro Rossi, Rome: Riuniti.

———— 1977, 'Gramsci e il Pci', in *Egemonia e democrazia*, Mondoperaio, 7.

———— 1985, *Stato, governo, società. Per una teoria generale della politica*, Turin: Einaudi.

———— 1990 [1958], 'Gramsci e la dialettica', in *Saggi su Gramsci*, Milan: Feltrinelli.

Bodei, Remo 1999, 'Colonizzare le coscienze. Forme della politica e società di massa in Gramsci', in Vacca (ed.) 1999b.

Boothman, Derek 1995, 'Scienza e traducibilità nei «Quaderni» di Gramsci', *Critica marxista*, 2.

Boudon, Raymond 1991, *L'ideologia. Origine dei pregiudizi*, Turin: Einaudi.

Broccoli, Angelo 1971, *Antonio Gramsci e l'educazione come egemonia*, Florence: La Nuova Italia.

Buci-Glucksmann, Christine 1980, *Gramsci and the State*, London: Lawrence & Wishart.

Burgio, Alberto 2002, *Gramsci storico*, Bari: Laterza.

———— 2005, '*Il Labriola di Gramsci*', in *Antonio Labriola nella storia e nella cultura della nuova Italia*, Macerata: Quodlibet.

Buttigieg, Joseph A. 1999, 'Sulla categoria gramsciana di «subalterni»', *Gramsci da un secolo all'altro*, edited by Giorgio Baratta and Guido Liguori, Rome: Editori Riuniti.

Cacciatore, Giuseppe 1999, 'Gramsci: problema di etica nei *Quaderni*', in Vacca (ed.) 1999b.

Caracciolo, Alberto and Gianni Scalia (eds.) 1959, *La città futura. Saggi sulla figura e il pensiero di Antonio Gramsci*, a cura di Alberto Caracciolo e Gianni Scalia, Milan: Feltrinelli.

Caramella, Santino 1932, 'Senso comune: teoria e pratica', *Ricerche filosofiche*, 1.

———— 1933, *Senso comune. Teoria e pratica*, Bari: Laterza.

Cavallaro, Luigi 1997, 'L'economia politica di Gramsci', *Critica marxista*, 4.

Centi, Beatrice 1984, *Antonio Labriola dalla filosofia di Herbart al materialismo storico*, Bari: Dedalo.

Chiarotto, Francesca 2011, *Operazione Gramsci. Alla conquista degli intellettuali nell'italia del dopoguerra*, Milan: Mondadori.

Ciliberto, Michele 1982 'La fabbrica dei Quaderni', in *Filosofia e politica nel Novecento italiano. Da Labriola a «Società»*, Bari: De Donato.

Cohen Jean L. 1999, 'La scommessa egemonica: l'attuale dibattito americano sulla società civile e i suoi dilemmi', in Vacca (ed.) 1999b.

Colletti, Lucio 1974, *Intervista politico-filosofica*, Bari: Laterza.

———— 1977, *Gramsci e il Pci*, in *Egemonia e democrazia*, Mondoperaio, 7.

Cospito, Giuseppe 2004, 'Egemonia', in Frosini and Liguori (eds.) 2004.

Coutinho, Carlos Nelson 1998, 'Attualità e limiti del «Manifesto»', *Critica marxista*, 5.

———— 1999, 'Volontà generale e democrazia in Rousseau, Hegel e Gramsci', in Vacca (ed.) 1999b.

———— 2009, 'Volontà collettiva', in *Dizionario gramsciano 1926–1937*, edited by Guido Liguori and Pasquale Voza, Rome: Carocci.

———— 2012, *Gramsci's Political Thought*, Leiden: Brill.

Cox, Robert 1999, 'Il pensiero di Gramsci e la questione della società civile alla fine del XX secolo, in Gramsci e il Novecento', in Vacca (ed.) 1999b.

Croce, Benedetto 1918, *Conversazioni critiche*, II, Bari: Laterza.

———— 1928, 'Filosofia come vita morale e vita morale come filosofia', *La Critica*, 2.

———— 1947, 'Come uomo di pensiero egli fu dei nostri', *Quaderni della "Critica"*, 8.

———— 1951, 'Filosofia americana e filosofia europea', *Quaderni della "Critica"*, 19–20.

———— 1968 [1900], *Materialismo storico ed economia marxistica*, Bari: Laterza.

Daniele, Chiara (ed.) 1999, *Gramsci a Roma, Togliatti a Mosca. Il carteggio del 1926*, Turin: Einaudi.

De Felice, Franco 1972, 'Una chiave di lettura in «Americanismo e fordismo»', Rinascita, 29.

De Giovanni, Biagio 1977, 'Gramsci e l'elaborazione successiva del partito comunista', in *Egemonia Stato Partito in Gramsci*, Rome: Editori Riuniti.

Dewey, John 1988, *The Later Works of John Dewey*, Vol. 13, Carbondale: Southern Illinois University Press.

Dizionario gramsciano 1926–1937, edited by Guido Liguori and Pasquale Voza, Rome: Carocci.

Donzelli, Carmine 1981, 'Introduzione', in Antonio Gramsci, *Quaderno 13. Noterelle sulla politica del Machiavelli*, Turin: Einaudi.

D'Orsi, Angelo 2004, 'Introduzione', in Antonio Gramsci, *La nostra città futura. Scritti torinesi (1911–1922)*, Rome: Carocci.

Dubla, Ferdinando 1986, *Gramsci e la fabbrica*, Rome: Lacaita.

Eagleton, Terry 1991, *Ideology*, London: Verso.

Ferri, Franco (ed.) 1977–9, *Politica e storia in Gramsci*, 2 vols., Rome: Editori Riuniti.

Finelli, Roberto 1992, 'Antropologie della politica', *Democrazia e diritto*, 2.

————— 1997, 'Introduzione', in Louis Althusser, *Lo Stato e i suoi apparati*, edited by Roberto Finelli, Rome: Editori Riuniti.

————— 2005, 'Antonio Labriola e Antonio Gramsci: variazioni sul tema della «prassi»', in *Antonio Labriola nella storia e nella cultura della nuova Italia*, edited by Alberto Burgio, Quodlibet, Macerata.

Fiori, Giuseppe 1991, *Gramsci Togliatti Stalin*, Bari: Laterza.

Fontana, Benedetto 1999, '"Che cos'è la verità?" Modernità ed egemonia in Gramsci', in Vacca (ed.) 1999b.

Forenza, Eleanora 2012, 'Nuovo senso comune e filosofia della praxis', in *Domande dal presente. Studi sul Gramsci*, edited by Lea Durante and Guido Liguori, Rome: Carocci.

Francioni Gianni 1984, *L'Officina gramsciana*, Naples: Bibliopolis.

————— 2009a, 'Nota introduttiva a Quaderno 2', in *Quaderni del carcere. Edizione anastatica dei manoscritti*, Vol. 5, Rome: Treccani.

————— 2009b, 'Nota introduttiva a Quaderno 8', in *Quaderni del carcere. Edizione anastatica dei manoscritti*, Vol. 13, Rome: Treccani.

————— 2009c, 'Nota introduttiva a Quaderno 9', in *Quaderni del carcere. Edizione anastatica dei manoscritti*, Vol. 6, Rome: Treccani.

Francioni, Gianni and Giuseppe Cospito 2009, 'Nota introduttiva a Quaderno 13', in *Quaderni del carcere. Edizione anastatica dei manoscritti*, Vol. 14, Rome: Treccani.

Frosini, Fabio 2003, *Gramsci e la filosofia. Saggio sui 'Quaderni del carcere'*, Rome: Carocci.

————— 2010, *La religione dell'uomo moderno. Politica e verità nei 'Quaderni del carcere'*, Rome: Carocci.

————— 2012, *Il 'Primo quaderno'*, available at: http://www.igsitalia.org/Seminario Quaderno 1 Relazione Frosini.pdf

————— 2013, *El Príncipe de Maquiavelo como 'auto-reflexión del pueblo': política, religión y mito en la interpretación de Gramsci*, talk at the Machiavelli seminar in Marilia, Brazil, 6–8 May. To be published.

Frosini, Fabio and Guido Liguori (eds.) 2004, *Le parole di Gramsci. Per un lessico dei 'Quaderni del carcere'*, Rome: Carocci.

Gallo, Elisabetta 2012, 'Un marxismo antidogmatico per la rivoluzione in Occidente', in *Domande dal presente. Studi sul Gramsci*, edited by Lea Durante and Guido Liguori, Rome: Carocci.

Garin, Eugenio 1975 [1962], 'Quindici anni dopo 1945/1960', in *Cronache di filosofia italiana 1900/1943*, Bari: Laterza.

————— 1997 [1958], 'Gramsci nella cultura italiana' in *Con Gramsci*, Rome: Editori Riuniti.

Gentile, Giovanni 1931, 'La concezione umanistica del mondo', *Nuova Antologia*, 1421.

George, Susan 1998, 'La mondializzazione e i pericoli per la democrazia', *Critica marxista*, 4.

Gerratana, Valentino 1969, 'Intervento', in *Gramsci e la cultura contemporanea*, Vol. 1, edited by Pietro Rossi, Rome: Editori Riuniti.

———— 1972 [1963], 'Sulla «fortuna» di Labriola', in *Ricerche di storia del marxismo*, Rome: Editori Riuniti.

———— 1977, 'Stato, partito, strumenti e istituti dell'egemonia nei «Quaderni del carcere»', in *Egemonia Stato Partito in Gramsci*, Rome: Editori Riuniti.

———— 1985, 'Introduzione' to Friedrich Engels, *Anti-Dühring*, Rome: Editori Riuniti.

———— 1997, 'Le forme dell'egemonia', in *Gramsci. Problemi di metodo*, Rome: Editori Riuniti.

Gerratana, Valentino and Antonio A. Santucci (eds.) 1987, *L'Ordine Nuovo 1919–1920*, Turin: Einaudi.

Gill, Stephen (ed.) 1993, *Gramsci, Historical Materialism and International Relations*, Cambridge: Cambridge University Press.

———— 1999, 'Gramsci, modernità e globalizzazione', in Vacca (ed.) 1999b.

Gramsci, Antonio 1950, *Americanismo e fordismo*, edited by Felice Platone, Milan: Universale economica.

———— 1964, *2000 pagine di Gramsci*, edited by Giansiro Ferrata and Niccolò Gallo, Milan: Il Saggiatore,

———— 1966, *Socialismo e fascismo. L'Ordine Nuovo 1921–1922*, Turin: Einaudi.

———— 1971a, *Selections from the Prison Notebooks*, translated by Quintin Hoare and Geoffrey Nowell-Smith, London: Lawrence & Wishart.

———— 1971b, *La costruzione del partito comunista 1923–1926*, Turin: Einaudi.

———— 1975, *Quaderni del carcere*, critical edition edited by Valentino Gerratana, Turin: Einaudi.

———— 1980, *Cronache torinesi 1913–1917*, edited by Sergio Caprioglio, Turin: Einaudi.

———— 1982, *La città futura 1917–1918*, edited by Sergio Caprioglio, Turin: Einaudi.

———— 1984, *Il nostro Marx 1918–1919*, edited by Sergio Caprioglio, Turin: Einaudi.

———— 1987, *L'Ordine Nuovo, 1919–1920*, edited by Valentino Gerratana and Antonio A. Santucci, Turin: Einaudi.

———— 1992a, *Prison Notebooks*, translated by Joseph A. Buttigieg, Vol. 1, New York: Columbia University Press.

———— 1992b, *Lettere 1908–1926*, edited by Antonio A. Santucci, Turin: Einaudi.

———— 1995, *Further Selections from the Prison Notebooks*, edited by Derek Boothman, Minneapolis: University of Minneapolis Press.

———— 1996a, *Lettere dal carcere 1926–1937*, Palermo: Sellerio.

———— 1996b, *Prison Notebooks*, translated by Joseph A. Buttigieg, Vol. 2, New York: Columbia University Press.

———— 2007, *Quaderni di traduzione (1929–1932)*, edited by Giuseppe Cospito, Rome: Istituto della Enciclopedia italiana.

———— 2009, *Quaderni del carcere. Edizione anastatica dei manoscritti*, 18 Vols., Rome: Treccani.

———— 2011, *Prison Notebooks*, translated by Joseph A. Buttigieg, Vol. 3, New York: Columbia University Press.

Gruppi, Luciano, 1967, 'Il concetto di egemonia', in *Prassi rivoluzionaria e storicismo in Gramsci, Critica Marxista*, Quaderni, 3.

———— 1972, *Il concetto di egemonia in Gramsci*, Rome: Editori Riuniti.

Hardt, Michael and Toni Negri 2000, *Empire*, Cambridge, MA: Harvard University Press.

Haug, Wolfgang Fritz 1995, 'Tradurre Gramsci', in *Gramsci nel mondo. Atti del convegno internazionale di studi gramsciani. Formia, 25–28 ottobre 1989*, edited by Maria Luisa Righi, Rome: Fondazione Istituto Gramsci.

Hirst, Paul and Grahame Thompson 1996, *Globalisation in Question*, London: Polity.

Horsman, Matthew and Andrew Marshall 1994, *After the Nation State*, London: Harper Collins, 1994.

Izzo, Francesca 2009, *Democrazia e cosmopolitismo in Antonio Gramsci*, Rome: Carocci.

Jaulin, Annick 1991, 'Senso comune e mondo oggettivo nei «Quaderni»', *Critica marxista*, 6.

Labica, Georges 1991, *Dopo il marxismo-leninismo*, Rome: Edizioni Associate.

Labriola, Antonio 1973, *Scritti filosofici e politici*, edited by Franco Sbarberi, Turin: Einaudi.

———— 2000, *Saggi sul materialismo storico*, edited by Antonio A. Santucci, Rome: Editori Riuniti.

Laclau, Ernesto and Chantal Mouffe 1985, *Hegemony and Socialist Strategy. Towards a Radical Democratic Politics*, London: Verso.

Lenin, Vladimir 1972, *Materialism and Empirio-Criticism*, Peking: Foreign Languages Press.

———— 1987, *'What is to be Done?' and Other Writings*, New York: Dover.

Liguori, Guido 2002a, 'Fine o Metamorfosi dello Stato-nazione?', *Trimestre*, 4.

———— 2002b, 'Lo Stato non è morto', *La rivista del manifesto*, 29.

———— 2011, 'Tre accezioni di "subalterno" in Gramsci', *Critica marxista*, 6.

———— 2012, *Gramsci conteso*, Rome: Editori Riuniti.

Lisa, Athos 1973, *Memorie. Dall'ergastolo di Santi Stefano alla casa penale di Turi di Bari*, Milan, Feltrinelli.

Lo Piparo, Franco 1979, *Lingua intellettuali egemonia in Gramsci*, Bari: Laterza.

Lukács, György 1981, *The Destruction of Reason*, New York: Humanities Press.

Luporini, Cesare 1967, 'Avvertenza' in Karl Marx and Friedrich Engels, *L'ideologia tedesca*, Rome: Editori Riuniti.

———— 1973, 'Il marxismo e la cultura italiana del Novecento', in *Storia d'Italia*, Vol. 5, *I documenti*, edited by Ruggiero Romano and Corrado Vivanti, Turin: Einaudi.

———— 1974, *Dialettica e materialismo*, Roma, Editori Riuniti.

———— 1987, 'Senso comune e filosofia', in *Antonio Gramsci. Le sue idee nel nostro tempo*, supplement to the 12 April 1987 issue of *L'Unità*.

Losurdo, Domenico 1990, 'Gramsci, Gentile, Marx e la filosofia della prassi', in *Gramsci e il marxismo contemporaneo*, edited by Biagio Muscatello, Rome: Editori Riuniti.

Mancina, Claudia 1976, 'Egemonia, dittatura, pluralismo: una polemica su Gramsci', *Critica marxista*, 3–4.

Medici, Rita 2009, 'Giacobinismo', in *Dizionario gramsciano 1926–1937*, edited by Guido Liguori and Pasquale Voza, Rome: Carocci.

Merker, Nicolao 1986, 'Introduzione' in Karl Marx and Friedrich Engels, *La concezione materialistica della storia*, Rome: Editori Riuniti.

Missiroli, Mario 1930, 'Religione e filosofia', *L'Italia Letteraria*, 23 March.

Montari, Marcello 1997, 'Introduzione', in Antonio Gramsci, *Pensare la democrazia*, Turin: Einaudi.

———— 1999, 'Crisi dello Stato e crisi della modernità. Gramsci e la filosofia politica del Novecento', in Vacca (ed.) 1999b.

Musto, Marcello 2004, 'Vicissitudini e nuovi studi dell'«Ideologia tedesca»', *Critica marxista*, 6.

Natoli, Aldo 1997, 'Introduzione', in Gramsci 1997.

Natoli, Claudio 1995, 'Gramsci in carcere: le campagne per la liberazione, il partito, l'Internazionale (1932–1933)', *Studi storici*, 2.

———— 1999, 'Le campagne per la liberazione di Gramsci, il Pcd'I e l'Internazionale (1934)', *Studi storici*, 1.

Natta, Alessandro 1977, 'Conclusioni', in *Egemonia, Stato, partito in Gramsci*, Rome: Editori Riuniti.

Nogueira, Marco Aurélio 1997, 'Gramsci e la nuova politica', *Critica marxista*, 5–6.

———— 2000, 'Riforma dello Stato e società in Brasile', *Critica marxista*, 3–4.

Ohmae, Kenichi 1990, *The Borderless World*, London: Collins.

———— 1995, *The End of the Nation State*, New York: Simon & Schuster.

Paggi, Leonardo 1970, *Antonio Gramsci e il moderno principe*, Rome: Editori Riuniti.

———— 1984 [1969], 'Il problema Machiavelli', in *Le strategie del potere in Gramsci*, Rome: Editori Riuniti.

Paulesu Quercioli, Mimma (ed.) 1977, *Gramsci vivo nelle memorie dei suoi contemporanei*, Milan: Feltrinelli.

Petrucciani, Stefano, 'Introduzione', in *Marx in America. Individuo, etica, scelte razionali*, Rome: Editori Riuniti.

Pistillo, Michele 1996, *Gramsci-Togliatti. Polemiche e dissensi nel 1926*, Rome: Lacaita.

Portinaro, Pier Paolo 1999, *Stato*, Bologna: Il Mulino.

Poulantzas, Nicos 2008, 'Political Power and Social Classes', in *The Poulantzas Reader*, London: Verso.

Prestipino, Giuseppe 2000, *Tradire Gramsci*, Milan: Teti.

Preti, Giulio 1946, 'Il pragmatismo, che cos'è', *il politecnico*, 33–4.

————— 1975 [1957], *Praxis ed empirismo*, Turin: Einaudi.

Prezzolini, Giuseppe 1923, *La coltura italiana*, Florence: La Voce.

Racinaro, Roberto 1999, 'L'interpretazione gramsciana dell'idealismo', in Vacca (ed.) 1999b.

Ragazzini, Dario 2002, *Leonardo nella società di massa. Teoria della personalità in Gramsci*, Bergamo: Moretti Honegger.

Ragionieri, Ernesto 1976, *Palmiro Togliatti. Per una biografia politica e intellettuale*, Rome: Editori Riuniti.

Raimondi, Ezio 1988, *Letteratura e identità nazionale*, Milan: Bruno Mondadori.

Revelli, Marco 1997, *La sinistra sociale. Oltre la civiltà del lavoro*, Turin: Bollati Boringhieri.

————— 1998, 'Americanismo e fordismo: la lettura di Antonio Gramsci', in *Il giovane Gramsci e la Torino d'inizio secolo*, edited by the Fondazione Istituto Piemontese Antonio Gramsci, Turin: Rosenberg & Sellier.

Rossi-Landi, Ferruccio 1982, *Ideologia*, Milan: Mondadori.

Rusconi, Gian Enrico 1990, '*Egemonia e governo. Una rivisitazione di Gramsci*', in *Gramsci e l'Occidente. Trasformazioni della società e riforma della politica*, edited by Walter Tega, Bologna: Cappelli.

Russell, Bertrand 1967, *History of Western Philosophy*, New York: Simon and Schuster.

Russo, Luigi 1931, *Prolegomeni a Machiavelli*, Florence: Le Monnier.

Salvadori, Massimo L. 1977, 'Gramsci e il Pci: due concezioni dell'egemonia', in *Egemonia e democrazia*, Mondoperaio, 7.

Showstack Sassoon, Anne 1999, 'Indietro nel futuro: Gramsci e il dibattito sulla società civile in lingua inglese' in Vacca (ed.) 1999b.

Siciliani De Cumis, Nicola 1978, 'La «logica» di Dewey e la «praxis» di Gramsci', *Scuola e città*, 8.

Sobrero, Alberto M. 1976, 'Folklore e senso comune in Gramsci', *Etnologia e antropologia culturale*, 1.

————— 1979, 'Culture subalterne e nuova cultura in Labriola e Gramsci', in Ferri (ed.) 1977–9, Vol. ii.

Spriano, Paolo 1965, *Gramsci e l'Ordine nuovo*, Turin: Einaudi.

————— 1967, *Storia del Partito Comunista Italiano*, Vol. i, *Da Bordiga a Gramsci*, Turin: Einaudi.

————— 1977, *Gramsci in carcere e il partito*, Rome: Editori Riuniti.

————— 1988, *L'ultima ricerca di Paolo Spriano*, supplement to the 27 October 1988 issue of *L'Unità*.

Suppa, Silvio 1979, *Consiglio e Stato in Gramsci e Lenin*, Bari: Dedalo.

Tamburrano, Giuseppe 1959, 'Fasi di sviluppo del pensiero politico di Gramsci', in Caracciolo and Scalia (eds.) 1959.

———— 1973 [1958], intervention reproduced in *Studi gramsciani*, Rome: Editori Riuniti.

———— 1977, *Antonio Gramsci*, Milan: Sugarco.

Telò, Mario 1999, 'Note sul futuro dell'Occidente e la teoria delle relazioni internazionali', in Vacca (ed.) 1999b.

Texier, Jacques 1969, intervention reproduced in *Gramsci e la cultura contemporanea*, Vol. I, edited by Pietro Rossi, Rome: Editori Riuniti.

———— 1988a, 'Significati di società civile in Gramsci', *Critica marxista*, 5.

———— 1988b, *Révolution et démocratie chez Marx et Engels*, Paris: Presses Universitaires de France.

Togliatti, Palmiro 1967, *Opere*, Vol. I, Rome: Editori Riuniti.

———— 1974, *La politica culturale*, Rome: Editori Riuniti.

———— 1975, *Togliatti e il centrosinistra*, Florence: Istituto Gramsci.

———— 2013, *Scritti su Gramsci*, edited by Guido Liguori, Rome: Editori Riuniti.

Tortorella, Aldo 1997, 'Il socialismo come idea-limite', *Critica marxista*, 5–6.

———— 1998, 'Il fondamento etico della politica in Gramsci', *Critica marxista*, 2–3.

Tosin, Bruno 1976, *Con Gramsci. Ricordi di uno della «vecchia guardia»*, Rome: Editori Riuniti.

Trentin, Bruno 1997, *La città del lavoro. Sinistra e crisi del fordismo*, Milan: Feltrinelli.

———— 1999, *Autunno caldo. Il secondo biennio rosso 1968–1969*, interview with Guido Liguori, Rome: Editori Riuniti.

Tuccari, Francesco 2001, 'Gramsci e la sociologia marxista di Nikolaj I. Bucharin', in *Gramsci: il partito politico nei Quaderni*, edited by Salvo Mastellone and Giorgio Sola, Florence: Centro Editoriale Toscano.

Vacca, Giuseppe 1991, 'Egemonia e politica-potenza. La «filosofia della praxis» come programma' in *Gramsci e Togliatti*, Rome: Editori Riuniti.

———— 1994, *Pensare il mondo nuovo. Verso la democrazia del XXI secolo*, Milan: Edizioni San Paolo.

———— 1998, 'La crisi dello Stato-nazione e la democrazia: una nuova stagione di studi gramsciani', in *Il giovane Gramsci e la Torino d'inizio secolo*, edited by the Fondazione Istituto Piemontese Antonio Gramsci, Turin: Rosenberg & Sellier.

———— 1999a, *Appuntamenti con Gramsci*, Rome: Carocci.

———— (ed.) 1999b, *Gramsci e il Novecento*, Rome: Carocci.

———— 1999c, 'Gramsci a Roma, Togliatti a Mosca', in Daniele (ed.) 1999.

———— 2012, *Vita e pensieri di Antonio Gramsci 1926–1937*, Turin: Einaudi.

Vigna, Carmelo 1979, *Gramsci e l'egemonia. Una interpretazione metapolitica*, Rome: Città nuova.

Vittoria, Albertina 1992, *Togliatti e gli intellettuali. Storia dell'Istituto Gramsci negli anni Cinquanta e Sessanta*, Rome: Editori Riuniti.

Voza, Pasquale 1999, 'Gramsci e l'egemonia, oggi', in *Gramsci e l'Internazionalismo. Nazione, Europa, America Latina*, edited by Mario Proto, Rome: Lacaita.

———— 2004, 'Rivoluzione passiva', in Frosini and Liguori (eds.) 2004.

West, Cornel 1989, *The American Evasion of Philosophy*, Basingstoke: Macmillan.

———— 1992, 'Marxist Theory and the Specificity of Afro-American Oppression', in *Marxism and the Interpretation of Culture*, edited by Cary Nelson and Lawrence Grossberg, Urbana, IL: University of Illinois Press.

———— 2000, *Race Matters*, Boston, MA: Beacon Press.

Zanardo, Aldo 1986, 'Togliatti e Banfi sulla via di Labriola al marxismo', *Critica marxista*, 5.

———— 1988, 'Gramsci e la concezione della vita morale', *Critica marxista*, 5.

Name Index

Agosti, Aldo 160–2, 223
Alighieri, Dante 202
Althusser, Louis 17, 79, 129, 180, 225
Anderson, Perry 184–5, 223
Aristotle 105
Ascoli, Graziadio Isaia 185
Asor Rosa, Alberto 46–7, 223
Auciello, Nicola 179–80, 223

Badaloni, Nicola 186–7, 223
Balibar, Étienne 42
Balzac, Honoré de 139
Banfi, Antonio 231
Baratta, Giorgio 47, 223
Barbusse, Henri 68, 153
Barilli, Bruno 85
Bauer, Bruno 31
Bauer, Otto 45
Bentham, Jeremy 197
Bergson, Henri 60, 116, 194
Bernstein, Eduard 69
Bloc, Joseph 138, 149, 153
Bobbio Norberto 26–8, 30–4, 36, 40,
  48–9, 126, 137, 178, 178–80, 182, 223
Bodei Remo 39, 223
Bodin, Jean 219
Bogdanov Aleksandr 152, 229
Bonaparte, Napoleon 65, 76, 152
Boothman Derek 78, 136, 223, 226
Bordiga, Amadeo 56, 61, 64, 158–9, 161–2,
  179, 229
Borgia, Cesare ("Valentino") 204, 211
Borgius, Walther 138
Boudon, Raymond 65, 67, 223
Boullier Auguste 76
Broccoli, Angelo 179, 223
Bukharin Nikolaj (*Popular Manual*)
  21, 65, 73–4, 92–93, 95, 98–99, 121–2,
  128, 131–2, 134–6, 137, 139–40, 196
Buci-Glucksmann, Christine 1, 34, 51,
  180–181, 185, 223
Buonaiuti, Ernesto 142, 145, 166–7
Burgio, Alberto 47, 145, 190–1, 223,
  225
Buttigieg, Joseph A. 33, 223, 226–7

Cacciatore, Giuseppe 117, 223
Calderoni, Mario 194
Cammett, John M. 156
Caprioglio, Sergio 226
Caracciolo, Alberto 172, 223, 230
Caramella, Santino 94–5, 107–8, 223
Cavallaro, Luigi 6, 224
Cavina, Luigi 208
Centi Beatrice 117, 148, 150, 224
Chabod, Federico 205
Chiarotto, Francesca 167, 224
Ciliberto, Michele 130, 224
Cohen, Gerry 113
Cohen, Jean L. 36–7, 124
Colletti, Lucio 128, 182, 224
Cosmo, Umberto 202
Cospito, Giuseppe 9, 121, 191, 220, 224–5,
  227
Coutinho, Carlos Nelson 4, 36, 56, 126, 181,
  224
Cox, Robert 36–7, 189, 224
Craxi, Bettino 181
Croce, Benedetto 16, 23–4, 27, 60, 68, 70–1,
  77, 81–2, 90, 93–6, 98, 107, 121, 130, 134,
  138–39, 142–3, 153–4, 165–6, 169, 193, 196,
  203–6, 210–1, 217, 224

Daniele, Chiara 157–8, 224, 230
De Felice, Franco 167, 224
De Giovanni, Biagio 183, 224
De Man, Henri 58–9
De Sanctis, Francesco 144, 202, 204
Derrida, Jacques 199–200
Descartes, René 107
Destutt de Tracy, Antonine-Louis-Claude
  65, 146
Dewey, John 192–200, 224
Di Vittorio, Giuseppe 159
Dimitrov, Georgi M. 167
Donini, Ambrogio 170
Donzelli, Carmine 205, 214, 224
D'Orsi, Angelo 61, 224
Dühring, Eugen 134, 140
Dubla, Ferdinando 47, 224
Durante, Lea 53, 225

Eagleton Terry   66, 69, 75, 225
Eastman, Max   197
Elizabeth I (Tudor)   206
Elster Jon   114
Emerson, Ralph Waldo   192
Engels, Friedrich   x, 65–8, 72, 120–3, 125–41,
    145–6, 148–51, 153–4, 165, 194, 210, 219,
    226–8, 230
Ercole, Francesco   205

Ferdinand II (of Aragon)   206
Ferrata, Giansiro   226
Ferri, Franco   182, 225, 229
Feuerbach, Ludwig   30, 60, 65, 68, 70, 93, 111,
    121–2, 139, 146, 154
Finelli, Roberto   49, 67, 144, 225
Fiori, Giuseppe   159, 225
Fontana, Benedetto   39, 225
Foscolo, Ugo   210–1
Foucault, Michel   199–200
Fradeletto, Antonio   203
Francioni, Gianni   121, 184, 208, 213–4,
    219–20, 225
Frosini, Fabio   67, 72, 78, 85, 103, 110, 207, 211,
    221–5, 231

Galilei, Galileo   203
Gallo, Elisabetta   207, 225
Gallo, Niccolò   226
Garin, Eugenio   196, 202, 225
Gentile Giovanni   2, 16, 23–4, 60, 94–7, 101,
    116, 205, 226
George, Susan   44, 226
Gerratana, Valentino   29–31, 58, 76, 131, 140,
    144–5, 147, 168, 183, 194, 214, 220, 226
Giasi, Francesco   156
Gill, Stephen   36, 37, 189, 226
Giolitti, Giovanni   204
Giuliano, Balbino   194
Giusti, Giuseppe   101, 204
Gobetti, Piero   205
Grieco, Ruggero   159
Gruppi, Luciano   178–80, 227
Guicciardini, Francesco   16, 208, 218
Guiducci, Roberto   172

Hardt, Michael   43, 227
Haug, Wolfgang Fritz   28, 227
Hegel, Georg Wilhelm Friedrich   8–11, 15, 26,

29–31, 34, 39, 49, 70, 73, 122, 126, 128, 139–40,
    155, 159, 166, 195, 224
Hirst, Paul   43, 227
Hoare, Quintin   226
Horsman, Mathew   43, 227

Ivan IV (the Terrible)   206
Izzo, Francesca   66, 227

Jackson, Jesse   192
James, William   192, 194–5
Jaulin, Annick   92, 103, 227

Kant, Immanuel   90, 117–8
Korsch, Karl   45

La Rocca, Tommaso   100
Labica, Georges   132, 227
Labriola, Antonio   x, 68, 117, 133, 142–55, 167,
    223–7, 229, 231
Labiola, Arturo   204
Laclau, Ernesto   186, 227
Latouche, Serge   42
Lenin, Vladimir   2, 8, 33, 46, 50, 52, 55–60,
    69, 78, 111, 124, 127, 144, 152, 172, 176, 178–183,
    185, 192–3, 204, 222, 227, 230
Leonetti, Alfonso   160, 174
Liguori, Guido   ix, 58, 132, 143, 160, 163, 167,
    223–5, 227–8, 230–1
Lisa, Athos   161, 227
Lo Piparo, Franco   185, 227
Losurdo, Domenico   135, 228
Louis XI (of Bourbon)   206
Lukács, György   131, 136, 192–3, 197, 227
Luther, Martin   150
Luporini, Cesare   66, 88, 94, 144, 167, 227
Luxemburg, Rosa   45, 57

Macchierò, Vittorio   194
Machiavelli, Niccolò   x, 185, 202–22, 224–5,
    228–9
Malagodi, Giovanni Francesco   71, 77
Mancina, Claudia   79, 182, 228
Manzoni, Alessandro   83, 107–8, 185
Marshall, Andrew   43, 227
Marx, Karl   x, 2, 6, 8, 26–35, 42, 47, 49–50,
    52, 60, 65–74, 83, 93, 101–2, 111, 113–5, 118,
    120–23, 125–30, 132, 134, 138–40, 144–55, 193,
    197–9, 204, 209–11, 219, 226–8

Mastellone, Salvo   230
Mathiez, Albert   208
Mazzoni, Guido   208
Medici, Rita   204, 228
Mehring, Franz   67, 153
Merker, Nicolao   67, 147, 228
Mill, John Stuart   197
Missiroli, Mario   94, 107, 228
Mondolfo, Rodolfo   130–1
Montanari, Marcello   38, 51
Mosca, Gaetano   3, 217
Muscatello, Biagio   228
Mouffe, Chantal   186, 227
Mussolini, Benito   115, 161, 205
Musto, Marcello   146, 228

Natoli, Aldo   160, 228
Natoli, Claudio   158–9, 228
Natta, Alessandro   167, 228
Negri Antonio   43, 227
Neurath Otto   2
Nogueira Marco Aurelio   35–6, 54, 228
Nowell-Smith, Geoffrey   226

Ohmae Kenichi   43, 228
Ojetti Ugo   75

Paggi Leonardo   68, 145, 150, 203, 207, 228
Papini Giovanni   116, 195
Pareto Vilfredo   60, 68, 153
Paulesu Quercioli, Mimma   61, 228
Petri Carlo   46
Petrucciani Stefano   60, 114, 228
Pirandello Luigi   92, 107
Portinaro Pier Paolo   29, 228
Poulantzas, Nicos   181, 229
Prestipino Giuseppe   65, 229
Preti, Giulio   191, 229
Prezzolini Giuseppe   116, 168, 229

Racinaro, Roberto   39–40, 229
Ragazzini, Dario   79, 187, 229
Ragionieri, Ernesto   160, 229
Raimondi, Ezio   53, 229
Rathenau, Walther   2, 34
Ravazzoli, Paolo   160
Rawls, John   114
Revelli, Marco   45–7, 229

Ricardo, David   2
Righi, Maria Luisa   156, 227
Roemer, John   114
Romano, Ruggiero   228
Roosevelt, Franklin Delano   197
Rorty, Richard   192
Rossi, Pietro   223, 226, 230
Rossi-Landi, Ferruccio   75, 229
Rousseau, Jean-Jacques   224
Rovatti, Pier Aldo   27
Royce, Josiah   194
Rusconi, Gian Enrico   187, 229
Russell, Beltrand   196, 229
Russo, Luigi   205, 218, 229

Salvadori, Massimo L.   181–2, 229
Santhià, Battista   61
Santucci, Antonio A.   226–7
Savonarola, Girolamo   218
Sbarberi, Franco   153, 227
Scalia, Gianni   172, 223, 230
Schmidt, Conrad   138
Schucht, Tat'jana (Tania or Tatiana)   8, 17, 95, 111, 131, 158, 160, 178, 194, 202, 205, 207–8, 212
Scoccimarro, Mauro   174
Showstack Saassoon Anne   36, 39, 229
Siciliani de Cumis, Nicola   229
Sobrero, Alberto M.   94, 229
Soderini, Pier   211
Sola, Giorgio   230
Sorel, Georges   39, 56, 60, 62, 68–9, 130–1, 153, 222
Spirito, Ugo   5, 23
Spriano, Paolo   61, 64, 158–9, 162, 229
Sraffa, Piero   158–60, 202, 205, 212
Stalin, Iosif   52, 159, 161, 166, 169, 172, 181, 225
Suppa, Silvio   50, 230

Tambuttano, Giuseppe   172, 176–7, 230
Tasca, Angelo   162, 174
Telò, Mario   38–9, 189, 230
Terracini, Umberto   174
Texier, Jacques   4, 32, 141, 230
Thompson, Grahame   43, 227
Tocqueville, Alexis Charles de   36
Togliatti, Palmiro   x, 26, 32, 116, 132, 142–5, 156–77, 179, 217, 223–5, 228–31
Tolstoy, Lev   83
Tortorella, Aldo   117, 230

Tosin, Bruno 161, 230
Trentin, Bruno 45–9, 230
Tresso, Pietro 160
Treves, Paolo 205, 218
Trotsky, Leon 143, 158, 161, 204
Tronti, Mario 172
Tuccari, Francesco 65, 230
Turati, Filippo 139

Vacca, Giuseppe 27, 36, 38, 51, 157, 159, 167, 187–9, 223–6, 228–30
Vailati, Giovanni 194
Veca, Salvatore 113

Vigna, Carmelo 185, 230
Vittoria, Albertina 170, 231
Vivanti, Corrado 228
Volney, Constantin-François de Chasseboeuf conte di 65
Voza, Pasquale IX, 6, 48, 190, 224, 228, 231

Weil, Simone 45
West, Cornel X, 192, 194, 197–201, 231
Wilson, Thomas Woodrow 69

Zanardo, Aldo 116, 143, 231
Zini, Zino 66

Subject Index

Americanism and Fordism   45–7, 167
Anti-Croce   133
Anti-determinism   138–41, 148–50, 154
Anti-Dühring   128–138, 140, 149, 226
Anti-Fascist unity   163–5

Civil society   4–10, 16–20, 22–4, 26–41, 44, 48, 79, 178, 213
Citizenship   47–8
Common sense   10, 58, 62, 77, 80–112
Communist Party   55–7, 62–4, 80, 86, 209, 213, 217
Conformism   80, 83, 116
Conscious Leadership   55–57, 62–4
Conceptions (or vision) of the world   80–3, 86, 88–102

Economism   3–4, 74
Egemony   12, 24–5, 106, 176

Folklore   77, 80–2, 85, 88

Globalisation   42–4, 49–51, 123, 189
Good sense   87–8, 92, 94–6, 105–110

Hegemony   9, 12, 16, 18, 24–5, 63, 81, 86, 106, 124, 176–81, 191
Hegemonic apparatuses   9, 180
Hermeneutics (of Gramscian texts)   ix–x
Historical bloc   28, 32, 118
Human nature   210–1

Ideology   65–84, 88–9, 102, 118–9, 121–3, 142–55
Intellectuals   7–8, 86, 166–9
Italian road to socialism   172, 175

Jacobinism   208, 216, 220

Language   80, 103
Leninism   172, 176, 208
Lexicon (of Gramsci)   ix–x
Liberalism   48–9

Machiavellianism (and Anti-Machiavellianism)   202–2, 206, 219

Mass movements   55–6, 60–4
Modern Prince (or New Prince)   209–22
Monocausalism   123, 197–200
Morality   113–9
Mundialisation   42–4, 51

National State   38, 42–3, 49–52, 123–5, 187–9
New Deal   5–6

Objectivity of the real   135–6
Ordine Nuovo (L')   46–7, 55–8, 60–3, 89–90, 169–70, 181

Philosophy   80–2, 88, 91, 99, 102–4
Passive Revolution   53
Philosophy of praxis   105
Political party   209, 213
Political realism   217–8
Political society   8–9
Politics   118, 125–7, 187, 209–11, 217
Pragmatism   192–97
Preintentionality   111–2
Prestige   185
Public opinion   19

Quality/quantity   136–7

Religion   77–8, 80–2, 94, 99, 102–3, 106

Salerno policy   164
Second International   132, 139, 151, 196
Soviet Union   11, 20–1
Spirit of cleavage   35, 69, 79, 112
Spontaneity   56–8, 62–4, 89–90
Stalinism   156–9, 166–7, 169–70
State (and extended state, integral state)   1–8, 11–13, 15–25, 36–40, 79, 125–7, 190, 213
State, ethical   18–20, 35, 39–41
Statolatry   20–2
Stenterello   204
Structure/ Superstructures   6–8, 10, 71, 149–51, 200
Subaltern classes   57–9
Subject and subjectivity   79–84, 89, 85, 116, 121

Taylorism 45–7
Theses on Feuerbach 60, 93

War of moviment/war of position 14–15

Will 84, 89, 118

Zhdanovism 166, 168–9